OCT   2001 $ 24.95

Heartbreakers

Heartbreakers

BASEBALL'S MOST AGONIZING DEFEATS

John Kuenster

 Ivan R. Dee Chicago 2001

HEARTBREAKERS. Copyright © 2001 by John Kuenster. All rights
reserved, including the right to reproduce this book or portions thereof
in any form. For information, address: Ivan R. Dee, Publisher,
1332 North Halsted Street, Chicago 60622. Manufactured in the United
States of America and printed on acid-free paper.

Library of Congress Cataloging-in-Publication Data:
Kuenster, John.
　　Heartbreakers : baseball's most agonizing defeats / John Kuenster.
　　　p. cm.
　　Includes index.
　　ISBN 1-56663-366-4 (alk. paper)
　　1. Baseball—United States—History. I. Title.

GV863.A1 K85 2001
796.357'0973—dc21   00-050435

To all major league players,
past and present,
who have honored the game
by always giving
their best efforts on the field,
even when their teams lost

Contents

Acknowledgments

This book would have been difficult to complete without the generous cooperation of former and current players and managers who took time to dredge up memories of heartbreaking defeats.

Thanks also are due to my publisher Ivan Dee for his original suggestion for the theme and title of the book, and for his skillful editing of each chapter.

Appreciation likewise goes to the following for their special assistance along the way: Dick Bresciani, vice president of public affairs for the Boston Red Sox; W. C. Burdick of the Baseball Hall of Fame photo department; Ned Colletti, assistant general manager of the San Francisco Giants; Benjie de la Fuente, media relations assistant with the Chicago Cubs; Paul Hoynes, baseball writer for the *Cleveland Plain Dealer*; Desta Kimmel, media services coordinator for the Houston Astros; Bob Kuenster, managing editor of *Baseball Digest*; Tim Mead, vice president of communications for the Anaheim Angels; Sally O'Leary, a vital link in the Pittsburgh Pirates Alumni Association; Arthur Richman, senior adviser with the New York Yankees media relations department; Chris Stathos, media relations coordinator of the Kansas City Royals; and Bart Swain, director of media relations for the Cleveland Indians.

As sources I have used the *Baseball Biographical Encyclopedia*, produced by the editors of *Total Baseball; Baseball Digest; Baseball Encyclopedia*, published by Macmillan, and various *Baseball Guides*, published by *The Sporting News*.

J. K.

Chicago, January 2001

The game breaks your heart.

It is designed to break your heart.

—A. Bartlett Giamatti

Heartbreakers

Introduction

After a night game at old Comiskey Park in the long ago, members of the Chicago White Sox were trying to shrug off an agonizing defeat they had suffered at the hands of the New York Yankees. It was a tug-of-war they should have won, but through several botched opportunities to score the tying and go-ahead runs, their efforts in the end only added another digit to the team's loss column.

Upstairs in the park's Bards Room, an after-game haunt of writers and other media folks, Bill Veeck was holding forth as usual. The gregarious Sox owner was noted for his mirth, but during this round-table discussion he was not so mirthful. "Baseball," he sighed, "is a boy's game that makes grown men cry."

Veeck never really cried over the misfortunes that befell his players on the field. He enjoyed life too much. But his mournful comment reflected a truism that has been part of major league history ever since baseball made a serious impact on the public's consciousness.

Although Veeck was in a philosophical mood that night, he had a hard time trying to conceal his dismay over the quirks of the game that often turn joy to grief in a heartbeat. These quirks are almost countless—a curve ball that doesn't break and instead enters a hitter's power zone; a line drive that skips off a shortstop's glove; a double play thwarted because the second baseman juggles the ball; a well-timed bunt that rolls foul by an inch; a sure-out grounder that unexpectedly bounces over an infielder's head. Such maddening malfunctions are all woven into the capricious and unpredictable nature of baseball and often lead to stinging defeats.

Since the baseball season runs so long, individual failures do not always create lasting feelings of remorse. In spring and midsummer, losers can say, "We'll get 'em tomorrow." But when it comes down to pivotal games late in a pennant race, in division and league playoffs, and finally in the World Series, the bitterness of coming off second best has a sharper edge to it.

Perhaps in this era of huge salaries, that edge has been blunted a bit because the extra money earned for winning championships doesn't mean as much as it once did when paychecks were relatively skimpy by today's standards. Nonetheless the edge is still there because most major leaguers have a strong competitive drive, otherwise they wouldn't be playing at the game's highest professional level. A hardened cynic may deride richly paid players as lacking in desire but, cynicism aside, let it be said that most every one of them really does want to win, sometimes at any cost. Their pride and sometimes their sense of self-worth are at stake.

While the print and electronic media continually lionize baseball's winners, sometimes to the point of overkill, many fascinating stories of losers go untapped. The vanquished in critical games generally include excellent as well as less talented players who tried their best but fell short. They deserve a hearing.

In determining the scope of this book I decided to forgo retelling the experiences of some ancient baseball figures who were smeared as losers in big games, victims such as first baseman Fred Merkle of the New York Giants, outfielder Fred Snodgrass, also of the Giants, and catcher Mickey Owen of the Brooklyn Dodgers, whose ill-timed mistakes, in order, involved a failure to touch second base, a dropped fly ball, a passed ball. Through the years many authors have described the circumstances that forced these men to endure extended disgrace for their lapses, so their particular on-field woes—in memorable games against the Cubs in 1908, against the Red Sox in 1912, and against the Yankees in 1941—need not be recounted again.

Here I try to bring to life the stories of players who took part in some poignant losses over the last half-century, beginning with the traumatic elimination that stunned the Dodgers in the final National League playoff game against the Giants in 1951, seven years before both of those clubs moved to the West Coast.

When my baseball writing adventures started regularly with the *Chicago Daily News* in 1957, major league venues included such historic and challenging facilities as the Polo Grounds in New York, Ebbets Field in Brooklyn, Sportsman's Park in St. Louis, Forbes Field in Pittsburgh, Crosley Field in Cincinnati, Shibe Park in Philadelphia, and Griffith Stadium in Washington—now all long gone. At the Polo Grounds it was a mere 257 feet down the line from home plate to the right-field stands. The distance down the left-field line was only 279 feet. On the other hand, the deepest outfield corner in Forbes Field, just left of straightaway center at the flagpole, was a daunting 457 feet from the plate. And it took a monstrous home run to clear the back of the left-field bleachers at Griffith Stadium; Mickey Mantle and Josh Gibson were the only two players ever to do it.

Press boxes in those days were often cramped and uncomfortable. The one at Forbes Field had a foul aroma near its entrance during warm weather, and as writers moved to their assigned areas they had to duck to avoid hitting their heads on low, overhanging girders. The press box at the Polo Grounds was reached by gingerly walking down a spiral staircase. Typewriter-lugging writers, once seated, felt as though they were ensconced in a compact submarine.

At Boston's Fenway Park the closeness of the press box to the field enabled local writers to vent their sarcasm and shout loud insults at the players and umpires, a rather disturbing, provincial practice performed with notable regularity by Dave Egan of the *Boston Record*. In Cleveland's Municipal Stadium the open press box behind home plate had no protective barrier and could be a dangerous place to work when foul balls came whistling back. In Philadelphia's Shibe Park (also known as Connie Mack Stadium) the height of the press box from the field below could lead to a queasy stomach for those afflicted with acrophobia.

In those days the Yankee Stadium press row was frequented

by a distinguished cast of New York wordsmiths, including Red Smith of the *Herald-Tribune*, Dick Young of the *Daily News*, Jimmy Cannon of the *Post*, Milt Richman of United Press, and Arthur Daley of the *Times*. Smith, a Pulitzer Prize–winner, could often be seen bent over his typewriter, suffering the pangs of generating his beautiful prose. Daley, another Pulitzer recipient, was frequently spotted in or near the home dugout before games, jotting notes on a legal-sized pad of paper. And Young could be heard delivering choice wisecracks most any place on most any subject.

Once, former Japanese premier Nobusuke Kishi was invited to attend a game at Yankee Stadium. He was seated next to Edna Stengel, wife of Yankee manager Casey Stengel, who was noted for speaking a hard-to-decipher form of fractured English. Someone in the press box said, "I wonder if Mrs. Stengel can understand what that Japanese premier is saying to her."

"She ought to be able to," Young responded, "she's listened to Casey long enough."

Bench jockeying in that era was a prevalent and occasionally virulent art form that would cause today's politically correct practitioners to bristle. It was a time when skinny shortstops didn't hit 20 home runs a year. The ball wasn't juiced up, and a pitcher could actually manipulate the cover to raise the seams and get a better grip for throwing a curve. Hitters didn't stroll around outside the batter's box between pitches, boring the living daylights out of the plate umpire and everyone else. There were no muscle-toning and exercise rooms adjoining clubhouses or nearby special indoor areas for batting practice. When it came to compensating players, owners and general managers, particularly Branch Rickey, squeezed the dollar with a death grip. Greedy agents hadn't discovered how easy it was to siphon money out of the game.

In a way it was a simpler time, though not necessarily a better time. Most players were mere chattels. The game was less democratic, and black and Latin players were just beginning to gain widespread recognition.

Since then the growth of major league baseball from 16 to 30 teams has brought with it many changes, including the introduction of the designated hitter, division playoffs, the League Championship Series, World Series games played at night, a greater reliance on relief pitching, interleague competition during the regular season, indoor stadiums with retractable roofs, artificial turf, and games that count in the pennant race being staged in such countries as Mexico and Japan.

And in recent years individual records once thought to be unreachable have been blown away by such performers as Nolan Ryan (most lifetime strikeouts and no-hit games), Mark McGwire (most home runs in a season), and Cal Ripken (most consecutive games played). Today players are bigger and faster than they once were. They also have the benefit of vastly improved equipment, including batting gloves, specialized sunglasses, and elaborate protective gear for catchers.

Yet one aspect of big league baseball has never changed and probably never will: the disappointments, frustrations, and, yes, heartbreaks of losers in games that may determine the ultimate success or failure of their teams for an entire season.

There is no consistent assurance of success in baseball. Hitting a 95-mile-an-hour fastball or a deceptive slider down and away, catching a slicing line drive to right field, or throwing out a sliding runner at home plate can never be taken for granted. Winners and losers should be equally appreciated. When Sandy Koufax pitched a perfect game for the Dodgers against the Cubs in 1965, he outdueled Bob Hendley who gave up only one hit and one unearned run in getting beat 1–0. It hardly seems fair that Hendley should be labeled a loser on that September night in Los Angeles.

Years afterward, Ralph Branca, the Dodger pitcher who yielded Bobby Thomson's famous playoff home run that won the pennant for the Giants in 1951, still couldn't shake off the opprobrium that shadowed him. "If you kill somebody," he lamented, "they sentence you to life; you serve 20 years and you get paroled. I've never been paroled."

1951

Dodgers Crushed by the "Shot Heard 'Round the World"

"Those Dodger-Giant games weren't baseball. They were civil war."—Andy Pafko

It was approaching four o'clock in the afternoon on October 3, 1951, when Russ Hodges made one of the most spine-tingling home-run calls in baseball history. Seated in the WMCA radio booth at the Polo Grounds in New York, he was watching a tall Giants hitter, Bobby Thomson, step into the batter's box to face Ralph Branca, a right-handed Brooklyn Dodger reliever who had come in from the bullpen to close out the ninth inning and wrap up the final game of the playoff series that would determine the National League pennant winner.

A native Kentuckian, Hodges was a soft-spoken, droll professional who had been broadcasting Giant games since 1949. He announced action on the field with a certain sense of dispassion, except when he called "Bye, bye, baby!" in describing a home run hit by a Giant player. At 3:58 p.m. on that memorable Wednesday, however, his passion exploded. What transpired at that moment became known as the "Miracle of Coogan's Bluff" and turned into one of the dominant news stories of the year.

While baseball unquestionably remained America's game in 1951, it shared the public's attention with events that were making headlines as the second half of the twentieth century unfolded: the Korean War, Harry Truman's firing of General Douglas MacArthur, the powerful new influence of television.

In baseball, Joe DiMaggio signed a $100,000 contract with the Yankees for the third straight year; a 20-year-old rookie named Willie Mays made his debut with the Giants; Bob Feller pitched his third no-hitter for the Cleveland Indians; Bill Veeck sent up a midget, Eddie Gaedel, to pinch-hit for the St. Louis Browns against the Detroit Tigers; and Ford Frick was elected to a seven-year term as baseball commissioner.

Less than two weeks after Frick's election, the Dodgers and Giants finished the season tied for first place in the National League, necessitating a three-game playoff to decide who would face the Yankees in the World Series.

Both clubs had completed their regular 154-game schedules with identical 96–58 records, though the standings were still in doubt until late the final day, Sunday, September 30. In Boston the Giants beat the Braves 3–2. The score was posted on the scoreboard at Philadelphia's Shibe Park, where the Dodgers were struggling against the Phillies in extra innings. It was getting dark, and players were having trouble following the ball, but league rules prohibited the lights from being turned on for a Sunday game. Finally Jackie Robinson, as he had done so often during the season, rescued the Dodgers by slamming a 14th inning home run into the left-field bleachers off Robin Roberts to give his teammates their needed victory, 9–8.

Although the Dodgers almost fell off the top rung of the ladder at the end, they entered the playoff series as favorites against a team that had fashioned an incredible rally to get as far as it did. As late as August 7 the Giants had trailed the Dodgers by 13-1/2 games.

Earlier, critics had claimed that the Giants had only a two-man pitching staff in Sal Maglie and Larry Jansen, and an infield that included an erratic shortstop in Alvin Dark, an aging second baseman in Eddie Stanky, and a converted outfielder at third base in Bobby Thomson. But as the season moved into July, starter Jim Hearn finally gained his control and began throwing strikes, giving manager Leo Durocher three consistently effective pitchers. Thus armed, and with some robust hitting by left fielder Monte Irvin, the Giants won 37 of their last 44 games to hit the wire in a dead heat with Brooklyn.

The rivalry between the two teams was fierce. "Those Dodger–Giant games weren't baseball, they were civil war," recalled Andy Pafko, who played for Brooklyn that year. While the rivalry had festered for years, it was magnified by the fact the Giants' give-no-quarter manager, Durocher, had piloted the Dodgers in the 1940s. There was no love lost between Durocher and Charlie Dressen, the egocentric manager of the Dodgers. Dressen, at 53, was seven years older than Durocher and considered himself one of the world's great baseball minds. Durocher also had a substantial ego and used every trick imaginable to gain an upper hand on the field.

When the season began, the Giants went into a swoon after winning their first two games. They lost their next 11, five of them to Brooklyn. During these April skirmishes, tempers flared on both sides, and the bench jockeying was fierce. Durocher's loud mouth and down-and-dirty tactics riled not only the Dodgers but other opponents as well.

On April 29 at Ebbets Field, Jansen knocked down Duke Snider with a high inside fastball, a pitch the Dodgers obviously felt had been called by Durocher—though pitchers on both sides didn't have to be told to intimidate batters. Snider retaliated by hitting a pair of home runs as the Dodgers went on to win 6–3. During the game Don Newcombe, Brooklyn's ace pitcher, kept yelling over to the Giants' dugout, "Eat your heart out, Leo! Eat your heart out!"

On April 30 the Giants finally ended their losing streak, beating the Dodgers 8–5, but not before Jackie Robinson tried to exact a measure of revenge for the knockdown pitches thrown by the Giants. On a bunt down the first-base line, Robinson hoped to draw Sal Maglie over to the base line to field the ball so that he could slam into him. The ball rolled foul, but Robinson bumped Maglie anyway. Durocher blasted Robinson's effort as a "bush stunt." Robinson retorted, "If it was a bush stunt, he's a bush manager, because he taught me to do it."

The Giants were lodged in eighth place as May arrived, and their fans and some local baseball writers thought they were finished. "It would take a miracle for them to win a championship now," wrote Arthur Daley of the *New York Times*. "Says who?" countered the combative Durocher. "There's a long way to go before the season is over."

Durocher's bravado, however, could not diminish the fact that the Dodgers had one of the National League's best teams in years. Their regular lineup included four future Hall of Famers: Jackie Robinson at second, Pee Wee Reese at short, Duke Snider in center, and Roy Campanella behind the plate. They had power in Gil Hodges at first, and two skilled defensive players in third baseman Billy Cox and right fielder Carl Furillo, a dangerous hitter with a tremendously strong throwing arm.

The only apparent soft spot in the Dodger lineup was left field. That weakness was addressed in June when Brooklyn acquired 30-year-old veteran Andy Pafko in an eight-player deal with the Cubs. Although his normal position was center field, Pafko was moved to left. He brought with him solid defensive credentials and extra-base hitting power.

On paper the Giants seemed decidedly overmatched by the Dodgers, who continued their mastery by sweeping three straight from Durocher's crew at Ebbets Field in early July, bolstering their first-place lead to seven and a half games. The sweep caused Charlie Dressen to overflow with optimism. "We knocked 'em out," he crowed. "They won't bother us any more." An old-time baseball warrior, Dressen should have known better than to say something like that, even though the Dodgers continued to pummel their enemies from upper Manhattan, wrapping up another three-game sweep against the Giants in early August.

When the Giants brought up Willie Mays from the Minneapolis Millers of the American Association in late May, he faltered at the plate in the early going, but he sparkled in center field and his presence gave the club a much-needed boost in morale. By midseason the Giants' pitching had come together, and Mays had found the range with his bat. The once seemingly insurmountable Dodger lead began to shrink as the Giants won 16 straight games from August 12 through August 27. On September 20 the Dodgers held first place, four and a

The Dodgers boasted a superb outfield: (from left) Carl Furillo in right, Duke Snider in center, and Andy Pafko, obtained from the Cubs in mid-season, in left.

half games ahead of the Giants. Brooklyn had ten games left to play, the Giants seven.

Dressen's club then unaccountably unraveled, losing six of its last ten games while the onrushing Giants won seven in a row, including their finale in Boston where they beat the Braves on a home run by Thomson and Jansen's five-hitter to assure themselves of at least a first-place tie. So what was once considered improbable became reality. A coin toss determined that the best-of-three playoff series would open in Ebbets Field, with the remaining two games, if both were needed, to be played in the Polo Grounds.

The Giants won the first game 3–1 behind the five-hit pitching of Hearn, aided by home runs by Thomson and Irvin. Pafko homered for the only Dodger run. Branca was charged with the loss.

In game two, Dressen chose as his starting pitcher Clem

Labine, a young rookie whom he had bypassed during the club's desperate stretch run. Dressen could be a punitive character, and he had a grudge against the brash Labine who had lost a critical game to the Phillies on September 21. Labine promptly made Dressen look foolish for his peevishness by shutting down the Giants in the second playoff game, 10–0. His six-hit masterpiece set the stage for the decisive third game, pitting Newcombe against Maglie at the Polo Grounds.

Early in the game the lights had to be turned on because of overcast skies. Newcombe had pitched 23-2/3 innings over the previous seven days but managed to hold the Giants in check. After the seventh inning, with the score tied 1–1, Newcombe walked into the Dodger dugout and confessed, "I've got nothing left." Jackie Robinson and Roy Campanella, who sat out the game because of a pulled thigh muscle, talked to Newcombe. The big right-hander complained, "My arm is tight."

"Bullshit," responded Robinson. "Go out there and pitch until your arm falls off."

"Roomie," said Campanella, "don't quit on us now."

In the top of the eighth the Dodgers punched over three runs to fatten their lead to 4–1. Newcombe set down the Giants one-two-three in the eighth, but in the bottom of the ninth, holding a three-run lead, weariness caught up with him. He yielded singles to Alvin Dark and Don Mueller. Then, after retiring Irvin on a foul caught by Gil Hodges, Brooklyn's workhorse pitcher was touched for a double by Whitey Lockman, making the score 4–2, with runners at second and third and one out.

Earlier Dressen had called the Dodgers' bullpen, asking coach Clyde Sukeforth for an evaluation of Ralph Branca and Carl Erskine, who were warming up for possible relief duty. Branca had been loosening up his arm since the fifth inning.

"Branca's popping the ball," Sukeforth reported. "Erskine's not at his best." Erskine had thrown one of his curveballs in the dirt. Branca had pitched just two days earlier, but he was now firing glove-smacking fastballs.

"Give me Branca," Dressen ordered.

So Branca, wearing number 13 on the back of his uniform, was summoned to relieve Newcombe and face Thomson, a

Brooklyn manager Charlie Dressen (right) went to right-hander Ralph Branca in the crucial ninth inning. *(Wide World)*

Scottish-born resident of Staten Island who, according to Dark, was "our best run-production hitter over the last two and a half to three months" of the season.

Shortly before the pitching change, an announcement came over the speaker in the Polo Grounds press box: "Attention, press. World Series credentials for Ebbets Field can be picked up at six o'clock at the Biltmore Hotel."

When Branca reached the mound, Dressen gave his pitcher just three words of advice on how to handle Thomson. "Get him out," the manager said, and walked back to the dugout.

As Thomson waited for Branca to finish his warm-up throws, Durocher said to him, "If you ever hit one, hit one now."

"Before I got in the batter's box, all I thought about was hitting the ball," Thomson later recalled. "I got mad at myself. I said to myself, 'Get in there, you so-and-so, and bear down. Watch for the ball. Wait for it. Don't swing at a bad pitch.' I guess my anger was a way of disciplining my anxiety, forcing me to concentrate on the pitch, making me be selective."

In the radio booth upstairs, Russ Hodges began his now-famous eyewitness account: "Bobby Thomson up there swinging. He's had two out of three, a single and a double, and Billy Cox is playing him right on the third-base line. One out, last of the ninth, Branca pitches. Bobby Thomson takes a strike call on the inside corner! Bobby hitting .292. He drove in the Giants' first run with a long fly to center. Brooklyn leads it, 4 to 2. [Clint] Hartung down the line at third, not taking any chances. Lockman without too big a lead at second, but he'll be running like the wind if Thomson hits one.

"Branca throws. There's a long drive! It's going to be . . . I believe! The Giants win the pennant! The Giants win the pennant! The Giants win the pennant! The Giants win the pennant! Bobby Thomson hits into the lower deck of the left-field stands!

"The Giants win the pennant! And they're going crazy! Oh-ho! I don't believe it! I don't believe it! I do not believe Bobby Thomson hit a line drive into the lower deck of the left-field stands, and this whole place is going crazy. The Giants won it 5 to 4, and they're picking Bobby Thomson up and carrying him off the field!"

"When Thomson came to the plate," Andy Pafko recalled, "I was playing straightaway in left field. In the Polo Grounds you more or less had to play straightaway because you had to protect that big gap between you and center field. And besides, I knew Bobby was more of a straightaway hitter because I had played against him for a number of years.

"But you had to be careful playing left or right field at the Polo Grounds because the angle of the walls caused balls to be deflected in odd ways. If the ball hit off the wall and you didn't play it properly, it'd get by you for a double or triple.

"I was thinking ahead, figuring what I would do if he hit in my direction. He represented the winning run. Would I throw

Branca heads for the clubhouse in despair as Jackie Robinson
watches to see that Bobby Thomson touches home plate.

to second to keep him from getting into scoring position, or
would I have a chance with a strong throw to the cutoff man
to keep the tying run [Whitey Lockman] from reaching home?

"After Branca's first pitch, Thomson hit the next one, a line
drive. I thought the ball might be sinking when it came my
way, but it just took off and sailed over my head and landed
in the fifth or sixth row. And of course the game was over.

"So I became part of a trivia question: 'Who was playing
left field when Thomson hit his homer off Branca?' Even after
all these years, I still say that when I looked up and saw that
ball go over my head, it was the biggest disappointment of my
life.

"My heart just sank," Pafko said. "I just could not believe

what happened. We had this 4–1 lead, and the whole ball game blew up in front of me, right there.

"I had been thinking, well, tomorrow we're going out to Yankee Stadium for the opener of the World Series. Here we had gone into the ninth inning with a three-run lead. I mean, everything was on our side. But like they say, the game isn't over until the last man is out.

"I just started heading for the clubhouse out there in center field. I don't even remember looking at them mobbing Thomson at home plate. By the time I got to the clubhouse steps, all of us outfielders were there together—Snider, Furillo, and myself. We followed each other up the steps to the clubhouse, and I still couldn't believe what had just happened.

"All bedlam broke loose because the Giants had won the pennant. We were the first ones in the clubhouse, and all the photographers and newspaper guys were there, expecting us to be the winners. As we started taking our gear down, the photographers were leaving, going to the Giants' side. We could hear the noise in the Giants' clubhouse next door. They were banging on the walls to remind us, I suppose, that they had won.

"In the meantime I looked out in center field and the playing field was full of people. They were all cheering for Bobby Thomson, Bobby Thomson. It just kept ringing in our ears. Bobby could have run for mayor or had anything he wanted at that moment because he was the hero."

In the Dodgers' clubhouse "everybody was subdued, in disbelief," Pafko recalled. "We all went by Ralph's locker, patted him on the back, and tried to console him. He just stood there, didn't move a muscle. I felt sorry for Ralph. I never saw him so dejected. He thought he had lost the pennant. But we told him, 'You didn't lose it, Ralph. We lost it, we lost it as a team.'

"We had a lot of chances to win the pennant during the summer. We had a 13-1/2 game lead, but we blew it. With a short time to go we played .500 baseball. Under normal conditions we still could have won it, but the Giants got awfully hot. They'd win three out of four, three out of three, and that's why it went down to the last day of the season when we had to beat the Phillies just to get into the playoffs."

Branca was inconsolable after the loss. Sal Maglie later told him he should have thrown a curve. *(Barney Stein)*

After Thomson dashed the Dodgers' hopes of going to the World Series, Pafko returned to the Hotel St. George in Brooklyn and phoned his wife, Ellen, in Chicago.

"She was ready to catch a train to come to New York for the Series," he said. "A cab had been waiting in front of our house in Chicago to take her to the train station. She had been

watching the game on TV, and the cab driver was blowing the
horn. So she went outside and told the driver, 'I'm watching
that playoff game in New York. Give me a few more minutes,
the game will be over soon.' She gets back into the house, the
TV is blaring, Bobby Thomson hits the 'shot heard 'round the
world,' and she knew she wouldn't be going to New York.

"So my wife goes out to the cab and tells the driver, 'Well,
you can be on your way. The Giants won the pennant.' She
gave him a few bucks for a tip and away he went. Instead of
her coming to New York to see the Yankees and Dodgers play,
I was coming back to Chicago by plane."

Not considering himself, Pafko insisted that the Dodgers,
man for man, were a better team than the Giants. "Campanella,"
he said, "was one of the best defensive catchers in all of baseball. You can name any of the good ones of the past, like Bill
Dickey or Birdie Tebbetts. Campy was right up there with them.
He was a power hitter. Pitchers liked to throw to him because
he knew the game. That year he hit around .325 and had 33
homers. You know, he missed the last two games of the '51
playoffs because he had pulled a leg muscle in the first game.

"At first base we had Hodges, one of the finest defensive
players I ever saw at that position. You find a lot of left-
handers at first. Gil was right-handed, but he adapted beautifully. He had a great pair of hands. He was a pull hitter. He
hit the long ball and drove in a lot of runs for us. He was quiet,
but every once in a while he'd show his temper.

"Jackie Robinson at second base—what can I say about
Jackie Robinson that hasn't already been said? He had speed.
He could upset the pitcher when he was on base. I'll never forget a game when I was with the Cubs, he stole second, third,
and home on three pitches. He produced one run all by himself. I don't know whether Curt Flood or Rickey Henderson ever
did that, but it was something to see. Jackie did so many things
to win games.

"Over at shortstop we had Pee Wee Reese, another great defensive guy. He knew the game, he was our captain. He positioned our players a lot. He was a good hit-and-run man. Just
an intelligent ball player. He would've made a good manager,
but he didn't want to manage.

"Billy Cox was just an average hitter, but he was one of the finest defensive third basemen of that time. As far as fielding is concerned, I'd rank him with Brooks Robinson. He was quick with his glove and just outstanding with his throws.

"In right field we had Furillo, who was a magician out there. Ebbets Field was tricky in right field because of the wall, but he knew how to play the angles, and runners didn't take risks against him. The wall was 30 feet high with a 28-foot screen above it. And there was a scoreboard in right center with a clock on top of it. It wasn't easy to play right because the ball would bounce off those things in crazy ways. But Furillo mastered the caroms. He was called the 'Reading Rifle' because he had such a great arm. He got that nickname when he played for Reading [Pennsylvania] in the Eastern League. There was a game I remember when he caught the ball on one hop in right field and threw out the runner before he reached first base. They say he did that at Reading six times.

"In center field there was Duke Snider, who gave us great power from the left side of the plate. He was the only left-handed hitter in our regular lineup that year. He was coming into his own, and I think there were five straight years later on that he hit 40 or more home runs, which was something in those days. He was one of the greatest outfielders of our time, a Hall of Famer, even though he was overshadowed by Mays and Mantle.

"And, of course, I played left field." In seventeen seasons from 1943 through 1959, Pafko played on four pennant-winning teams—the Cubs in 1945, the Dodgers in 1952, and the Milwaukee Braves in 1957 and 1958. He was on four National League All-Star teams, finished with a career batting average of .285, and has long been regarded as one of the best center fielders ever to wear a Cub uniform. He also had good bat control; in 1950, when he hit 36 home runs, he struck out only 32 times. In fact he never struck out more than 50 times in a season during his entire career.

While the Dodgers were set in center field with Snider early in the 1951 season, they traded for Pafko because they knew he was versatile enough to make the adjustment to left field. "I had played a little left field in the minors," he said, "but when I was coming up through the Cubs' farm system, I was strictly a center fielder. In my opinion, center field is the easiest outfield position to play because you're directly behind the pitcher and you can get a better break, left or right, on the ball. In left or right you have to wait to see if the ball is being hooked or sliced.

"But I adapted. It wasn't much of a transition for me when I was with the Dodgers."

What about the rivalry between Dressen and Durocher during the '51 season?

"They were both great baseball people," Pafko said with a knowing laugh. "They tried to outsmart, outthink each other. Leo had that crazy disposition. He was kind of a wild guy. I don't think he had too many friends in baseball. If you were on his side you admired the guy, but if you played against him it was different.

"I'll never forget my first game when I came up with the Cubs, and it was against the Dodgers. Leo was managing the Dodgers then. I was up to the plate for the first time, and Durocher is on the top step of the Dodgers' dugout, yelling, 'Ah, you busher, you'll be back in the minor leagues next year!' I got a couple of hits, and that quieted him down. He didn't say much after that."

Pafko recalls, "I once asked Bobby Thomson, 'How did it feel to hit that home run?' He said, 'Andy, that's history.' He didn't even want to talk about it. He was so humble. You'd think some players would gloat about that forever. It would go to their heads. That wasn't the case with Bobby."

Did that playoff heartbreaker darken Pafko's normally cheerful demeanor for long? "No," Pafko answered, "I managed to shake it off, but I think it was the beginning of the end for Ralph Branca. He was never the same after that. I could sense it hurt him emotionally. Maybe I'm wrong. Ralph was a great pitcher. He had good stuff. He just got one pitch in the wrong spot. We didn't want him to take it as a personal loss. As I said, it was a team loss, even though it's still hard to believe we got beat."

At the time of his crushing defeat, Branca was 25 years old, completing his eighth season with the Dodgers. He had won

76 games for Brooklyn from 1945 through 1951, but by 1956, when his playing career ended, he had gained only 12 more victories—four for the Dodgers, seven for the Tigers, and one for the Yankees.

Although Pafko didn't mention it, Branca broke down in the Dodgers clubhouse after the playoff game. He buried his head in his arms as he stretched himself face down on the stairs between the two levels of the dressing room. He then sat on the stairs for some time with his head bowed in misery.

One writer tried to talk to him, but he said, "Just leave me alone, just leave me alone."

Later Branca went to dinner with his fiancée, joined by his catcher that day, Rube Walker, and his wife. "We didn't talk about the game at all," Walker said. "But we were sure thinking about it. Heartbreak is the right word to describe how we felt. It hurt."

In one account after the game, Branca told of his reactions after Thomson hit the ball. "I thought it was just a long fly at first," he said. "I thought it would be the second out and that one run would score. But then I saw he had pulled the ball more than I thought he had. I knew then that it was going to hit the fence and the score would be tied. But I was praying it wouldn't go in.

"And right up to the last second, I didn't think it would. I can still see Pafko right up against the wall and hear myself saying, 'Sink, sink, don't go over.'

"But it did, and all I could do was stick my glove in my pocket and head for the clubhouse." As he made his long walk across the field, Branca wished there were a large hole in the ground that would swallow him up.

Long after the game had been logged into the record books, Sal Maglie met Branca and asked him about his strategy in pitching to Thomson. "I wanted to get ahead of him, throw a strike," Branca said.

"You did get ahead of him," Maglie reminded him. "Then what?"

"I wanted to get him with a curve, so I threw the second fastball to set up the curve," answered Branca.

"If you wanted to get him with a curve in a spot like that," reasoned Maglie, "you should've thrown the curve. What were you waiting for?"

While Branca didn't take kindly to such cutting observations, he eventually learned to live with the stigma of losing the deciding playoff game.

In the clubhouse after the game, he kept saying "Why me? Why me?"

"When I left the ball park," he said later, "I knew I had done the best I could do. I went home and forgot. It's amazing, though, that other people didn't forget.

"I'd be walking down the streets in New York, and little kids would ask me if I was the guy who served up the big pitch. That didn't bother me. It was the season after that got me."

Before the 1952 pennant race Branca had slipped off a chair and injured his pelvis. He won only four games that year but didn't realize the extent of his injury until after the season.

"I didn't want to let on, I didn't want people to think that I was hurt by the home run," he admitted. "I used to stand in the shower for hours, rubbing my arm, not knowing that I needed serious treatment. The trainer, needless to say, did me no good.

"What most people don't remember about me," he said, "is that I taught myself to pitch. I won 21 games when I was 21 years old. At that time there were only six pitchers who had won 21 games at age 21: Lefty Gomez, Bob Feller, Wes Ferrell, Babe Ruth, Christy Mathewson, and me.

"If it hadn't been for that homer," he added wryly, "who would remember Ralph Branca?"

Critics have questioned Charlie Dressen's strategy in the historic playoff game. Why didn't the Dodger manager order Branca to walk Thomson, who had been swinging a hot bat, and take his chances against Willie Mays, the on-deck hitter? Mays had collected only four hits, all singles, in 22 at-bats for a .182 average in the three games against Brooklyn pitching. He might have been vulnerable as a rookie in a high-pressure situation, long before he became one of the greatest hitters in baseball history. Mays later admitted that he was happy he didn't have to bat when the entire season was on the line.

But Dressen discarded any thought of intentionally walking Thomson, who had hit a home run against Branca in the first game of the playoff series. The tying runs were already in scoring position. Why put the winning run on base—also filling the bases and forcing Branca to throw strikes?

The critics also wondered why Dressen chose Branca as his ninth-inning reliever. "I asked myself that question all winter," Dressen said six months later, "and I say, what else could I do? It had to be Branca.

"I had Labine in the bullpen, but I had in mind I might pitch him just to one hitter. If Branca walked Thomson or looked like he didn't have anything, I might've brought Labine in to throw curves to Willie Mays.

"But I hoped I wouldn't have to use Labine. He pitched the day before, and some of those curveballers, their arms tighten up and they can't pitch the next day."

Labine had joined the Dodgers late in the season, winning five crucial games while losing only one. "I didn't have Labine long enough to know if he was that way," said Dressen, "but I didn't want to take the chance.

"Peacher Roe couldn't do it. He pitched two days before. Only two innings, but for him pitching two innings is like pitching nine. He has to have rest after it. The morning of the last game, I asked him if he could relieve for me and he said, 'Charlie, if I had one more day . . .' He wasn't ready.

"Clyde King would've been my guy if he'd been right. But his arm was bad the last five weeks.

"When I called the bullpen and asked about Erskine, Sukeforth said, 'Erskine's ball is bouncing, but Branca's really got a fast one.' That was good enough for me.

"When Branca threw his first pitch to Thomson, I knew Sukey was right. I only wish Thomson would've swung at the first one. It had so much on it, he couldn't have done much with it. I think he wanted to swing, but he saw he couldn't get around on it.

"If I could've done anything different, I would've done it right there, after that first pitch. I'd have gone out to Branca and told him, 'That's it. Just fire it like that. Fire the ball.' But I didn't go out, and I think what happened was Ralph got wor-

Brooklyn Dodgers vs. New York Giants
at Polo Grounds, October 3, 1951

Brooklyn Dodgers	AB	R	H	RBI	New York Giants	AB	R	H	RBI
Carl Furillo, rf	5	0	0	0	Eddie Stanky, 2b	4	0	0	0
Pee Wee Reese, ss	4	2	1	0	Alvin Dark, ss	4	1	1	0
Duke Snider, cf	3	1	2	0	Don Mueller, rf	4	0	1	0
Jackie Robinson, 2b	2	1	1	1	Clint Hartung, pr (c)	0	1	0	0
Andy Pafko, lf	4	0	1	1	Monte Irvin, lf	4	1	1	0
Gil Hodges, 1b	4	0	0	0	Whitey Lockman, 1b	3	1	2	1
Billy Cox, 3b	4	0	2	1	Bobby Thomson, 3b	4	1	3	4
Rube Walker, c	4	0	1	0	Willie Mays, cf	3	0	0	0
Don Newcombe, p	4	0	0	0	Wes Westrum, c	0	0	0	0
Ralph Branca, p	0	0	0	0	Bill Rigney, ph (a)	1	0	0	0
					Ray Noble, c	0	0	0	0
					Sal Maglie, p	2	0	0	0
					Hank Thompson, ph (b)	1	0	0	0
					Larry Jansen, p	0	0	0	0
Total	**34**	**4**	**8**	**3**		**30**	**5**	**8**	**5**

(a) Struck out for Westrum in eighth; (b) Grounded out for Maglie in eighth; (c) Ran for Mueller in ninth

Brooklyn	1	0	0	0	0	0	0	3	0	—	4
New York	0	0	0	0	0	0	1	0	4	—	5

Brooklyn Dodgers	IP	H	R	ER	SO	BB
Don Newcombe	8.1	7	4	4	2	2
Ralph Branca (L)	0.0	1	1	1	0	0

New York Giants	IP	H	R	ER	SO	BB
Sal Maglie	8.0	8	4	4	6	4
Larry Jansen (W)	1.0	0	0	0	0	0

Errors—None. 2B—Thomson, Irvin, Lockman. HR—Thomson. Sac—Lockman.
DP—Brooklyn 2. LOB—Brooklyn 7, New York 3. Wild pitch—Maglie.
Umpires—Lou Jorda, Jocko Conlan, Bill Stewart, Larry Goetz.
Time—2:28. Attendance—34,320

ried because the first one was low when he was trying to make it high.

"Maybe he said to himself, 'Jeez, I made a mistake. I got that one in his alley.' So now he's going to make sure the next one is high inside, and he's trying so hard he ends up aiming the ball.

"I've seen Branca do that for years. He'll fire and fire, and then suddenly he starts aiming, and the ball has nothing on it.

"He got that second pitch where he wanted it, but there was nothing on it. I think it was because he aimed it."

Dressen paused and then said, "Come to think of it, there's one other thing I might've done different. Walk Thomson? No. Maybe it would've worked, but it's still the wrong play with a guy like Mays coming up.

"No, what I'd have done was let Roy Campanella hit for Walker in the eighth, and then keep Campy in to catch Don Newcombe, for psychology. Newcombe wanted to get out in the seventh inning, but Jackie Robinson made him stay in. I figure with Robinson and Campanella both working on him, the way they keep after him, Newcombe might've never got in trouble in the ninth.

"That was the big thought I had in mind. But Campanella couldn't run with his bad leg. So if a foul ball goes up and he limps and can't get it, the second-guessers would criticize me. That's why I didn't put him in.

"Then, I stayed with Newcombe as long as I could. But after Whitey Lockman hit the double, I asked Newcombe what the pitch was, and he said low and outside. If Newcombe has his stuff, Lockman won't hit that pitch for a double, so I had to take him out. No sane man would've left him in there after that."

While memories of the 1951 playoff game have dimmed with the passing of time, a happy note can be appended to the aftermath of the Dodgers' wrenching loss. Ralph Branca and Bobby Thomson became good friends and remained so long after that ball sailed over Andy Pafko's head near the 315-foot marker in a ball park once located beneath Coogan's Bluff. They appeared together at various speaking engagements and baseball card shows, manifesting warm respect for each other.

Be that as it may, a last piece of irony should be included in a wrap-up of the playoff game. Yankee catcher Yogi Berra was among the 34,320 spectators at the game, but he decided to leave the Polo Grounds before the Giants launched their ninth-inning rally. He wanted to beat the rush of fans out of the park. He never saw Thomson hit his homer. Perhaps that's why, as he gained in age and wisdom, he had good reason to coin the phrase, "It ain't over 'til it's over."

1960

The Yankees Walk the Plank in Pittsburgh

"After the last game, Mickey and me, we both cried like babies."—Bill "Moose" Skowron

In January 1960, John F. Kennedy, not yet 43, tossed his hat in the ring of presidential hopefuls, and thus began the "Age of Aquarius." Late in February that year, an iron ball was swung into action to begin the demolition of Ebbets Field, home of the Brooklyn Dodgers from 1913 through 1957. Wrecking crews were preparing the site for a housing project.

In baseball it was a year in which Willie Mays became the highest-paid player in the National League at $85,000. Mickey Mantle agreed to a contract for $65,000 while his pitching teammate Whitey Ford was happy to sign for $35,000. Stan Musial actually took a cut of $20,000 from the $100,000 he had received from the Cardinals in 1959.

White Sox owner Bill Veeck, a resolute believer in all sorts of merriment, unveiled an exploding scoreboard at Comiskey Park. It cost $300,000 and disturbed local residents as well as opposing players. When a Sox player hit a home run, the scoreboard would belch forth with loud music and noises, and erupt in a display of fireworks. When a player on an opposing team slammed a homer, the scoreboard remained silent.

Jimmy Piersall hated the scoreboard and its uncouth emanations, and once threw a baseball at it, a defiance that incensed Veeck. During a night game against the Yankees on June

17, after Clete Boyer hit a home run for the Yankees early in the game, manager Casey Stengel and a number of his players in the dugout lit sparklers and waved them derisively over their heads in view of Comiskey Park fans. They went through the same maneuver when Mickey Mantle unloaded a homer in the fifth inning.

Ted Williams ended the 1960 season and his magnificent career on September 28 by hitting his 521st and final home run in his last at-bat at Fenway Park in a game against the Orioles. He declined to tip his cap to the cheering Red Sox fans after he crossed home plate. "I thought about tipping my cap," Williams said, "but by the time I got to second base, I knew I couldn't do it. It just wouldn't have been me."

Despite Williams's dramatic exit, the biggest baseball story of the year was brewing in Pittsburgh where the Pirates were chasing their first pennant since 1927 and where "Beat 'em Bucs" signs popped up all over the city.

That story had its beginning in January when Casey Stengel predicted that the Yankees would win the American League pennant. In 1959 the Yankees had finished a distant third, 15 games behind the front-running White Sox. Speaking at a charity dinner in Manchester, New Hampshire, Stengel vowed, "The Yankees will bounce back bigger than ever and will win the pennant this coming season." In his inimitable style, Stengel explained, "Not until Christmas did most of my men realize they didn't win the pennant. They realized it at the time because they were reminded by their wives there were no new Cadillacs, fur coats, or deep freezers at Christmas."

With age sneaking up on him, Stengel drove his players hard during the 1960 season, his last at the Yankee helm. On July 30 he turned 71 and uttered his immortal line, "Most people my age are dead at the present time."

His club had plenty of long-ball power that year with the addition of Roger Maris, acquired from the Kansas City A's in a seven-player winter trade. By season's end Maris had delivered 39 homers, Mickey Mantle 40, and Bill Skowron 26. The Yankees scored the most runs, 746, and produced the most homers, 193, in the American League.

Yet during the pennant race Casey was critical of some of

his players in public. In turn, they felt that his long years of managing and his hard drinking were taking a toll on "the old man," and they occasionally talked back to him or muttered disparaging remarks about him when he was out of earshot.

Still, behind a pitching staff that included no starter with more than 15 victories and the established leader Whitey Ford with only a dozen wins, the Yankees breezed home to the pennant. They finished eight games ahead of the second-place Orioles and ten in front of the '59 champion White Sox.

At the start of the season George Weiss, the club's hard-headed general manager, entertained numerous doubts: Would first baseman Bill Skowron fully recover from the broken wrist he suffered in 1959? Would Mantle's tender right knee reduce his playing time? Would Whitey Ford and Bob Turley overcome arm injuries? Would Tony Kubek be better off playing short-stop or the outfield? And would catcher Yogi Berra, at 35, be able to play a full schedule behind the plate, or was it time to give the regular catching job to Elston Howard?

By mid-September all those questions had become irrelevant. Stengel was on his way to his tenth World Series, and Weiss, who hated to lose as much as anyone, could take satisfaction in helping shape a winning team from the club that had disappointed him so much the year before.

Although the Pirates of 1960 could scarcely be considered a super team, they were tenacious, winning 23 games in their last at-bats. In capturing the pennant they finished a comfortable seven lengths ahead of the second-place Milwaukee Braves. Yet by the end of the season they had scored more runs, 734, than any other team in the National League, hit the most doubles, 236, and completed the most double plays, 163. The last statistic was due primarily to the slick glove work of their middle infielders, shortstop Dick Groat and second baseman Bill Mazeroski. As the pivot man on the double play, Mazeroski was so quick in catching the ball from Groat and relaying it to first, it seemed the ball barely touched his glove.

While Groat and Mazeroski were solid on defense, the Pirates also had two outstanding outfielders in Bill Virdon in center and Roberto Clemente in right. Clemente was 26 and coming into his own as one of the game's brightest young stars. He had a tremendous arm and in 1960 collected 19 assists, the most credited to any right fielder in the league.

Don Hoak, a battler who constantly tried to rouse his teammates when they were losing, nonetheless committed more errors, 25, than any other third baseman in the league. First base too was a troublesome spot for manager Danny Murtaugh, who relied basically on Dick Stuart but also used Rocky Nelson as a backup. Stuart could hit a long ball and unloaded the most homers, 23, during the club's pennant run. But as a fielder he was less than adequate, eventually earning the nickname "Dr. Strangeglove." He also was a free spirit.

Once, Murtaugh became angered over Stuart's failure to follow orders when he was at bat. After the game Murtaugh confronted Stuart and lambasted his first baseman. "Remember, Stuart," Murtaugh said, "I'm the manager, and you're nothin'! You got it? I'm the manager and you're nothin'!"

As Stuart was leaving the room, Murtaugh asked, "Did you get the message?"

Stuart turned and responded, "Yeah, you're the manager of nothin'."

Murtaugh was the manager of much more than that in 1960. He boasted several strong pitchers, including Vernon Law (20–9), Bob Friend (18–12), Vinegar Bend Mizell (13–5), and a superb reliever in ElRoy Face who piled up 24 saves. He also directed a team that never quit, that always seemed to get the run it needed to win close games. It was, in retrospect, a team of destiny. And its rendezvous with destiny materialized on a bright, sunny day in Pittsburgh on October 13 in game seven of the World Series against the Yankees.

Going into the Series the Yankees were heavily favored over the Pirates. They had won the American League pennant with a 97–57 record, eight games in front of the second-place Baltimore Orioles. They had a deep bench, including such players as Gil McDougald, John Blanchard, Hector Lopez, and Bob Cerv, along with an impressive bullpen featuring Bobby Shantz, Luis Arroyo, and Ryne Duren, who together accounted for 13 victories and 27 saves. Their infield of Clete Boyer at third, Tony Kubek at short, Bobby Richardson at second, and Bill Skowron at first helped the pitchers with steady defensive work.

Elston Howard, the first black player ever signed by the Yankees, was gradually assuming regular catching duties, allowing Yogi Berra to play left field and spend less time in the grueling work behind the plate. And there were the special hitting and defensive talents of center fielder Mickey Mantle and right fielder Roger Maris.

With the Series opening in Pittsburgh, it was assumed that Stengel would give the starting assignment to Whitey Ford, his "money" pitcher. But Casey decided to hold Ford back until the Series returned to New York for game three. One former Yankee thinks George Weiss influenced Stengel to make that decision so that Ford could pitch the Yankee Stadium opener and assure a sellout crowd of seventy thousand or more. "If that wasn't the case," said the former player, "maybe Casey was overconfident." Whatever the reason, the decision prevented Stengel from pitching Ford in a seventh game if necessary. It proved to be a costly miscalculation.

The Series seesawed back and forth, with the Yankees pounding Pittsburgh pitching in winning three games, 16–3, 10–0, and 12–0, while the Pirates eked out their three victories by scores of 6–4, 3–2, and 5–2.

It came down to game seven, with Bob Turley starting for the Yankees and Vernon Law for the Pirates. In the eighth inning, with both starters long gone, the Yankees took a commanding 7–4 lead. In the bottom of the eighth, however, Pittsburgh staged one of its typical rallies. With Bobby Shantz, the third Yankee pitcher on the mound, pinch-hitter Gino Cimoli delivered a single to right center. Bill Virdon also singled on a bad-hop ball that struck Kubek in the throat. Dick Groat then singled past third, scoring Cimoli with Virdon stopping at second.

At that point Stengel waved in his fourth pitcher, Jim Coates, who retired Bob Skinner on a sacrifice that moved both runners up a base. Coates retired Rocky Nelson on a fly to right but yielded a single to Clemente on a slow chopper to first, scoring Virdon and leaving the Pirates only one run down 7–6. Up stepped Hal Smith who slammed a three-run homer over the left-field wall to put Pittsburgh in front 9–7.

That was enough for Stengel, who summoned his fifth

pitcher, Ralph Terry, from the bullpen. Terry ended the inning by retiring Don Hoak on a fly to left.

Now the Pirates were only three outs from winning the World Series. But the Yankees weren't going down quietly. They tied the game, 9–9, with two runs in the ninth. Thus the stars were aligned in the baseball heavens for drama in Pittsburgh. More specifically, the alignment pitted leadoff hitter Bill Maze-roski against Ralph Terry in the bottom of the ninth inning.

"I was up and down in the bullpen five times during that game," said Terry. "I had almost thrown a full game in the bullpen. I got up when Turley got in trouble in the first inning. I got up when [Bill] Stafford got in trouble. And then I got up for Shantz and again for Coates. By the time they called me in, I had nothing left. I couldn't blacken your eye if I hit you with a fastball."

Terry's second pitch to Mazeroski was a hard one, but he didn't get it down. Mazeroski belted it for the game-winning home run. "I thought the ball might hit the top of the fence in left," said Terry, "but it carried over."

As Mazeroski connected, the clock above the left-field score-board read 3:36 p.m. The line on the scoreboard read N.YORK 9, PITTS. 9, and told that the batter was number 9. As Maze-roski raced around the bases, waving his cap and being chased by delirious fans who rushed onto the field, the final score be-came 10–9.

"That Series," said Skowron, "was a heartbreaker, for us to lose to a team like that.

"After the last game, Mickey and me, we cried like babies.

"Mazeroski was a fastball hitter. Terry never should've thrown him a fastball. He was better throwing sinkers and curveballs. They got more dingers, I mean bleeders, than any-body. Don Hoak. Gino Cimoli.

"The guy we worried about in the Series was Bob Friend. We figured he was the pitcher who was going to stop us. He and Law were their big winners that year. As it turned out, we knocked Friend out after he pitched only four innings in the second game, and in the sixth game he lasted only a couple of innings."

Whitey Ford shut out the Pirates twice, 10–0 in game three

Bill Mazeroski, mobbed at home plate after hitting the Series-winning home run against the Yankees. *(UPI)*

in New York and 12–0 in game six in Pittsburgh. His second victory was his seventh in World Series competition but his first away from Yankee Stadium.

Why didn't Ford start game one in Forbes Field, and then be available, if needed, for game seven?

"He should've pitched the first game," Skowron said. "That was a mistake we made. I have no idea who made that decision, but he should've started the first game."

Skowron began leafing through a Yankee encyclopedia, soaking up the 1960 World Series numbers. "When you look at the stats," he said, "the Yankees won games two, three, and six by overwhelming scores. We set World Series records with the highest batting average, .338; most runs scored, 55; most RBIs, 54; most total bases, 142; most hits, 91, and most extra-base hits, 27. All right? Mickey Mantle, three home runs, 11 RBIs, hit .400. I hit .375. And Richardson had a good Series too.

"After the game Mr. [Joe L.] Brown comes next to me and taps me on the shoulder. I didn't know who the hell Mr. Brown was, but I found out later he was the Pirates' general manager, [movie actor] Joe E. Brown's son.

"I told him that was the worst team I ever played against in a World Series. I didn't give a damn. And when I went to the Dapper Dan dinner in Pittsburgh that winter, they booed the hell out of me. I didn't care. I told 'em the truth. I had nothing to hide. I had been through all that.

"Cimoli hit some dying quails out there. Dick Groat did too, but I'll tell you the guy who really gave us a hard time was their [relief] pitcher, ElRoy Face. He was tough."

When Mazeroski connected for his decisive home run, what was Skowron's reaction?

"I just saw $3,000 going over the fence," Skowron said. "Mazeroski hit the hell out of that ball. I looked at Yogi Berra's number 8 out there in left field, saw him look up, and knew it was over. The winners' share was $8,000 and the losers' share $5,000. So we're out $3,000 a man."

Mantle and Skowron had been on many championship teams. They were both proud, experienced professionals. Did their loss to the Pirates really shake them emotionally?

"Yeah," Skowron said. "We sat next to each other in the clubhouse. We both cried. We should've won that damn Series. We had a great club—Roger, Mickey, Yogi."

How was Casey Stengel's managing that year? Was he losing his managerial touch?

"He was sharp," Skowron said, "but he sent a letter of resignation before the Series. That was going to be his last year. When we lost he tried to retract and come back, but they wouldn't let him because Ralph Houk was in line to get the job. Casey wanted to redeem that loss in the Series.

"In the clubhouse afterward, Ralph Terry took it hard," Skowron said. "Kubek was in the trainer's room. He had ice on his throat before they took him to the hospital. But Terry, all of us, were in the dumps. That was the feeling we had. We beat the hell out of them and we lost the last game. But that happens in baseball, right?

"I went back to New Jersey, that's where I was living then.

Bill Skowron (left) and Mickey Mantle, shown here in 1960 with John Kuenster, both cried after losing the Series to Pittsburgh.

And, that was it. It was a bad time for me. That's when I was going through my problems. I was going through a divorce from my first wife."

Skowron talked about the Yankee pitching staff, especially Whitey Ford. "Whenever he pitched, we always felt the other team had to beat us," he said. "He was a real pro. If you made an error behind him, he'd say, 'Moose, get the next one.' Whitey always gave 100 percent. He wouldn't get pissed off if you made an error. Certain pitchers, if you made an error, they acted like the roof fell in."

The $3,000 that Skowron and other Yankees lost for not winning the Series wasn't exactly petty cash. "The most I ever made with the Yankees was thirty-seven grand," Skowron said, "but that was in 1962, my last year with them. In 1960 I was making about twenty-something thousand. Yogi wasn't making much either."

Up two games to one, the Yankees could have virtually put the Pirates away had they won game four on their home field. But they didn't, losing to Vernon Law, 3–2, despite Skowron's home run and double that resulted in both New York scores.

"I hit two home runs in that Series," Skowron said, "both

to right field, one in New York in game four and one in Pittsburgh in game seven, and both off Law." A right-handed batter, Skowron was noted for hitting with power to the opposite
field. "Ted Williams once told me that I was trying to pull the
ball too much. 'You should try to hit to the opposite field,' he
said. So in a game at Fenway I hit two home runs into the
bullpen in right center. Afterward Ted said, 'Don't tell any of
the Boston writers what I told you.'"

What about the critical eighth inning in game seven when
Pittsburgh, trailing 7–4, rallied with five runs to take a 9–7 lead
going into the ninth inning? "That was the turning point," said
Skowron. "The guy who beat us was Hal Smith, their catcher.
He was once in the Yankees' farm system. Maybe that gave him
some extra incentive. Jim Coates had two strikes on him and
he hits a three-run homer to give them the lead."

Skowron figured Smith never should have come to bat. "Before Smith's homer," he said, "there were a couple of plays that
changed the game. Cimoli led off for them in the bottom of
the eighth and got a single off Bobby Shantz. Then Bill Virdon
comes up and hits a double-play ball to Tony Kubek at short.
That damn infield at Forbes was hard as a rock. I remember
that because Virdon was my roommate when I was in the Pied-
mont League. The ball takes a bad hop and hits Kubek in the
throat, and he has to come out of the game.

"I was standing there when Kubek was sitting on the ground,
and he was trying to tell Casey he wanted to stay in the game
but no words came out of his mouth. His throat was so bruised,
he couldn't talk.

"Now, instead of two outs, they've got two men on base. The
next hitter, Groat, hits a single, scoring a run, and Stengel comes
out to the mound, takes out Shantz, and brings in Coates.

"Then we get a couple of outs, and Clemente comes up. He
hits the ball to me, and I made a helluva play on it and went
to throw the ball to Coates at first base, but he didn't come
over to cover first. If he had, that would've been the third out.
The inning would've been over. I tried to get to the base before Clemente, but he beat me. They scored a run on that play,
making it 7–6, so the table was set for Hal Smith."

Down 9–7 in the ninth inning, the Yankees managed to close

the gap to 9–8, and had pinch-runner Gil McDougald on third with the tying run and Mantle on first with one out.

"That's when we got our only break of the Series," Skowron said. "Yogi hit a shot to first where Rocky Nelson fielded the ball. Instead of throwing to second to start a double play that would've ended the game, he steps on first. That took the force off at second.

"Mickey was a few feet off first, and made a helluva move in getting back to the base before Nelson could tag him. If Nelson tags him, the game is over."

After Mazeroski crushed his dramatic homer, Terry and the rest of the Yankees quickly left the field.

"I was just trying to make good pitches," Terry said later about his short duel with Mazeroski. "The first pitch I threw was high, and [catcher John] Blanchard came out to the mound and told me to keep the ball down. I threw another hard slider, but it didn't come down, and Mazeroski hit it good. I didn't think it was going to clear the fence."

Later, in the Yankee clubhouse, Terry expressed his regrets to Casey Stengel. "Casey," he said, "I really feel bad it ended this way."

Stengel asked Terry how he was trying to pitch to Mazeroski. The pitcher said he was trying to keep the ball down, low and away. "You're not always going to get the ball where you want to," Casey said. "If you went against the scouting reports and tried to throw him high fastballs, I wouldn't sleep good tonight. So forget it. Don't let it bother you."

But the loss did fester in the minds of players other than Skowron. "The Pirates never should have beaten us," said Roger Maris. "I think if we played them all season, we'd beat them real bad. They were real lucky."

Mantle had pretty much the same opinion. Years later he said, "That was the one time in my career I thought the better team had lost."

Bobby Richardson echoed similar sentiments. The little second baseman had driven in 12 runs for the Yankees and had been voted the Most Valuable Player in the World Series. "It was my biggest disappointment," he said about the defeat. "We felt like the best team had lost. That's because we had scored

New York Yankees vs. Pittsburgh Pirates at Forbes Field, October 13, 1960

New York Yankees	AB	R	H	RBI	Pittsburgh Pirates	AB	R	H	RBI
Bobby Richardson, 2b	5	2	2	0	Bill Virdon, cf	4	1	2	2
Tony Kubek, ss	3	1	0	0	Dick Groat, ss	4	1	1	1
Joe DeMaestri, ss	0	0	0	0	Bob Skinner, lf	2	1	0	0
Dale Long, ph (d)	1	0	1	0	Rocky Nelson, 1b	3	1	1	2
Gil McDougald, 3b (e)	0	1	0	0	Roberto Clemente, rf	4	1	1	1
Roger Maris, rf	5	0	0	0	Smoky Burgess, c	3	0	2	0
Mickey Mantle, cf	5	1	3	2	Joe Christopher, pr (b)	0	0	0	0
Yogi Berra, lf	4	2	1	4	Hal Smith, c	1	1	1	3
Bill Skowron, 1b	5	2	2	1	Don Hoak, 3b	3	1	0	0
Johnny Blanchard, c	4	0	1	1	Bill Mazeroski, 2b	4	2	2	1
Clete Boyer, 3b/ss	4	0	1	1	Vernon Law, p	2	0	0	0
Hector Lopez, ph (a)	1	0	1	0	Gino Cimoli, ph (c)	1	1	1	0
Bobby Shantz, p	3	0	1	0					
Total	**40**	**9**	**13**	**9**		**31**	**10**	**11**	**10**

(a) Singled for Bill Stafford in third; (b) Ran for Smoky Burgess in seventh; (c) Singled for ElRoy Face in eighth; (d) Singled for Joe DeMaestri in ninth; (e) Ran for Dale Long in ninth.

New York	0	0	0	0	1	4	0	2	2	—	9
Pittsburgh	2	2	0	0	0	0	1	5	1	—	10

New York Yankees	IP	H	R	ER	SO	BB
Bob Turley +	1.0	2	3	3	0	1
Bill Stafford	1.0	2	1	1	0	1
Bobby Shantz +++	5.0	4	3	3	0	1
Jim Coates	0.2	2	2	2	0	0
Ralph Terry (L) +++++	0.1	1	1	1	0	0

Pittsburgh Pirates	IP	H	R	ER	SO	BB
Vernon Law ++	5.0	4	3	3	0	1
ElRoy Face	3.0	6	4	4	0	1
Bob Friend ++++	0.0	2	2	2	0	0
Harvey Haddix (W)	1.0	1	0	0	0	0

+ Pitched to one batter in the second
++ Pitched to two batters in the sixth
+++ Pitched to three batters in the eighth
++++ Pitched to two batters in the ninth
+++++ Pitched to one batter in the ninth

Errors—Maris. **2B**—Boyer. **HR**—Berra, Mazeroski, Nelson, Skowron, Smith. **Sac.**—Skinner.
DP—New York 3. **LOB**—New York 6, Pittsburgh 1.
Umpires—Bill Jackowski, Nestor Chylak, Dusty Boggess, Johnny Stevens, Stan Landes, Jim Honochick.
Time—2:36. **Attendance**—36,683

so many runs. But we let some easy games slip by, and then all of a sudden the Series was tied."

Mazeroski was the number eight hitter in the Pirates' lineup. "When we trotted off the field for our turn at bat in the ninth," Mazeroski recalled, "I was thinking, 'I'd like to hit a home run and win it all.' The time before, in the seventh inning, I had gone for the long ball and I overswung. I grounded into a double play. So against Terry I kept saying to myself, 'Don't overswing. Just meet the ball.'

"I thought I'd be more nervous, but I wasn't a bit. I wanted a homer, but I didn't want to overswing. I was guessing all the way. As Terry wound up, I was saying to myself, 'Fastball! Fastball!' That's what I wanted. The first one was a high slider. The next one was down a little, but still high—a fastball right into my power.

"A moment after I hit that ball, a shiver ran down my back. We always felt we could pull it out—even after the Yankees tied it up in the ninth—but I didn't think I'd be the guy to do it."

As Mazeroski made his joyous run around the bases, fans in Forbes Field erupted as though they had each won a million dollars. Thirty-three years after losing the 1927 World Series to the Yankees in four games, and after finishing in last place six times during the 1950s, the Pirates had finally redeemed themselves.

In the Pirate clubhouse after the game, a teenager who had retrieved Mazeroski's home-run ball beyond the left-field fence brought the prized souvenir to him. Mazeroski signed the ball and then gave it to the boy. "Here," he said, "you keep it. The memory is good enough for me."

Away from the park, drivers leaned on their car horns and people snake-danced in the streets. In downtown Pittsburgh, fans stood atop streetcars and waved "Beat 'em Bucs" signs. The partying continued into the early hours of the next morning.

The Yankees headed for the airport for their trip back to New York. "I got on the plane with the rest of the guys," said Terry. "I wasn't a drinker, but I knocked down a few. I was in a daze for a couple of weeks. But losing to the Pirates gave me motivation. I was pissed off. I thought I had gotten a bad rap.

I knew I had good stuff and what I needed to do was work on my control. By spring training the next year, I had forgotten that game, but some writers wanted to know if I had suffered any trauma from getting beat in the big one. I said, 'No, why should I? It was my first World Series.'

"That year [1961] I missed part of the season with a sore shoulder. I was out from June 5 to July 21, but I still finished with a 16–3 record. And then the next year I won 23 games. I think I'm one of the few pitchers whose career took off after losing a big game like that one against the Pirates." In 1962, Terry won the final game of the World Series against the San Francisco Giants.

"After the Pirates game, when I went to see Casey Stengel in his office, I felt bad for him because we figured it was his last season with the Yankees," Terry recalled. "I was only 24 at the time. He could've hung a guilt trip on me, but he didn't. He was great. I loved that man."

Terry's thinking about Stengel's departure was correct. The Yankees announced the retirement of their manager two days after the close of the World Series. It was an awkward situation, and the irrepressible Stengel let it be known that he was not leaving of his free will. "I guess," he said, "this means they fired me."

He had won ten American League pennants and seven world championships with the Yankees, a record that stamped him as one of the game's all-time great managers. After a few seasons of guiding the newly formed and forlorn New York Mets, he ended his active career in baseball in 1965 at age 76. Many years later he admitted he had made a mistake in starting Art Ditmar instead of Whitey Ford in the first game of the 1960 World Series.

1962

A Line Drive Spells the End of the Giants

"If it had been a foot higher or two feet either left or right, I would've been a hero."—Willie McCovey

On September 30, 1962, James Meredith became the first black student to be admitted to the University of Mississippi, stirring up a hornet's nest of segregationists and causing President Kennedy to send U.S. troops into the area to force compliance with the law. On October 28, after a week of showdown diplomacy between Kennedy and Soviet Premier Nikita Khrushchev, the Cuban missile crisis ended. Khrushchev agreed to remove Soviet nuclear weapons from missile sites in Cuba.

That year Bob Feller, Jackie Robinson, and Edd Roush were elected to the baseball Hall of Fame in January. And as summer made way for fall, baseball fans turned their eyes to a torrid National League pennant race between the Los Angeles Dodgers and the San Francisco Giants.

The race went down to the last day of the season and ended in a tie, both the Dodgers and Giants finishing with identical 101–61 records, forcing a three-game playoff series that opened in Candlestick Park on October 1.

Managed by Walter Alston, the Dodgers featured an offense that centered on the base-stealing skills of Maury Wills and the clutch hitting of Tommy Davis. Wills finished the season with a record-setting 104 stolen bases while Davis led the league in hitting with a .346 mark and in RBI with 153.

Alston, as was customary during his tenure as Dodger manager, directed a strong pitching staff that included starters Don Drysdale, 25–9; Johnny Podres, 15–13; Stan Williams, 14–12; and Sandy Koufax, 14–7, along with relievers Ed Roebuck, 10–2, and Ron Perranoski, 6–6, who earned 20 saves and appeared in more games, 70, than any other major league bullpen specialist. Roebuck posted nine saves and made 64 appearances.

Stan Williams recalled, "Wills and Tommy Davis were our offense. Wills would walk or get an infield single, steal second, and keep going to third when the catcher threw the ball into center field. Then, after the next guy popped out. Davis would come through with a two-out RBI single. That's how it worked."

The Giants, on the other hand, had some big run-producers in their lineup, including center fielder Willie Mays, first baseman Orlando Cepeda, right fielder Felipe Alou, and backup outfielder/first baseman Willie McCovey. Mays hit 49 home runs in 1962; Cepeda, 35; Alou, 25; and McCovey, 20. That year the Giants out-homered the Dodgers 204 to 143, but in addition to this power advantage, manager Alvin Dark, like Alston, also had at his disposal a proficient pitching staff, including starters Jack Sanford, Billy O'Dell, Juan Marichal, and Billy Pierce.

A hard-throwing right-hander, Sanford struggled with his control at the start of the season and was 6–6 before he settled into a winning groove. He went 18–1 the rest of the way, including a club record of 16 straight victories. "I guess I got mad after that," he said of his slow start. "I don't just *throw* my fastball anymore. I have an idea of what I want to do with it, and I'm getting so I can do it. I could always throw hard, but I threw high."

To Dark's credit, Sanford played a crucial role in the Giant's pennant rush. Sanford had been National League Rookie of the Year in 1957, winning 19 games for the fifth-place Phillies. Yet Philadelphia management dealt him to the Giants in December 1958 for washed-up pitcher Ruben Gomez and a mediocre catcher, Valmy Thomas. In his first season with the Giants, Sanford was less than spectacular, and the club considered leaving him unprotected for the 1961 expansion draft. But Dark talked the front office out of it.

That move worked to the Giants' benefit, but other of Dark's actions generated controversy during his managerial stay in San Francisco from 1961 through 1964. On the plus side, he made a strong effort to bridge the cultural gaps among the team's white, black, and Latino players when he first came on the job, and to heal the club's factionalism. Dark attempted to break up cliques by mingling players of different ethnic backgrounds so that their lockers were next to each other in the clubhouse. He wanted the team to pull together.

On the negative side, he reaped criticism for his comments to a national magazine writer who allegedly twisted Dark's "off-the-record" remarks around so that it appeared the manager was prejudiced against black and Latin players. The article seriously damaged Dark's credibility, and he was let go by the Giants after the 1964 season, when the club finished in fourth place.

But 1962 was a year for him to remember. He was in charge of a splendid array of talent that included five future Hall of Famers: Willie Mays, Willie McCovey, Juan Marichal, and Orlando Cepeda, in addition to rookie pitcher Gaylord Perry.

Billy Pierce was a key member of the pitching staff, having been acquired by the Giants the previous November in a six-player trade with the White Sox. Pierce turned 35 that April and was on the down side of a long and successful career in the American League, where he was twice a 20-game winner. The Sox evidently felt their once highly prized left-hander was at the end of the line, but he wasn't. He had one more good season left in him.

"In spring training that year," he recalled, "I got absolutely nobody out. I had an earned run average of over 16! Finally, in the last game of spring training in Salt Lake City, I pitched in relief. I came in at the end of the game and got three guys out in a row. Al Dark says to me, 'You've found it. You're going to be my pitcher for the home opener in San Francisco.'

"As it turned out, I won my first eight decisions during the regular season. In fact I won 13 games in a row at Candlestick Park. I can't explain why. But the ball there carried to right field, so I pitched to right-handers inside and to left-handers outside, making all the batters hit the other way."

During his years with the White Sox, Pierce pitched for

Billy Pierce pitched the
ninth inning of the
deciding playoff game,
helping win the pennant
for San Francisco.

teams that sparkled on defense but were generally weak on offense. "I was helped," he said, "by having Mays, McCovey,
Cepeda, Harvey Kuenn, and Felipe Alou knocking in runs for
me, and having Jose Pagan at short, Jim Davenport at third,
and Mays in center catching everything. I was finally pitching
for a team that had a tremendous offense, but I didn't change
my style. I pitched with everything I had all the time, though
I knew I'd probably get more runs to work with than I'd had
with the White Sox. I didn't believe in pacing myself."

Billy O'Dell, at 29, was another veteran left-handed pitcher
who produced a stellar season for the Giants, his 19 victories
being the most he would ever post in the majors. He had been
dealt to San Francisco by the Orioles in November 1959. "We
had so many guys having great years," O'Dell said, "that it
looked like we were going to win it early in the season. Then
we fell far behind but came back to win it. In the last two
weeks of the season, I think I pitched in six games."

The Giants trailed the Dodgers by four games with seven to
play, but they caught the leaders on the final day of the season, beating Houston 2–1. O'Dell started the game and was relieved by Stu Miller, with Willie Mays hitting a home run in
the eighth inning to seal the victory. After the game, Giant play-

ers listened to the radio in their clubhouse as the Dodgers lost 1–0 to the Cardinals.

So the pennant race ended in a tie. In the opener of the playoff series, Billy Pierce shackled the Dodgers on three hits as the Giants won 8–0. Sandy Koufax, who had been winless since July 12 after suffering numbness in his pitching hand, absorbed the defeat, lasting less than two innings.

"Winning that game," Pierce said, "gave me the greatest satisfaction of my career to that point."

There would be another big moment for Pierce in game three, but in the meantime the Dodgers evened the series, winning the second game 8–7 in four hours and 18 minutes of tension-packed baseball on their home grounds in Los Angeles.

The teams returned to Dodger Stadium the next day to determine who would face the Yankees in the World Series. On the same date, October 3, 11 years earlier, another Dodger team had lost to the Giants in the final playoff game to decide the National League pennant winner and opponent of the Yankees in the World Series. Pessimistic Dodger fans could have pointed to that coincidence as a forewarning of what was to befall their team in 1962.

Juan Marichal and Johnny Podres were the starting pitchers. The Dodgers held a 4–2 lead going into the top of the ninth inning when Matty Alou led off for the Giants with a single. After a forceout, Dodger reliever Ed Roebuck walked pinch-hitter Willie McCovey and right fielder Felipe Alou, filling the bases. Willie Mays hit a line drive back at Roebuck that tore through the webbing on the pitcher's glove and landed behind the mound for an infield single, scoring a run and closing the gap to 4–3. Stan Williams then relieved Roebuck, yielding a sacrifice fly to Orlando Cepeda that tied the score, 4–4. Ed Bailey was given an intentional walk, loading the bases again, and Williams then walked Jim Davenport, putting the Giants ahead 5–4.

The Giants added another run on an error by second baseman Larry Burright on Jose Pagan's grounder, and held a 6–4 margin as the Dodgers came to bat in the bottom of the ninth inning.

Alvin Dark summoned Billy Pierce from the bullpen to close

out the game, though Pierce had pitched only two days earlier. "When the pennant is on the line," Pierce said, "it's a long walk from the bullpen to the mound. The main thing I didn't want to do was walk somebody. Walks had gotten the Dodger pitchers in trouble in the top of the inning.

"I'd be facing two switch-hitters, Maury Wills and Junior Gilliam, and their right-handed pinch-hitter Lee Walls. I threw sliders, down and in, to get both Wills and Gilliam to ground out, and then I got Walls to fly out to Mays to end the game.

"One, two, three—I got them out. That was my biggest thrill in baseball. We won the pennant, the place goes crazy. Everybody's jumping on each other. We get to the clubhouse, yelling and celebrating. There was champagne, reporters, and [Richard] Nixon came in to congratulate us."

Later Stan Williams talked about his duel with Jim Davenport when the score was tied and the bases loaded in the top of the ninth inning. "John Roseboro [Dodger catcher] asked me how we should pitch him, and I said low and away," Williams commented. "We started him low and away, and I missed with two pitches. They were close, but it was a 2-and-0 count. All of a sudden the realization hits me that there's no place to put him, so I suddenly felt the pressure. I threw a strike, and then threw two more balls and forced in the lead run. They weren't far off the plate, but they were balls. Davenport had a good eye."

Williams admittedly was tired when he failed to get the ball over the plate against Davenport, but he was able to shrug off his failure. "It didn't bother me that much," he said, "because I gave it all I had and it didn't work out. If I had let up and thrown him a half-assed fastball and he had gotten a base hit, I never would have forgiven myself. But I walked him, giving him my best shot. It was the best I could do."

Going into the playoffs, the Dodgers had been in a slump, losing six of their last seven games, and Sandy Koufax had not regained his effectiveness after suffering a strange numbness in his throwing hand in mid-July. The Giants, on the other hand, had won 16 of their last 19 games in a sensational race down the stretch.

While the playoffs did not offer a particularly dramatic ending, such as a game-winning home run, the loss still stung the Dodgers. Lee Walls, for one, confessed that he buried his woes in drinking in the days that followed.

It was an hour and a half or so before the Giants began clearing out of their clubhouse for the triumphant plane ride back to San Francisco, where thousands of fans flocked to the airport to greet them. Pierce remembers the scene vividly. "We couldn't land on the regular runway," he recalled. "So the plane taxied to the front of the United Airlines maintenance base where we got on a bus. The people were so excited, they almost turned the bus over, and they broke a couple of windows."

Pierce and his teammates had little time to regroup and savor their playoff victory. The Yankees were waiting for them, and the World Series opened the next day, October 4, at Candlestick Park. It turned out to be the longest World Series in history, stretching over 13 days when rainy weather caused one postponement in New York and three days of idleness in San Francisco. It was also the first Fall Classic requiring teams to travel from coast to coast to settle their differences. And it came down to a final scorching line drive in the bottom of the ninth inning of game seven.

The Yankees were pretty much the same club in 1962 as they had been in 1960 and 1961 when they won American League pennants. After they dismissed Casey Stengel as their manager at the end of the 1960 season, they replaced him with Ralph Houk, who had been with the organization as a third-string catcher, coach, and minor league manager. In World War II, Houk had earned the Silver Star during combat in Europe and had advanced to the rank of major before his discharge from the army. His leadership qualities made him a logical candidate to succeed Stengel, and in his first year as manager in 1961 the Yankees jelled into a powerhouse, winning 109 games and the first of three successive pennants under their tobacco-chewing manager.

Houk was not in Stengel's class as a storyteller, but he had a dry sense of humor and was not above playing tricks on unsuspecting writers. During conversations on the bench when an innocent reporter was sitting next to him, Houk would spit tobacco juice as close as possible to the writer's shoes without getting a direct hit. A splash off the dugout surface was good enough for Houk. It was a game "the major" liked to play, and it kept some writers ill at ease when talking with him.

In 1961 the Yankees finished eight games ahead of the second-place Detroit Tigers and swept the Cincinnati Reds in the World Series. The team produced 240 home runs, led by Roger Maris with 61; Mickey Mantle, 54; Bill Skowron, 28; Yogi Berra, 22; and John Blanchard and Elston Howard with 21 apiece. Whitey Ford had his greatest season ever, finishing with a league-leading 25–4 record which he compiled with the help of reliever Luis Arroyo, who had 29 saves.

Now, in 1962, Houk had brought his troops home in front again with virtually the same cast of high-level performers except for rookie Tom Tresh, who filled in at shortstop for Tony Kubek while Kubek was in the military. When Kubek returned to the team in August, Houk moved Tresh to left field, where he finished his season with 20 home runs, 93 RBI, and a .286 batting average.

Defensively the Yankee infield was solid, with Skowron at first, Bobby Richardson at second, Kubek at short, and Clete Boyer at third. Mantle and Richardson both won Gold Gloves for their defensive skills, and Elston Howard led all American League catchers in fielding.

The pitching staff helped the club waltz to its third straight pennant and second for Houk with a 96–66 record and a five-game margin over the second-place Minnesota Twins. The workhorse starters for the Yankees were Ralph Terry, 23–12; Ford, 18–8; and Bill Stafford, 14–9.

Before the World Series started in San Francisco, a reporter asked Willie Mays if he was as tense as he had been at the opening of the 1951 and 1954 Series in which he also played. "Man," responded Willie, "after that playoff in Los Angeles, I'm all out of tense."

The favored Yankees won the first game at Candlestick Park, 6–2, behind Whitey Ford. Then the Giants won games two, four, and six while the Yankees took games three, five, and seven.

In game two, Jack Sanford shut down the Yankees 2–0 on three hits as Ralph Terry absorbed the loss. One of the runs off Terry came on Willie McCovey's seventh-inning homer.

The Series moved to New York for game three, which drew 71,434 fans to Yankee Stadium. Billy Pierce lost 3–2, but the Giants bounced back the next day to even the Series at two games apiece, pounding out a 7–3 decision with the help of a grand slam by Chuck Hiller, the first in World Series competition by a National League player.

Rain postponed the next game a day, and once again the Yankees took command, winning 5–3 behind Terry.

The two teams then headed back to San Francisco for game six, which was delayed by three days of torrential rains. The pitching matchup for game six was Pierce versus Ford. "During that rain," Pierce recalled, "I remember Ford and myself doing some throwing beneath the stands at the park." On Sunday, October 15, the two teams traveled a hundred miles by bus from San Francisco to sun-kissed Modesto for brief workouts.

Finally the Series resumed on Monday, October 15, and Pierce turned in a masterpiece, a three-hitter, beating the Yankees 5–2 and setting up the deciding seventh game the next day. It was a Tuesday afternoon game on October 16 at Candlestick Park, with Terry starting for the Yankees against Sanford.

The game was a nail-biter all the way. The Yankees scored a lone run in the fifth inning. Skowron, batting in the seventh slot, and Boyer, batting eighth, singled to open the inning. That brought Terry to the plate, and Sanford walked him to load the bases with none out.

Long after the game was over, Sanford, still partially dressed in the clubhouse, moaned, "That walk to Terry did it."

With the bases filled, the next batter, Tony Kubek, bounced into a double play, and Skowron scored from third.

Terry, meanwhile, muzzled the Giants' offense. He allowed only two runners to reach base until the bottom of the ninth inning when the Giants, as they had done so often during the season, appeared poised to snatch victory from defeat.

Pinch-hitter Matty Alou led off with a drag bunt past Terry, reaching first base safely with the potential tying run. Terry then settled down and struck out Felipe Alou and Chuck Hiller, and got a strike on Willie Mays. Later, Mays conceded, "I was going for the bomb. We needed a home run. I was going for it, but I was a little behind the pitch." He was talking about the outside pitch that Terry threw him next. He slashed the ball to the right-field corner. Alou was off with the drive, racing around second and heading into third. Maris came up with the bouncing ball quickly, and in one motion threw it to Richardson, the cutoff man.

Alou made a short turn around third, but third-base coach Whitey Lockman signaled him to stop. In Lockman's mind it would have been foolhardy to send him home. Mays reached second base.

Now, with the tying and winning runs in scoring position and first base open, the Yankees had to make a decision on the next batter, Willie McCovey: walk him or pitch to him.

Houk went to the mound and asked Terry what he wanted to do.

"I want to pitch to him," Terry said.

McCovey swung at the first pitch and hit a long drive foul. On the next pitch he hit a screaming line drive toward right— but it was right at Bobby Richardson. In the blink of an eye the World Series was over and the Yankees had won, 1–0.

Watching McCovey slam the ball for what he thought might be the game-winning hit, Sanford jumped up from his dugout seat and hit his head of the top of the dugout. "It knocked me right back down," he said. "I was with Harvey Kuenn in the clubhouse afterward. He got a bottle of Crown Royal from somebody, and we must've stayed in the clubhouse until around midnight. I think we finished the bottle. We were the last two there, and we just talked about the year we had, about finally getting into the World Series."

"When McCovey came to the plate, I was in the bullpen," Billy Pierce recalled. "Alvin Dark had asked me, 'Bill, can you go in and pitch the tenth inning if we tie the game up?'

"And, I said yes, so I'm in the bullpen along the left-field side, and I had a pretty good view of Mays's ball when he hit it into the right-field corner. Maris fielded it well and got the relay in to Bobby Richardson, so Matty Alou had to stop at third.

"Some people criticized Whitey Lockman for not sending

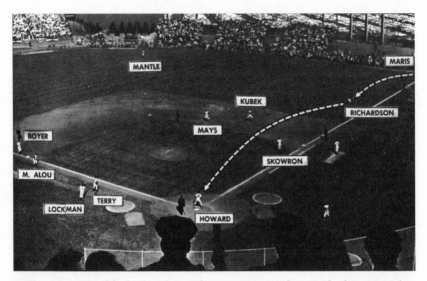

Willie Mays doubled to right with two outs in the ninth, but Maris's relay to Richardson, who threw to the plate, held base-runner Matty Alou at third base. *(AP)*

Alou home with the tying run, but he made the right decision in holding him up. Alou would've been out, and it would've been an awful way to end the Series.

"We were all surprised that they didn't walk McCovey, a left-handed hitter, against Terry, a right-hander. McCovey had hit very well in the clutch for us all year long. We thought for sure they'd walk him, then pitch to Cepeda, the next batter, who hit right-handed, and go with the percentage. When McCovey hit that shot right at Richardson, the game ended so quickly. It was kind of a shock—bingo! It was over.

"Remember, that year we were three or four games behind the Dodgers with a week to go. We didn't even think we were going to get into the World Series. Then we tied it on the last day, beat the Dodgers in the playoffs, and then lost to the Yankees on the first day after we got home. We were on such a mental and emotional high during the playoffs and all the way through the sixth game of the World Series, when we tied it up, it's hard to describe how we felt when we lost game seven.

"Sure, we felt bad we didn't win it, but we knew we'd had a great season, and had a chance to take it all, right down to

New York Yankees vs. San Francisco Giants at Candlestick Park, October 16, 1962

New York Yankees	AB	R	H	RBI	San Francisco Giants	AB	R	H	RBI
Tony Kubek, ss	4	0	1	0	Felipe Alou, rf	4	0	0	0
Bobby Richardson, 2b	2	0	0	0	Chuck Hiller, 2b	4	0	0	0
Tom Tresh, lf	4	0	1	0	Willie Mays, cf	4	0	1	0
Mickey Mantle, cf	3	0	1	0	Willie McCovey, lf	4	0	1	0
Roger Maris, rf	4	0	0	0	Orlando Cepeda, 1b	3	0	0	0
Elston Howard, c	4	0	0	0	Tom Haller, c	3	0	0	0
Bill Skowron, 1b	4	1	1	0	Jim Davenport, 3b	3	0	0	0
Clete Boyer, 3b	4	0	2	0	Jose Pagan, ss	2	0	0	0
Ralph Terry, p	3	0	1	0	Ed Bailey, ph (a)	1	0	0	0
					Ernie Bowman, ss	0	0	0	0
					Jack Sanford, p	2	0	1	0
					Billy O'Dell, p	0	0	0	0
					Matty Alou, ph (b)	1	0	1	0
Total	**32**	**1**	**7**	**0**		**31**	**0**	**4**	**0**

(a) Fouled out for Jose Pagan in eighth; (b) Singled for Billy O'Dell in ninth.

New York	0	0	0	0	1	0	0	0	0	—	1
San Francisco	0	0	0	0	0	0	0	0	0	—	0

New York Yankees	IP	H	R	ER	SO	BB
Ralph Terry (W)	9.0	4	0	0	4	0

San Francisco Giants	IP	H	R	ER	SO	BB
Jack Sanford (L)	7.0	7	1	1	3	4
Billy O'Dell	2.0	0	0	0	1	0

Errors—Pagan. **2B**—Mays. **3B**—McCovey. **DP**—San Francisco 2. **LOB**—New York 8, San Francisco 4.

Umpires—Al Barlick, Charlie Berry, Ken Burkhart, Stan Landes, Jim Honochick, Hank Soar.

Time—2:29. **Attendance**—43,948

the last at-bat. After sitting around for a while consoling our-
selves, we started talking about it having been a good year. How
often does it come down to a 1–0 ball game? And the only run
scored was on a double play?

"McCovey was down," said Pierce. "Willie was such a nice,
easygoing guy. He wanted to knock in runs. He wanted to help
win ball games. He was down because he hit the ball as hard
as he could hit it, and it just happened to be in the wrong spot.
It comes down to an inch or so. If that ball had hit the bat an
inch or so from the spot it did hit, it would've made a difference of two feet on that line drive, and Richardson might not
have caught it. But that's baseball."

"I didn't think they were going to pitch to me," McCovey
said regarding his final plate appearance in game seven. "With
first base open, I thought they'd pitch to Cepeda. I'd had a
fairly good Series, especially against Terry. I hit a home run off
him in the second game and a triple against him earlier in the
seventh game. For that reason alone I thought they'd put me
on, but they elected to pitch to me.

"It was one of those situations you dream about all your
life. You're at the plate with a chance to win the World Series,
and you're going to deliver a home run. I thought about that
when I went to the plate. And I was thinking they'd pitch around
me. When Terry's first pitch came across the plate, it surprised
me. I got out in front of it and hit it foul into the stands. If I
had been thinking they'd pitch to me instead of walking me, I
would've hit that ball out of the park. It was right in my wheel-
house.

"The second pitch was a fastball, and I hit it right at Richardson."

The Yankee second baseman said he felt he was actually out
of position on the play. "A yard to one side or another," he admitted, "and I wouldn't have had a chance at that ball."

From his vantage point in the Giants' dugout on the first-
base side of the field, Jim Davenport saw Richardson snare Mc-
Covey's drive. "It was a terribly disappointing moment for us,"
he said. "It was over so doggone quickly.

"Still, that was a great club we had in '62. It seems like
everybody had their best year that season. I know I did. So did

McCovey figured the
Yankees would walk him
in the bottom of the
ninth.

Pagan and Hiller. It was an exciting time, and we didn't have
to apologize for anything after it was all over."

For Ralph Terry it was a delicious moment of redemption.
When he was on the mound facing McCovey, he said his mind
flashed back to the 1960 World Series when he gave up the
winning home run to Bill Mazeroski in the ninth inning of
game seven.

After retiring McCovey, he said, "A man rarely gets a second chance like I did."

After the game, McCovey sat around with his teammates in
the clubhouse. "I know I didn't leave early," he said. "Later, I
went home and then to dinner at a night club in San Francisco. When I entered the place, Duke Ellington was playing
his famous song, 'Take the A Train.' When he saw me walk in,
he looked at me and then improvised some lyrics: 'You hit it
good, and that ain't bad.'

"That pretty much summarized my feelings. Once you hit
the ball good, you've done your job."

1965

Koufax Throws Strikes in Taming the Twins

"We helped create the legend of Sandy Koufax."
—Joe Nossek

Social unrest was widespread in the United States in 1965, with destructive riots in the Watts section of Los Angeles underlining serious racial tensions facing the country. These tensions were manifested in a peaceful way in late March when an estimated 25,000 civil rights activists marched, under the leadership of Martin Luther King, Jr., from Selma, Alabama, to the state capitol in Montgomery, to protest racial discrimination in the state.

Baseball, meanwhile, got a new and unusual stadium. Built on what was once grazing land, the Houston Astrodome opened on April 9 when the New York Yankees and the Astros played a pre-season exhibition. It was the first major league game held indoors, with Mickey Mantle hitting the first home run in an enclosed arena.

Age finally caught up with the irrepressible Casey Stengel, and on August 30 the 76-year-old baseball charmer stepped down as manager of the tenth-place New York Mets. Although the last four seasons of his managerial career were spent trying to build a fan base for the losing Mets and cope with the team's lack of talent, Stengel had enjoyed great success during his tenure with the New York Yankees, adding an unforgettable personal touch to the club's major league dominance. In later years he remained a favorite with the media and was elected to the Hall of Fame in 1966.

As contenders entered the last lap of the pennant races in 1965, Sandy Koufax did something no other major league pitcher had ever done. The Dodgers' 29-year-old left-hander threw his fourth no-hitter, a perfect game, on September 30, beating the Cubs 1–0. His achievement surpassed the three no-hitters pitched by Larry Corcoran, Cy Young, and Bob Feller.

In January that year Koufax had attended the baseball writers' annual Diamond Dinner in Chicago and rolled up his shirt-sleeve to show a reporter his left elbow, which was grossly swollen because of arthritis. When he showed up for spring training in Vero Beach, Florida, Koufax was suffering from the same condition and was promptly put on a plane for Los Angeles and serious medical treatment.

Only three seasons earlier, Koufax had thought the circulatory problem in his left index finger would end his career. Now, in 1965, he overcame his arthritic elbow and was working with deadly proficiency. By the end of the season he had won pitching's "Triple Crown," leading the league in wins, 26; in strikeouts, 382; and in ERA, 2.04. He also led the league in most complete games, 27; in most innings pitched, 336; and in most strikeouts per game, 10.2.

He and Don Drysdale formed a fearsome lefty-righty tandem on the mound and practically carried the light-hitting Dodgers to the pennant by themselves. Manager Walter Alston could relax a bit when they were pitching.

An imposing 6–5 right-hander, Drysdale intimidated batters. Teammate Willie Davis remarked that when it came to brushing back hitters, Big D had few equals. "Don didn't like guys crowding the plate," Davis said. "Of course, he figured you were crowding the plate the minute you left the on-deck circle!"

Drysdale finished with a 23–12 record in 1965; Koufax, 26–8. Between them they accounted for 49 of the Dodgers' 97 wins that year. They also combined for 15 shutouts.

Their work on the mound was backed up by left-handed starters Claude Osteen and Johnny Podres who added 22 more victories between them, and another southpaw, reliever Ron Perranoski, the staff's leader in saves with 17.

Only a year earlier the Dodgers had finished in sixth place with one of the poorest-hitting teams in the club's history. They didn't have a regular who hit .300, ranked eighth in the league in runs scored with 614, ninth in home runs with 79, and ninth in slugging percentage at .340. Without much offensive support, Koufax still managed to win 19 games, but he had to do it the hard way, with the league's lowest earned run average, 1.74. Drysdale's ERA ranked second to Koufax that season at 2.18.

After Koufax pitched one of his no-hitters in 1964, an amusing story circulated about the Dodgers' lack of scoring punch. With the Dodgers on the road, Drysdale, so the tale went, had been sent ahead of the team to get ready for his next pitching assignment. When Drysdale received a phone call and learned about Koufax's no-hitter, he allegedly cracked, "Did he win?"

While the Dodgers weren't much better swinging their bats in 1965, they again were fortified with a pitching staff that was downright stingy in allowing runs. Their starters recorded 23 shutouts, most in the majors, and the staff's ERA of 2.81 was the lowest in both leagues.

Six days after the season's opener, Koufax tossed a five-hitter against the Phillies while striking out seven batters, a performance that allayed fears that his arthritic elbow would curtail his service.

The Dodgers suffered a serious blow on May 1, however, when Tommy Davis, the team's strongest and most consistent hitter, sustained a severe injury that would affect the balance of his career. In a night game against the Giants, he was attempting to break up a double play at second base when his spikes caught on the base. He fractured and dislocated his ankle on the play. Davis was hospitalized for six weeks and wore a cast on his leg for more than three months. His place was taken by Lou Johnson, who had been in the Dodger farm system for the two previous seasons but had first seen major league action with the Cubs in 1960. Johnson filled the vacancy in left field and contributed many clutch hits and a dozen homers.

Without much power, the Dodgers relied heavily on their running game to manufacture runs. They led the league in stolen bases, with Maury Wills piling up 94 thefts, most in the majors.

In September the National League pennant race found manager Walter Alston's charges battling the Giants for the lead. The rivalry hit a sour note when Giant pitcher Juan Marichal struck Dodger catcher John Roseboro in the head with his bat during a heated exchange near home plate. The two teams staged long winning streaks during the final month, but the Dodgers came home in front, two games ahead of the Giants.

In the American League the Minnesota Twins cruised to the pennant, finishing seven games ahead of the second-place White Sox with 102 wins against 60 losses. Unlike the Dodgers, the Twins brought to the World Series an assortment of long-ball hitters in Harmon Killebrew, Bob Allison, Jimmie Hall, and Don Mincher, plus a productive offensive combination in right fielder Tony Oliva and shortstop Zoilo Versalles.

And the Twins too were fortified with competent pitching, including starters Jim "Mudcat" Grant, Jim Kaat, Camilo Pascual, and Jim Perry, and a well-stocked bullpen headed by Al Worthington. By the end of the pennant race, Grant entered the record book as the first black pitcher in American League history to win 20 games. He finished 21–7 while Kaat was 18–11.

Behind the plate the Twins counted on the smooth defensive work of Earl Battey, who had been obtained, along with Mincher, in a 1960 trade with the White Sox. The Twins then had been the Washington Senators and were perennial noncontenders. Other teams would steal them blind because they didn't have a catcher who could make hard, accurate throws to second base. Battey changed all that and with his hitting helped the club gain respectability.

"Battey was the best all-around catcher the organization ever had," said Jim Kaat. "I know he was a calming influence on me when I was on the mound."

While the Dodgers featured a certain amount of pizzazz with the base-running of Maury Wills and the pitching of Koufax and Drysdale, their counterparts in the World Series weren't particularly flashy. And they commanded less national attention because they had not reached the Fall Classic since being moved from Washington to the upper Midwest in 1961. The Twins' owner, Calvin Griffith, was an impassive, business-oriented man, and manager Sam Mele was low-key. While Harmon Killebrew became the team's acknowledged leader as the '65 season moved along, he led not by being talkative but by his quiet example and willingness to do what was best to help the team win.

"Harmon was calm, unemotional," added Kaat. "If he struck out, popped up, or got a big hit, you couldn't tell the difference by the expression on his face."

In one game in mid-June the Twins were playing Detroit in Tigers Stadium, which had a short right-field front porch. It was an inviting target for left-handed hitters. At the time, Killebrew, a right-handed hitter, was playing first base, but the club had an able backup first baseman in Don Mincher who was sitting on the bench. Mincher hit left-handed.

"Sam," Killebrew said to Mele in Detroit, "if you think Mincher would help the club with his left-handed swing, I'll be glad to switch to third base so he can play first." Mele made the switch a few days later. The incident reflected Killebrew's unselfish approach to the game, and his example was not lost on his teammates.

With a rash of physical problems that plagued them in 1965, the Twins had to rely heavily on team unity. Mudcat Grant, who was bothered with arthritis in his knees, volunteered to start and relieve. Kaat insisted on taking his regular turn on the mound even though he had tendinitis in his arm. Zoilo Versalles ranged far and wide at shortstop despite having to deal with a pulled groin muscle, leg bruises, and a sore foot. Although suffering terrible back pains that forced him out of action for a while, 31-year-old Camilo Pascual still managed to make 27 starts and finished with a 9–3 won-lost record. And Tony Oliva kept playing despite swollen knees, and in only his second full season in the majors won his second straight league batting title.

So the Twins continued to win, with every player contributing a share to the club's success. At one point the team's

injuries were so numerous that Mele began using relief pitchers as starters. He once went eight successive days with a different infield alignment each game.

If there was a turning point in the Twins' season it came in
a game against the Yankees on July 12 at Metropolitan Stadium in Bloomington. With two out in the ninth inning and
the Yankees leading 5–4, the Twins had Rich Rollins on base
when Killebrew came to the plate against Pete Mikkelson.

A right-handed reliever, Mikkelson worked Killebrew to three
balls and two strikes, then tried to throw a fastball by him.
Killebrew drove the pitch into the left-field seats for a game-
winning homer. Players in the Twins dugout stood and cheered
as Killebrew circled the bases, and mauled him with congratulations as he entered the dugout.

Winning that critical battle stretched the Twins' first-place
lead to five full games. By August 1 they still were ahead of
their closest rivals, the Orioles and Indians, by five games but,
as so often happens in baseball, they were about to suffer a
cruel blow with the loss of Killebrew through a freakish injury.

On August 2 against the Orioles at Metropolitan Stadium,
the Twins were leading 2–1 in the sixth inning when Baltimore's
Russ Snyder came to the plate. Snyder hit a slow roller down
the third-base line. Rich Rollins charged the ball and fired it
to Killebrew at first. The throw was wide, on the home plate
side of first base, and Killebrew reached out with his left arm
to grab it. The ball and Snyder arrived at the same time, and
Snyder crashed into Killebrew's outstretched arm. In the collision, Killebrew suffered a full dislocation of his left elbow.

After X-rays, a doctor patted Killebrew on the back and said,
"Don't worry, you'll be back in the lineup in a couple of weeks."
Nonetheless Killebrew entertained serious doubts about his re-
covery. "My swinging power comes from my left arm," he said,
"and I just use the right one to guide my bat. It was really bad.
It was the most painful thing I ever experienced. All the nerves
were torn in the elbow, right where the crazy bone is located.
I thought I might be through as a player."

Instead of a two-week layoff, Killebrew sat out the next 48
games. If any good came from his disablement, it might be

said that Killebrew's injury served to unite the Twins even further. At the time he led the league in RBI with 70 and in home runs with 22. Also out of action then was Camilo Pascual, sidelined with torn back muscles.

Sam Mele gave his players a pep talk to boost their spirits. "We can still win," he said. "We'll just have to try harder."

In commenting on Mele's talk, one Minneapolis baseball writer observed, "Mele telling the team to win without Killebrew was like King Arthur telling his knights to go into battle without Sir Lancelot."

But the Twins continued to win. Their motto, pasted on the clubhouse bulletin board, read: "A hero a day keeps the contenders away." And they lived up to it. In each game it seemed that a different player did what was needed to win. Don Mincher took over at first base. Lesser-known players, including outfielders Joe Nossek and Sandy Valdespino, second basemen Jerry Kindall and Frank Quilici, and catcher Jerry Zimmerman all contributed to the Twins' final record of winning 34 games by one run, many of them in the team's final at-bat.

Killebrew returned to the club on September 23. His elbow was mended, but he had lingering doubts whether he had lost his home-run touch. He erased those doubts when he hit three homers in the final days of the regular season.

Before the World Series opened in Bloomington on October 6, the oddsmakers posted the Dodgers as 7-to-5 favorites. Those odds were based on the expected supremacy of Koufax and Drysdale during the course of the Series.

Drysdale started the opening game and was pounded by the Twins who won 8–2 behind Mudcat Grant. Koufax, who had been given the day off to observe Yom Kippur, took the mound in game two against his left-handed opponent Jim Kaat and lasted only six innings, losing 5–1.

"I remember sitting on the bench next to our pitching coach Johnny Sain and watching the way Koufax was throwing in the first inning," Kaat said. "I marveled at the stuff he had.

"I told Sain, 'I better not give up a run or the game will be over. If he keeps throwing like that, we'll be lucky to get a hit.'

"Before the game, I didn't even bother to go over the scouting reports on the Dodgers. I knew they were a lowball-hitting team. I was a lowball pitcher. That was my strength. If I pitched high, I'd be going with my weakness.

"So I went with my strength. Sain always told me, 'Rely on your natural stuff and throw strikes. Don't be a defensive pitcher.'

"Working against a pitcher like Koufax tended to take some pressure off me. I knew nobody expected me to beat him. But our hitters got to Sandy for a couple of runs in the sixth inning, and he was taken out of the game after that. I was keeping the ball down on them and didn't run into much trouble the rest of the way. The two runs we got off Koufax were enough for us to win.

"Afterward Sandy said he pitched a poor game, but he still struck out nine men in his six innings."

In beating both Drysdale and Koufax in games one and two, the Twins shocked the baseball public as well as the oddsmakers. But when the Series moved to Los Angeles, they learned something that National League opponents of the Dodgers already knew: it might be possible to beat Drysdale and Koufax in succession once, but not twice.

In game three Claude Osteen shut out Minnesota 4–0. Drysdale earned a 7–2 decision against Grant in game four, and Koufax came back to win game five in typical fashion, pitching a four-hit, ten-strikeout, 7–0 victory. Kaat was the loser against Koufax, lasting only two and a third innings.

The Twins invigorated their followers when they rebounded in game six with a 5–1 triumph at home behind the six-hit pitching of Grant.

Before game seven in Minnesota, Dodger manager Alston faced a dilemma. Should he start Drysdale or Koufax in the finale? Koufax would be going on only two days' rest, but Alston decided for him. "I'd rather have Drysdale in the bullpen," he said, "because he warms up faster." He also reasoned that if the Dodgers were behind when Drysdale went in, he could keep him in the game because of his strong bat and he wouldn't have to take him out for a pinch hitter."

Although Drysdale warmed up six different times during game seven, his services were not required. Koufax shut down the Twins 2–0 on three hits, a work of art that featured ten strikeouts and only one scoring threat by the losers.

That threat occurred in the fifth inning. The Dodgers had taken the lead on a pair of runs scored in the fourth—Lou Johnson pulled a homer against Kaat, and the other run scored on a double by Ron Fairly and a single by Wes Parker.

Jim Gilliam was playing third base for the Dodgers. Some years ago he recalled the situation in the fifth inning.

"Sandy got into trouble," Gilliam said, "when he gave up a double to Frank Quilici, then walked Rich Rollins. The next batter, Versalles, hit a shot down the third-base line. People who saw it told me later that it looked like a sure double that would have tied the game.

"I didn't have time to think about it. I just dove to my right, backhanded the ball, scrambled to my feet and stepped on third for the force on Quilici. That was two outs, and Koufax got Joe Nossek to ground out to end the inning.

"That play saved the game and maybe the Series. It's one play I won't ever forget because it meant so much."

In completing his masterpiece, Koufax twice struck out Allison, Battey, and Oliva, and fanned Versalles, Mincher, Quilici, and Kaat once each. He ended the game by getting Battey on a called third strike and whiffing Allison for the final out.

His dominance in the money game of the Series inspired one wag to comment, "All baseball, like Ceasar's Gaul, is divided into three parts—the American League, the National League, and Sandy Koufax."

How did the Twins feel about the matter?

"It was a disappointing loss," said Jim Kaat, "but I can't say it was shocking. I knew if I gave up a run or two, my chances of winning were slim. If it was against any mortal pitcher, instead of Koufax, then being down one or two runs might not have made much difference. But when I gave up those two runs in the fourth inning, Sam [Mele] went to the bullpen right away and brought in Worthington. Being down 2–0 to Koufax was like being down five or six runs against another pitcher."

How about the pitch Kaat threw to Lou Johnson?

"Johnson really hit a pretty good pitch," Kaat said. "The ball was actually outside, and he hooked it down the left-field

Jim Kaat (left) started but didn't last in the Series finale. Like the other Twins, rookie Joe Nossek was shut down by Koufax in game seven.

line. From a pitcher's standpoint, the pitch was not a bad location."

After being removed from the game, Kaat sat on the Twins' bench. "I had sort of a helpless feeling, watching Koufax," he recalled. "You knew he wasn't going to give them anything good to hit. If he had been facing a lineup of hitters that included guys like Gehrig and Ruth, he would've been the same way. He was masterful.

"It was sort of an overcast, gloomy day, and from the sixth inning on it seemed hopeless for us, like we were behind 10–0 instead of 2–0. When the game neared the end, there was a funereal atmosphere in the park.

"With two outs in the ninth, though, the fans got up and gave us an appreciative round of applause. That was nice."

Kaat said there was not much show of emotion in the Twins' clubhouse after the game. "We had a lot of young players, and I think their mind-set was that we had won the pennant, which was a big deal in those days, and here we stretched the World Series out to seven games but lost to a great pitcher. It's too bad we lost, but we'll be back. Little did I know then that I would become part of baseball trivia: the player who went the longest between World Series appearances, with the Twins in '65 and the Cardinals in '82."

"That was my rookie year, '65, and I platooned in center all year long with Jimmie Hall," said Joe Nossek. "He was a left-handed hitter and, of course, I was right-handed. That was probably why I played so many games in the World Series, because they had Koufax and Osteen, two left-handers who pitched five games between them in the Series. Jimmie had trouble with left-handers, so that got me in there a little bit."

Nossek was still relatively untested in critical major league situations that might dictate the outcome of an entire season. What was it like for him to face Koufax in the deciding game of a World Series?

"If I remember correctly, he got off his curve ball early in the game," Nossek said. "I guess his arm was a little tender. I think he beat us in that seventh game with just fastballs and change-ups. I don't know whether we were looking for too many breaking balls at times, or what, but he never served them up. And he shut us down pretty good. That's what those great pitchers do even if they don't use all their stuff. They rise to the occasion.

"Koufax had the ability to ride that fastball up high, which is a very difficult pitch for any hitter to get to, especially as hard as he threw it. Then he had that change-up—sometimes they call it a BP fastball today—but I remember him getting me out a couple of times when he would turn the ball over. It wasn't a legitimate change-up, it was a little harder, but he would turn the ball over and it would be what we call a sinker now. He would get you trying to pull the ball. You'd be so geared for that good fastball, you had a tendency to get out in front. You'd end up rolling over and pulling the ball on the ground for an easy out. I did that a couple of times.

"Koufax was a very smart pitcher. I've heard many people say that about guys like Tom Seaver, and Koufax was the same way. They had the ability to get into a hitter's mind and work accordingly."

Despite losing to the Dodgers in the World Series, Nossek still has fond memories of the Twins' pennant season.

Koufax gets congratulations from Dodgers manager Walter Alston and teammates after beating the Twins in game seven. *(AP)*

"It was one of those magical years for me," he said. "I was on cloud nine most of the year. We had good starting pitching with Grant, Kaat, and Perry. Camilo Pascual was in his thirties, but he won about nine games for us. Worthington and Johnny Klippstein gave us good innings out of the bullpen. Bill Pleis, a left-handed reliever, helped us too.

"And we had some power with Killebrew, Allison, and Mincher. Our right fielder, Tony Oliva, won the batting championship that year, and our shortstop, Zoilo Versalles, was voted the MVP in the American League. He was a great player for us, both offensively and defensively. He was our leadoff hitter and drove in 77 runs that year. He hit about .270, which wasn't bad back then.

"I looked it up, and our team led the league in hitting with a .254 average. Compared to nowadays, that's quite a difference, but that's the way it was. Oliva was our top hitter with .321, and there were only two other regular players in the American League who hit over .300.

"That was in the heyday of the Yankees, who were expected to win every year. They had won five pennants in a row, but in 1965 they slipped. Some of them were hurting with injuries, especially Mantle.

"I didn't play in the first game of the Series when we faced Drysdale, but I remember us coming out pumped, and we won it big, 8–2. That gave us a lift for the next day, with Sandy pitching, and we went out and beat him too.

"I was out in center field getting ready before game two when Koufax was coming in from the bullpen after he had warmed up. He walked past me and said, 'Hi, Joe. Good luck.' That was a big thrill for a kid like me—that he even knew my name."

After beating Koufax 5–1, it appeared the Twins had the Dodgers on the brink of defeat. "We went out to LA," Nossek recalled, "and lost the next three games. I remember one of our guys saying how tough it was playing them at Dodgers Stadium, that we might not have won a game before Christmas if we had to keep playing there. But we bounced back when we returned to Bloomington. Mudcat pitched a great sixth game, hit a three-run homer, and that tied the Series.

"We had won all three games at home to that point and felt pretty good going into the seventh game. But here comes Sandy again, and he shut us down. And he did it without his curveball. You might say we helped create the legend of Sandy Koufax."

After the final loss in game seven, Nossek said, "There was a lot of disappointment. But, again, it was a great season for the Twins, who had just moved to Minnesota in '61 and had made it to the World Series in four years. That was quite an accomplishment. They didn't do it again until 1987 with [manager] Tom Kelly.

"I headed back home pretty quick, to Euclid, Ohio, relishing the fact that I got to play in a World Series in my first year in the big leagues. The Dodgers got $10,000 for the winning share, and we got $6,600 for the losing share. That was big

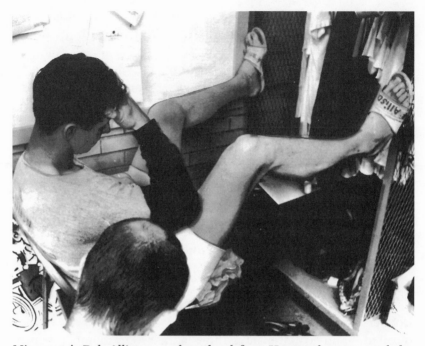

Minnesota's Bob Allison ponders the defeat. He struck out to end the Series.

bucks for me—my *season's* salary was $6,000—the minimum salary for a first-year player back then. So I doubled it by getting to the World Series."

Reliever Johnny Klippstein made two pitching appearances for the Twins in the World Series, including an inning and two-thirds of game seven. "In '65, I was 38 years old and glad to be pitching anywhere," he said. "I was with the Dodgers in '58 and '59, so I knew Koufax quite well. The thing I remember about him is what he told me once. He said that when his arm was really tired the ball moved better for him. That proved out in the last game of the Series."

Los Angeles Dodgers vs. Minnesota Twins
at Metropolitan Stadium, October 14, 1965

Los Angeles Dodgers	AB	R	H	RBI	Minnesota Twins	AB	R	H	RBI
Maury Wills, ss	4	0	0	0	Zoilo Versalles, ss	4	0	1	0
Jim Gilliam, 3b	5	0	2	0	Joe Nossek, cf	4	0	0	0
John Kennedy, 3b	0	0	0	0	Tony Oliva, rf	3	0	0	0
Willie Davis, cf	2	0	0	0	Harmon Killebrew, 3b	3	0	1	0
Lou Johnson, lf	4	1	1	1	Earl Battey, c	4	0	0	0
Ron Fairly, rf	4	1	1	0	Bob Allison, lf	4	0	0	0
Wes Parker, 1b	4	0	2	1	Don Mincher, 1b	3	0	0	0
Dick Tracewski, 2b	4	0	0	0	Frank Quilici, 2b	3	0	1	0
Johnny Roseboro, c	2	0	1	0	Jim Kaat, p	1	0	0	0
Sandy Koufax, p	3	0	0	0	Al Worthington, p	0	0	0	0
					Rich Rollins, ph (a)	0	0	0	0
					Johnny Klippstein, p	0	0	0	0
					Jim Merritt, p	0	0	0	0
					Sandy Valdespino, ph (b)	1	0	0	0
					Jim Perry, p	0	0	0	0
Total	32	2	7	2		30	0	3	0

(a) Walked for Al Worthington in the fifth; (b) Fouled out for Jim Merritt in the eighth.

Los Angeles	0	0	0	2	0	0	0	0	0	—	2
Minnesota	0	0	0	0	0	0	0	0	0	—	0

Los Angeles Dodgers	IP	H	R	ER	SO	BB
Sandy Koufax (W)	9.0	3	0	0	10	3

San Francisco Giants	IP	H	R	ER	SO	BB
Jim Kaat (L) +	3.0	5	2	2	2	1
Al Worthington	2.0	0	0	0	0	1
Johnny Klippstein	1.2	2	0	0	2	1
Jim Merritt	1.1	0	0	0	1	0
Jim Perry	1.0	0	0	0	1	1

+ Pitched to three batters in the fourth inning.

Errors—Oliva. **2B**—Fairly, Quilici, Roseboro. **3B**—Parker. **HR**—Johnson. **SH**—Davis.
LOB—Los Angeles, 9, Minnesota, 6. **Hit by pitch**—Davis (by Klippstein).
Umpires—Ed Hurley, Tony Venzon, Red Flaherty, Ed Sudol, Bob Stewart, Ed Vargo.
Time—2:27. **Attendance**—50,596

1969

Mets Deflate the Cubs' Pennant Hopes

"I put the tag on Agee so hard the ball almost popped out of my glove."—Randy Hundley

In 1969, news of noble achievement was offset by reports of chaos on college campuses, horror in Mylai, South Vietnam, and massive protests against war and racial inequities. If the Mylai massacre of civilians shrouded Americans in shame, they swelled with pride when Neil Armstrong and Buzz Aldrin landed on the moon on July 20. After they had piloted the Apollo lunar module named Eagle to a safe touchdown, Armstrong walked on the moon's surface and uttered his famous line, "That's one small step for man, one giant leap for mankind."

Another entry in the 1969 logbook of memorable events should include a rather whacky but mostly harmless gathering that took place on a 600-acre dairy farm in Bethel, New York, where the three-day Woodstock music festival in August attracted an estimated 400,000 young people. The festival featured endless traffic jams, food and water shortages, torrential downpours, drugs, open lovemaking, and poor sanitation. In a way, the festival typified the unrest and anti-establishment fervor that were sweeping the nation.

Not to be outdone by unexpected happenings, baseball witnessed the historically woeful New York Mets winning not only the National League pennant but the World Series as well. The Series victory, it might be noted, was earned at the expense of the highly regarded Baltimore Orioles, who were a firm pick of the oddsmakers to win the Fall Classic.

Before the season opened, Yankee idol Mickey Mantle announced his retirement from the game. Mantle, 37, told newsmen, "I just can't play anymore. I can't hit, I can't go from first to third, I can't steal second, and I can't score from second on a single. I figured it's best for the team I stop now."

During his spectacular 18-year career with the Yankees, Mantle hit 536 home runs and played on 12 pennant winners. The club retired his uniform number 7 on June 8, paying tribute to him on "Mickey Mantle Day" at Yankee Stadium.

On August 11 another future Hall of Famer, Don Drysdale of the Dodgers, also retired. The 33-year-old right-hander was sidelined much of the season with chronic soreness in his shoulder. He was the last active front-line player among the Dodgers who had been with the team when it was located in Brooklyn.

Major league baseball, under the leadership of fledgling commissioner Bowie Kuhn, expanded from 20 to 24 teams in 1969, the new entries being the Montreal Expos and San Diego Padres in the National League, and the Kansas City Royals and Seattle Pilots in the American League.

With pitchers having dominated hitters in 1968, the new season began with a pair of rules changes that were expected to create a better balance between the two forces. The pitching mound was lowered from 15 to ten inches; the strike zone was shortened vertically, from the top of the knees to the armpits.

In July, in connection with the annual All-Star Game, baseball celebrated one hundred years of professional existence, the occasion being highlighted by a special reception for many present and former players who were welcomed by President Richard Nixon at the White House. "I like the job I have now," Nixon said, "but if I had my life to live over again, I'd like to have ended up as a sportswriter." The remark was widely quoted, and Dick Young of the *New York Daily News*, president of the Baseball Writers Association of America, promptly announced that Nixon would receive a lifetime membership card in the association.

During the summer Stan Musial, Roy Campanella, Stan Coveleski, and Waite Hoyt were enshrined in the Baseball Hall of Fame in Cooperstown, New York. And while the ten-inch pitching mound may have been a factor in higher earned run averages being posted in both leagues, it did not prevent an astonishing number of six no-hit games being hurled in the majors.

As the season moved into its final month, the Baltimore Orioles were running away with the East Division title. They would finish with a resounding 109–53 record under manager Earl Weaver, 19 games ahead of second-place Detroit, then sweep the Minnesota Twins in the league playoffs and go on to the World Series.

In the National League, interest in the East Division race remained at a high pitch. The battle was spirited between the front-running Chicago Cubs and the fast-closing New York Mets.

The Cubs were a piece of work in 1969. Controversy swirled around them, primarily through the behavior and caustic remarks of their 64-year-old legendary manager, Leo Durocher, who berated some of his own players and constantly fought with the press.

The Cubs that season featured an All-Star infield—Ernie Banks at first, Glenn Beckert at second, Don Kessinger at short, and Ron Santo at third. They had three future Hall of Famers in Banks, left fielder Billy Williams, and starting pitcher Fergie Jenkins. They had a durable, savvy catcher in Randy Hundley, who also made the National League All-Star lineup that year.

They were lionized by the print and electronic media. They inspired the formation of the "Bleacher Bums," a boisterous bunch of fans who sat in the left-field bleachers at Wrigley Field, liked to wear yellow hard hats, and cheered wildly throughout the games. They even had their own unofficial theme song that featured the memorable refrain, "Hey, hey! Holy mackerel! No doubt about it! The Cubs are on their way!"

In short, they roused hopes among their faithful fans that maybe, just maybe, they were headed for their first pennant in 24 years—which included many seasons of dismal performances.

They never reached their goal, however, and their failure

haunted the club for the next decade. Players involved in that disappointing venture have provided various reasons why the 1969 Cubs staggered home eight games behind the Mets and in the process became the most celebrated second-place team in the history of the game.

"We had played out the string," said 21-game winner Fergie Jenkins. "We were tired. Leo played the regulars almost the whole season without any rest."

Ron Santo cited the team's lack of aggressiveness after it hit a bump in the road. "For much of that season," he said, "we couldn't lose. Then there came a time after the losing started that we were waiting for something to happen."

Left-hander Ken Holtzman, who won 17 games, said the '69 Cubs did not intimidate opponents. "I think that team simply wasn't ready to win," he commented. "There is a feeling about winning, a certain amount of intimidation which didn't exist with the Cubs."

Ernie Banks, at 38, played 153 games at first base that season. He hit only .253 but drove in 106 runs, unleashed 23 homers, and led all National League players in fielding at his position. Nonetheless his immense popularity with Chicago fans and the fact he had been dubbed "Mr. Cub" did not set well with the egocentric, hard-bitten Durocher.

Although age was taking its toll on his knees, Banks played hard and contributed to the club's rise as a pennant contender. But even when the Cubs had a comfortable first-place lead, Banks said to a teammate, "We're not going to win it because we've got a manager and three or four players who are out there waiting to get beat."

In addition to his thinly veiled dislike of Banks, Durocher further damaged team morale by openly ripping Fergie Jenkins, Ken Holtzman, and rookie center fielder Don Young. He called Jenkins a "quitter" in front of teammates. He reportedly called Holtzman "a gutless Jew." He crucified Young for messing up two plays in the outfield. His sharpness as a tactician was also questioned, and critics in the media felt his managerial style left a lot to be desired.

Still, a hard look at the '69 Cubs reveals certain weaknesses that figured in their eventual doom. Outside of utility infielder

Manager Leo Durocher
drove his '69 Cubs—
perhaps too hard.

Paul Popovich, they did not have a particularly strong bench. They lacked a proven center fielder. They were a slow, station-to-station team on offense, with only one player, Don Kessinger, stealing bases in double figures—a mere 11 thefts. Behind Jenkins, Hands, and Holtzman, the starting pitching was mediocre, and the bullpen was thin, so much so that primary reliever Phil Regan was overused and lost some crispness on his pitches, which included the spitter, late in the season.

During the early months of 1969, though, the Cubs sent their fans into a frenzy with their winning ways. They occupied first place for 155 consecutive days beginning with their home opener on April 8 when they beat the Phillies 7–6 on an 11th-inning two-run, pinch-hit homer by Willie Smith into the right-field bleachers.

With the Cubs down 6–5 and Hundley on first base, Durocher had called on Smith, a 30-year-old reserve and left-handed batter, to pinch-hit for Jim Hickman against Barry Lersch.

When Smith's drive landed in the bleachers, Wrigley Field, packed with 40,796 paying customers, exploded. "We felt right

The Cubs' winning habits prompted third baseman Ron Santo to click his heels. *(Ronald L. Mrowiec)*

then," said Santo, "that this was the season we were going to win."

By the end of April the Cubs were 16–7; by May 31 they were 32–16, and by June 30 they were 49–27, seven games ahead of the New York Mets. On June 19 Durocher entered into his fourth marriage, this time to Lynne Walker Goldblatt. On June 22 after the Cubs beat the Montreal Expos in the first game of a double header, 7–6, on a Jim Hickman home run, Ron Santo leaped in the air and clicked his heels in joy as the players headed to the clubhouse. Durocher liked Santo's uninhibited exhibition, which became customary after the Cubs won a game—but opponents frowned on it as hotdogging.

Controversy and dissension continued to mark Durocher's tenure. After Don Young misplayed two balls in center field in a game the Mets won 4–3 on July 8 at Shea Stadium, Durocher scorched his young outfielder. "It's tough to win," he said, "when your center fielder can't catch a f—— fly ball! It's a disgrace!"

Durocher, in turn, was torched by the print media for openly ravaging Young.

Then, on July 26, the Cubs manager created more fodder for his press critics when he left a nationally televised game at Wrigley Field against the Dodgers in the third inning, complaining of a stomach problem. His excuse fell flat when it was learned he was merely going AWOL to visit his stepson on parents' weekend at Camp Ojibwa in Eagle River, Wisconsin, some four hundred miles away. Owner Phil Wrigley almost fired Durocher over his manager's sneaky departure from the team.

Despite all these disconcerting incidents, the Cubs rolled through early August with six straight wins. By the morning of August 14 they held a nine-and-a-half-game lead over the third place Mets, and on August 19 their spirits were lifted further when Ken Holtzman pitched a 1–0 no-hitter against the Atlanta Braves.

But from August 16 through 31 the pitching-rich Mets won 14 out of 17 games to close the gap on the Cubs. By the time the two teams met for the opener of a crucial two-game series at Shea on September 8, the Cubs held a slim two-and-a-half-game margin over the surging Mets. Before their trip to New York, Durocher's forces had gone into a tailspin, losing four straight games, including an extra-inning battle with the Pirates on September 7.

"That last loss to the Pirates hurt," said Santo, "but we were still ahead of the Mets and thought we could bounce back behind Bill Hands, who had already beaten them three times that year."

So the pitching matchup for what was destined to be a turning point in the season for the Cubs pitted Hands versus Mets' left-hander Jerry Koosman.

Managed by Gil Hodges, whose composure was a direct opposite to the volatile Durocher's, the Mets were rated a long shot to win the National League pennant before the start of the 162-game campaign. But with superb pitching by Tom Seaver, who would finish with a record of 25–7, and Koosman, 17–9, and with Hodges adroitly platooning at least four position players, by season's end they would earn the title of the "Miracle Mets."

"Other than their pitching, we were a better team, man for man, than the Mets," said Santo. "They had only three regulars—Tommie Agee in center, Cleon Jones in left, and Bud Harrelson at short—who could have played for anybody in the league. The other guys were utility players.

"That was a pivotal game we lost to the Pirates [7–5 in 11 innings] at home. In the ninth inning we were one out from winning the game. Phil Regan had two strikes on Willie Stargell, and there was a 30-mile-an-hour wind blowing in from right field. So you figured the odds were against him hitting a homer in that direction. But sure enough, Stargell belts one onto Sheffield Avenue to tie the game, and then we go on to lose it in extra innings.

"When that happened I remember asking myself, 'What's going to happen next?' After that Pirates game, that's when we started going downhill."

Before the Mets' game the following Monday night, Hands promised that "Agee is going on his ass the first pitch." He made that hostile vow because Agee, the Mets' leadoff man, had been hitting him pretty well.

"I used to own him all through the minor leagues," said Hands, "but in the majors I just couldn't make good pitches against him. I was constantly hanging sliders over the middle of the plate, and he was constantly hitting the shit out of them."

Living up to his promise, Hands sent Agee sprawling with his first pitch in the bottom of the first inning. The pitch whizzed just beneath Agee's chin. "That woke me up," said Agee, who was not intimidated even though he grounded out to Santo in his first at-bat. His sweet revenge would come later.

With still no score in the game, Santo led off the top of the second inning for the Cubs, and for Koosman it was time for payback.

The Mets' left-hander threw a hard, inside fastball that struck Santo just above the right wrist. The Cubs' third baseman grabbed his injured wrist and danced around the plate in pain.

The Cubs did not so much as lift a finger in protest against

Bill Hands promised to
put Tommie Agee "on his
ass the first pitch."
(Ronald L. Mrowiec)

Koosman's retaliation pitch. They just sat on the bench. Nobody yelled at Koosman. Santo himself didn't think he was de-
liberately hit, but Koosman later admitted the pitch was
intended to send a message.

"I was keyed up for this game," said Koosman. "I'd been
thinking about it for several days. I had met Ernie Banks earlier in the day, and he was teasing me, saying, 'I'm going to hit
five home runs off you,' and things like that. I kidded him right
back—'Are you in the lineup? How'd you manage to break in?'
That exchange helped key me up even more."

After hitting Santo, Koosman escaped trouble in the second
inning by striking out the side.

Neither team crossed the plate until the bottom of the third
inning. With two out and Bud Harrelson on first base, Agee
came up again to face Hands.

"When Koosman retaliated (against Santo), it gave me great
incentive to win the game for him," Agee said. "I don't mind
being hit by a pitch as long as I know that our pitcher is going
to protect me.

"I don't like to see any batter get hit with a pitch, and when I saw Santo get it, I hoped he wasn't hurt bad, because he's a nice fellow. I've always liked him. But, if you keep getting hit by pitches and your team doesn't do anything about it, that's when you get disgusted. You ask yourself why you are going down, and the other guys never go down. Koosman had protected me."

Now Agee was ready as a World Series atmosphere enveloped Shea Stadium along with the mist and rain. He took ball one and then lashed Hands's second pitch, a high, hanging curve, over the 396-foot sign in left center for his 26th homer of the season, giving the Mets a 2–0 lead.

The Cubs finally reached Koosman in the sixth inning, tying the game at 2–2 on successive singles by Don Kessinger, Glenn Beckert, and Billy Williams, plus a sacrifice fly by Santo whose wrist was so sore he couldn't get a good grip on the bat. "I just couldn't pop my wrists," Santo admitted.

It appeared the Cubs had Koosman on the ropes, especially after he threw a wild pitch into the dirt that moved Williams to third, and then walked Jim Hickman. But Randy Hundley, the next batter, hit a short fly to Ron Swoboda in right field to end the rally.

Once more Agee was the focal point of the Mets' attack in the bottom half of the sixth inning. He hit a shot past Santo at third and the ball rolled into short left, slowed down by the wet grass. By the time Billy Williams hustled his throw to second base, Agee was sliding in safely, head first.

"Agee was fast," said Williams, "but I thought I might have a chance to get him at second. The grass in left field slowed the ball just enough to keep me from getting the throw off quick enough."

Agee was fully aware of the field condition in left. "I decided to try for second when I saw Williams would have to go to the ball instead of having the ball come to him," he said. "The grass was awfully slow out there because of the rain, and the ball wasn't moving."

The gamble paid off. It put Agee in scoring position with the lead run. At the same time it created the situation for one of the most controversial umpiring calls of the season. The next batter, Wayne Garrett, singled to right field. Jim Hickman fielded the ball and made a strong throw slightly to the third-base side of home plate, where the waiting Hundley swipe-tagged the onrushing Agee.

The throw had Agee beat. Rookie plate umpire Dave "Satch" Davidson was not in the best position to make the call because Agee's body blocked his view of Hundley's tag. Davidson was standing some distance from the right-side batter's box, looking in the direction of first base. Hundley tagged Agee on Agee's left side, a spot difficult for Davidson to see from where he had positioned himself.

When Davidson ruled Agee safe, Hundley went ballistic, jumping in the air in protest. Leo Durocher joined his catcher in challenging the call.

"I put the tag on Agee so hard the ball almost popped out of my glove," Hundley said. "I couldn't believe he was safe. I tagged him about six feet up the line, and then turned to first to make sure Garrett wasn't running. When the crowd roared, I turned around and couldn't believe Davidson was giving the safe sign."

As Agee headed to the plate, Glenn Beckert was sure the Mets center fielder would be thrown out. "I thought to myself," said Beckert, "'He's dead at home. We got him.' When he was called safe, I thought, 'What the hell's going on now? Is this going to happen to us all the time?'" Had Agee been called out, Beckert felt, the play would have changed the course of the game and swung the momentum to the Cubs.

Hickman had made a perfect throw to the plate. "I think that tag play was crucial to our entire season," the rangy right fielder said. "But, to be honest, all of those big games we lost to the Mets made the difference."

After Agee scored, the Mets' 3–2 lead held up, though the Cubs threatened in the eighth inning when Beckert and Williams led off with singles. But the wrist-impaired Santo hit into a double play. Then, with the tying run on third, Koosman struck out Banks.

"That double play was a key play of the game," said Koosman. "I threw him a fastball and he hit it just where I wanted."

Cubs catcher Randy Hundley tags Agee on a crucial play at the plate. Umpire "Satch" Davidson called Agee safe. *(UPI)*

The end of Koosman's mission came in sight at the start of the ninth inning when Hickman struck out. Hundley singled, but the Mets' lefty then fanned pinch-hitters Ken Rudolph and Randy Bobb.

With the tying run on base and the game on the line, Durocher was later asked why he used two virtually untried rookies in Rudolph and Bobb as pinch-hitters.

"It was as good a gamble as anything else," said Durocher. "All I had left were Paul Popovich and Nate Oliver, and these boys had a little more power."

This decisive victory left the Mets only a game and a half out of first place. Koosman yielded only seven singles and struck out 13 batters in notching his 13th win of the season. Hampered by a sore arm earlier in the year, he relied heavily on his fastball. "Everybody's been wondering why I haven't been striking out a lot of guys lately," he said after the game. "I had a photographer take pictures of me and I studied them. They showed I wasn't snapping my wrist, and I wasn't putting my body behind my pitches."

The Cubs never recovered from the loss to Koosman. The next night they caved in to Tom Seaver, 7–1. Their nosedive continued until September 10 when the Mets took over first place, then wiped out the Atlanta Braves in the League Championship Series, and followed that sweep with a surprising victory over the Orioles in five games in the World Series.

"That year," Santo insisted, "the Cubs were the best team in the National League, the Orioles were the best team in baseball, and the Mets beat everybody. I can't explain how that happened except that maybe God lived in New York."

Looking back on the '69 season, Billy Williams lamented, "I thought we were good enough to win, especially after we got that big lead. The game against Koosman was a hard one to lose because of that bad call.

"Koosman never gave you a good pitch to hit. For a left-handed hitter like me, he'd throw fastballs in and sliders away, most of them down at the knees. It was tough to pick up his pitches at Shea because when he threw the ball it seemed to be coming right out of his white jersey.

"On that play at the plate, Hickman charged the ball well and made an accurate throw just a little bit up the line to Randy, who made the swipe-tag. When the ump called Agee safe, I can still see Randy jumping up and down, and I remember Leo running off the bench to join him.

"When you lose a game because the other pitcher throws a one-hitter, or when you get beat by five or six runs, that's one thing, but when you lose because of something you can't control, like an umpire's call, that hurts.

"In the clubhouse afterward, we sat around longer than usual, going over the game, and the only thing we could say was, 'Well, we're still in first place, let's go get 'em tomorrow.' But in the end that game was a turning point."

Regarding Agee's decisive run, Hundley recalled, "That was the biggest play of the year. It was a gift for the Mets. When they win a game like that they start believing things are going their way and no one can stop them."

"That first game we played in New York was as big as any game we played all year," said Don Kessinger. "The next time Tom Seaver just beat us. A great pitcher can do that to you

"I can still see Randy jumping up and down," Billy Williams recalled.
(Ronald L. Mrowiec)

anytime. But when the umpire missed that play on Agee and
we lost the game, it took a lot out of us."

It came as little consolation to the Cubs years later when
Agee talked to Glenn Beckert about the play at the plate. "You
guys had me," he confessed. Even if Agee had been called out,
it still would not have ensured the Cubs of winning the game,
nor would it have prevented them, in all likelihood, from falling
apart the rest of the season. Their collapse during September,
when they lost 17 of 25 games, has been dissected many times,
and critics seem justified in pointing to team fatigue as a chief
reason for the Cubs' general deterioration in all phases of the
game. Only Billy Williams and Bill Hands seemed to continue
performing at a high level.

"What I remember most," said Kessinger, "is that we were
a tired ball club. A lot of it had to do with playing day baseball in Wrigley Field. It's the sun that does it. I feel that when
you play eight guys in the hot sun most every day, you have
to be a lot better than anybody else to win."

Chicago Cubs vs. New York Mets
at Shea Stadium, September 8, 1969

Chicago Cubs	AB	R	H	RBI	New York Mets	AB	R	H	RBI
Don Kessinger, ss	4	1	2	0	Tommie Agee, cf	3	2	2	2
Glenn Beckert, 2b	4	1	2	0	Wayne Garrett, 3b	4	0	1	1
Billy Williams, lf	4	0	2	1	Donn Clendenon, 1b	4	0	0	0
Ron Santo, 3b	2	0	0	1	Art Shamsky, lf	2	0	1	0
Ernie Banks, 1b	3	0	0	0	Rod Gaspar, lf	0	0	0	0
Jim Hickman, rf	3	0	0	0	Ken Boswell, 2b	3	0	0	0
Randy Hundley, c	4	0	1	0	Al Weis, 2b	0	0	0	0
Don Young, cf	3	0	0	0	Ron Swoboda, rf	3	0	0	0
Ken Rudolph, ph (a)	1	0	0	0	Jerry Grote, c	3	0	0	0
Randy Bobb, ph (b)	1	0	0	0	Bud Harrelson, ss	3	1	1	0
Bill Hands, p	3	0	0	0	Jerry Koosman, p	3	0	0	0
Total	32	2	7	2		28	3	5	3

(a) Struck out for Don Young in the ninth; (b) Struck out for Bill Hands in the ninth.

Chicago	0	0	0	0	0	2	0	0	0	—	2
New York	0	0	2	0	0	1	0	0	x	—	3

Chicago Cubs	IP	H	R	ER	SO	BB
Bill Hands (L, 16-13)	8.0	5	3	3	5	2

New York Mets	IP	H	R	ER	SO	BB
Jerry Koosman (W, 13-9)	9.0	7	2	2	13	2

Errors—Kessinger. **DP**—Chicago, 1; New York, 1. **2B**—Agee. **HR**—Agee. **SF**—Santo. **LOB**—Chicago, 7; New York, 3. **Hit by pitch**—Santo (by Koosman). **WP**—Koosman.
Umpires—Satch Davidson, Paul Pryor, Frank Secory, Tony Venzon
Time—2:09. **Attendance**—43,274

Night baseball at Wrigley Field was still a long way off when Durocher summarized the ineffectiveness of his weary troops in the final month of the season. "It was a composite slump," he growled. "The hitting, the pitching, the fielding all went bad at the same time. If we had played .500 ball or a little better, we might've made it, but the Mets kept winning, winning, winning."

In addition to the debilitating effects of Durocher's refusal to rest his regulars when they needed it, one other factor figured strongly in the Cubs' fadeout. Simply put, the Mets were deeper in quality pitching. Manager Gil Hodges had enough talent available to employ a five-man rotation, and he could reach deep into his staff without a falloff in efficiency.

In addition to Seaver, 24, and Koosman, 25, the Mets' young arms included Gary Gentry, 22, Jim McAndrew, 24, Nolan Ryan, 22, Tug McGraw, 24, Cal Koonce, 28, and Ron Taylor, 28. Don Cardwell was the old man on the staff at 33. They produced a major league–leading 28 shutouts and a skimpy ERA of 2.99.

"Their pitching was awesome," said Paul Popovich.

So, in the final analysis it might be said that Mets pitching rather than umpire Satch Davidson or even Tommie Agee vaporized the Cubs' dreams of glory in 1969.

As Durocher mellowed with age, he expressed regrets that he couldn't have won at least a division title for owner Phil Wrigley. Before he died in 1991 in Palm Springs, California, he also admitted that he should have given some of the regulars brief reprieves during the tension-packed '69 season. "If I'd only given Beck [Beckert] and Kess [Kessinger] a little rest," he said, "and given Randy a couple of days off, and spelled Billy in left field occasionally, and kept 'em strong, kept the pressure off them, we would have won the pennant if I did that."

Despite that bittersweet season, members of the '69 Cubs for years were so idolized by their fans that one would think they had actually won the pennant instead of finishing eight games behind the Mets.

Some years ago Bill Hands summed up the Cubs' fate in '69 in an interview with author Rick Talley. Hands had earned his $31,000 salary that year by winning 20 games, pitching 300 innings, and posting an ERA of 2.49, best on the staff.

"You gotta understand," Hands said, "that over the years certain plays are magnified—like the slide play at Shea Stadium in September. But we were already dead. We were already playing horseshit baseball. We weren't scoring runs, and we weren't pitching that great either. Somewhere from the middle of August on, we just weren't making it. And all that time the Mets were playing unbelievable.

"So we had so much pressure on us, we folded. It's that simple. We folded. I don't want to hear all the bullshit about day games and the guys being tired. I don't buy that crap.

"On paper, postionwise, we were better than the Mets, but they had an edge in pitching.

"I was proud of the year I had, but the losing was just a terrible, terrible letdown for all of us. It was awful."

Billy Williams still looks back with disappointment on the Cubs' failure in '69. "If we had won that year," he said, "I know we would have won two or three more times. We could have been recognized as one of the great teams in Cubs' history."

1972

A Wild Pitch Sinks the Pirates

"When I saw that ball bounce away from
Sanguillen, I said, 'No, this can't be happening.'"
—Steve Blass

In 1972, for the first time in major league history, the players set a general strike in motion. Before the start of the season, it momentarily turned the attention of players as well as baseball owners, fans, and writers away from the game itself and the forthcoming pennant races.

The strike involved a dispute over the expansion of the players' pension benefits. Through the persuasion of executive director Marvin Miller, the Baseball Players Association voted overwhelmingly to strike against club owners. The action delayed the opening of the season by eight days, until April 15, and resulted in the cancellation of 86 games. In the process, the players won their fight for greater pension benefits but lost public favor for their militant stance. Owners August Busch of the Cardinals and Gene Autry of the Angels were especially vehement in criticizing the action by the players' union.

Two highly regarded baseball writers held opposite views of the strike. Dick Young of the *New York Daily News* described Miller as a "Svengali" and accused him of mesmerizing the players. "Ball players," wrote Young, "are no match for him. He runs them through a high-pressure spray the way an auto goes through a car wash, and that's how they come out, brainwashed. With few exceptions, they follow him blindly, like zombies."

Red Smith of the *New York Times* sided with the players. "From time to time," he wrote, "owners and mouthpieces of the establishment have pictured Marvin Miller as a master pitchman who hypnotizes the players. The 663–10 vote in favor of a strike suggests that if the players aren't in earnest Miller has to be the glibbest con man this side of Soapy Smith."

While the players sought a larger slice of baseball's financial pie, it might be noted the highest-paid major leaguer in 1972 was Hank Aaron, who held a $200,000 annual contract with the Atlanta Braves. Next in line were Carl Yastrzemski, who was paid $167,000; Willie Mays, $165,000; and Roberto Clemente and Bob Gibson, $150,000 each.

General manager John Holland of the Cubs, who had the biggest payroll in the majors in 1972, warned that salaries had reached their limits. "I know we have reached a saturation point," said Holland. "If our payroll goes any higher, we just can't make it." In view of what happened to the big league pay scale in later years, Holland's lament proved to be ill founded.

In other baseball news, the San Francisco Giants said farewell to Willie Mays, dealing him to the New York Mets. The return of Mays, 41, to New York helped boost the Mets' attendance to 2,134,185 paid admissions, most in the majors.

The U.S. Supreme Court in June 19 delivered its decision in the Curt Flood case and by a 5–3 majority upheld baseball's unique exemption from anti-trust laws that bound a player to the team that held his contract. Flood had sued baseball in 1970 in protest of his being traded from the Cardinals to the Phillies, preventing him from bargaining with other clubs interested in his services.

Neither of the National League division races in 1972 was particularly close or exciting. In the East, the defending world champion Pirates ran away from the field, finishing 11 games ahead of the second-place Cubs. In the West Division, the Reds, after a slow start, also breezed to a title by a wide margin, ten and a half games ahead of the dual runners-up Astros and Dodgers.

The American League, however, was more competitive. The

Tigers beat out the Red Sox by a half-game in the East Division while the bickering, battling Oakland A's, who fought among themselves and with their manager Dick Williams and owner Charlie Finley, took the West Division crown with a more comfortable five-and-a-half-game edge over the White Sox.

In October the mustachioed, colorful A's gained entry to the World Series by beating the Tigers in five playoff games while losing the services of their top slugger Reggie Jackson for the Fall Classic. Jackson suffered a pulled hamstring muscle in a collision at home plate in game five. In doing so he scored the A's first run in their 2–1 tension-packed victory.

The Reds also reached the World Series in five playoff games, but they made it with a touch of good luck. They vanquished the Pirates in the deciding National League playoff game on one errant pitch.

In 1972 the Pirates were a close match for the Reds. They had four starting pitchers who won in double figures, including Steve Blass, 19–8; Dock Ellis, 15–7; Nelson Briles, 14–11; and Bob Moose, 13–10, plus tough relievers in Dave Giusti, Ramon Hernandez, and Bruce Kison.

The Bucs also had solid hitting, with Roberto Clemente and center fielder Al Oliver both batting .312; third baseman Richie Hebner, .300; left fielder Vic Davalillo, .318; catcher Manny Sanguillen, .298; and first baseman Willie Stargell, .293 with 33 home runs and 112 RBI.

As a team the Pirates outhit the Reds .274 to .251, and in staff ERA bettered them 2.81 to 3.21. Cincinnati held the edge in fielding, .982 to .974, but the Pirates completed more double plays, 171 to 143.

"I thought we were a better team in '72 than when we won it all in 1971," said Nellie Briles. "We were counting on going back to the World Series."

Danny Murtaugh had retired as Pittsburgh manager after the Pirates beat the Baltimore Orioles in the Series the previous October, and Bill Virdon had taken his place. Murtaugh was an easygoing skipper; Virdon was intense and more of a disciplinarian. "They were both good managers," said Al Oliver, "but no matter which one was running the team, you'd better hustle or you were in trouble."

No one knew that the Pirates' playoff loss to the Reds would be Roberto Clemente's last game. *(Ronald L. Mrowiec)*

"I remember Virdon saying that year we had the best all-around team he ever managed," added Steve Blass.

Testimony to the club's ability and staying power was the fact that Clemente, the Pirates' brightest star, played in only 102 games because of two rheumatic heels, tendinitis in his ankles, inflammation near both Achilles tendons, and repeated bouts with a viral infection. He played only 94 of those games in right field, the rest as a pinch-hitter.

By the All-Star break the Pirates had established a six-game lead and were never challenged the rest of the way as they rolled to their third straight East Division championship and a date with the Reds in the league playoffs.

Before the regular season ended, Clemente added a crowning touch to his Hall of Fame career. On September 30 he collected his three thousandth hit, a double off Jon Matlack of the Mets. It was his final hit before the playoffs began. He dedicated it to "the Pittsburgh fans and the people of Puerto Rico."

The first two playoff games were held at Three Rivers Stadium in Pittsburgh, with Blass winning the opener against Don

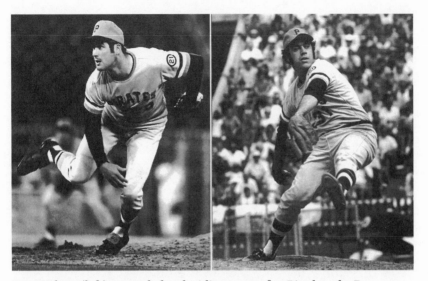

Steve Blass (left) started the deciding game for Pittsburgh. Dave
Giusti relieved in the ninth. *(Frank Bryan)*

Gullett, 5–1. In the second game the Reds rebounded and beat
Moose 5–3, moving the series to Cincinnati's Riverfront Stadium for the remaining three games if they were needed. They
were.

Pittsburgh won game three in a tight match, 3–2, behind
the pitching of Briles, Kison, and Giusti, while the Reds came
back in game four as left-hander Ross Grimsley smothered the
Bucs 7–1 on only two hits, an infield single and a home run,
both by Clemente. "This is a very surprising club," said Cincinnati manager Sparky Anderson of his Reds after game four.
"Whenever people think they're down, they always come back.
On the bench today, somebody must have fed those guys something. [Joe] Hague and [Hal] McRae were leading chants and
cheers from the first inning. Those guys were jumping up and
down. I wouldn't have used any of them as pinch-hitters. They
were too worn out from cheering."

In the game five showdown, Blass started against Gullett
before a crowd of 41,887 fans at Riverfront. Rain delayed the
start of the game for one hour and twenty-eight minutes, and
before the Reds took the field to begin the battle, Gullett and
Blass had both warmed up twice.

The Pirates jumped off to a 2–0 lead in the second inning on a single by Sanguillen, a double by Hebner, and another single by Dave Cash. In the bottom of the third, Darrel Chaney singled, moved to second on Gullett's sacrifice, and Pete Rose brought him home with a double, cutting the Pirates' lead to 2–1. Rose's double hit the edge of the artificial turf and bounced over first baseman Willie Stargell's head.

Pittsburgh, however, came right back with three straight singles by Sanguillen, Hebner, and Cash in the fourth inning, boosting its lead to 3–1. Sparky Anderson pulled Gullett.

Once more the Reds rebounded, this time with a home run to right field by Cesar Geronimo off a change-up curve from Blass in the fifth inning, closing the score to 3–2. It remained that way until the bottom of the ninth inning, leaving the Pirates only three outs away from the title.

Virdon had replaced Blass with left-hander Ramon Hernandez to get the last couple of outs in the eighth inning, but in the ninth he wanted his steady bullpen man, right-hander Dave Giusti, who had saved 22 games and notched seven victories for the Pirates during the season.

Hernandez that year had appeared in 50 games, won five, lost none, saved 14, and owned a miniscule ERA of 1.67. He was angry he wasn't pitching the ninth inning even though the first three Reds coming to the plate were right-handed hitters. Virdon was going with the percentages.

The first batter to face Giusti was Johnny Bench, who had led the National League with 40 home runs and 125 RBI. Giusti had the upper hand on Bench with one ball and two strikes when Bench sent his next pitch deep to the right-field seats for a home run that tied the score at 3–3.

"I felt ready against the Reds," said Giusti. "I had already done well against them in the third game when we won and I got the save. I had had some luck with Bench over the years until that time. I thought I had him set up with a fastball inside that he hit to the left, foul. Then I went with my best pitch, a palm ball. That was my out pitch. He waited on it so well, which was unusual for him. He was pretty much of a pull hitter, but he hit my best pitch to right center. I thought he'd swing and miss or try to pull it, but it didn't sink enough."

"When we took the field at the bottom of the ninth," said Al Oliver, "I was out there in center field counting my World Series share. I was confident we were going to win.

"When Bench hit that ball, I was running over to back up Roberto if the ball hit the wall, but as soon as I was half over there I knew it was gone. Bench was not known to hit to right field. He only hit two of them there all year, both against us."

As Bench stood at the plate facing Giusti, he looked over his shoulder. "I saw my mother leaning over the box-seat railing, shouting something," he said. "I couldn't hear what she was yelling, but I knew what she was saying, 'Hit one, John.'

"I told Pete [Rose] earlier in the game, I hoped there would be somebody on base in the ninth inning because I was going to hit one. It was a palm ball," he said, "and I was just lucky he got it up where I could hit it. For just a split second, when I had two strikes, I thought about going into that new defensive stance I used with two strikes. I usually spread my legs out more, brought my hands in, and shortened up my stroke. But, then I said, 'The hell with it. I'm going for the home run.' I just had that feeling.

"Before the game I looked at movies of myself and I saw the reason I wasn't hitting in the series was because I was crouching too much. That gave me confidence, plus the fact there were no shadows. It was still partly cloudy and I was seeing the ball. I don't care who's pitching, if there are no shadows I can hit the ball."

"I got so frustrated after Bench hit that homer," said Giusti, "I gave up hits to the next two batters [Tony Perez and Dennis Menke], and that's when Virdon took me out and brought in Moose."

A heavy-duty right-hander who had pitched 226 innings including 30 starts in 1972, Moose was summoned to the mound while Reds' manager Sparky Anderson sent George Foster in to run for Perez at second base with the potential winning run.

Moose got the next batter, Geronimo, on a fly to Clemente in deep right field, allowing Foster to advance to third on the play. Chaney then popped up to Gene Alley at short for the second out. Now Anderson sent Hal McRae up to pinch-hit for Cincinnati reliever Clay Carroll.

Bob Moose's slider bounced away from Sanguillen.

What happened next remains one of those oddities that make baseball such an unpredictable game.

With a one-ball, one-strike count on McRae, Moose threw a wide slider. It bounced away from catcher Manny Sanguillen who tried to backhand the ball but couldn't block it. Foster scored jubilantly from third base, giving the Reds a 4–3 victory and the National League pennant.

Steve Blass was in the Pirates' clubhouse after finishing his pitching. He was still in uniform and was watching the game on the TV monitor. "When I saw that ball bounce away from Sanguillen, I said, 'No, this can't be happening. We're supposed to be going to the World Series,'" Blass recalled.

"It was a shock, and I got that sick, empty feeling we might never get back to the Series. Moose's pitch took a funny bounce, wide of the plate. It was so quick, so unusual. Clemente was great afterward. He told us to keep our head up, that we had nothing to be ashamed of and that we had a great season. Little did we know that was his last game."

"I was in the dugout when Moose threw the wild pitch," said Giusti, "I saw the whole thing. It was not a good time for me. After the game, Roberto was one of the first to come over and pat me on the back. He said, 'It's just one game. You've got a long career ahead of you. If you and your family are doing well, that's the most important thing in life.'

"Most everybody came by and gave me a pat on the shoulder, but when you're down, a lot of things go in one ear and out the other. I do remember though what Clemente said.

"Strange, I still dream about that game once in a while. And I think about Moose. He did a helluva job for us that season except for that one pitch."

"I was getting ready in the bullpen in case I was needed," said Nellie Briles. "When Moose threw the wild pitch, and when it bounced over Sanguillen's shoulder, my heart sank to my feet. I just saw our World Series hopes bounce away."

The Reds swarmed over Foster as he crossed the plate with the winning run. The Pirates began leaving the field, but before they did Sanguillen retrieved the ball thrown by Moose and flung it to center field in a final gesture of frustration that gripped the defeated champions.

"It was a tough loss, but not a devastating loss because of the attitude we carried all year," said Al Oliver. "We always gave it our best shot, so I walked off the field with Roberto and kept my head up. It just wasn't meant to be.

"The Pirates and Reds were so close in talent in '72. Personally, I thought we had the edge that year even though they had more power in their lineup, but we had guys who hit the ball, put the ball in play. If not for that loss and we had gone on to the World Series again, they would've been talking about the Pirates and not the Big Red Machine.

"Moose threw a sinking fastball, a heavy ball, along with a sharp slider. To me, what cost us that game was not the wild pitch but the Bench home run. Bench wasn't known to hit to right field."

Dropping the League Championship Series to the Reds was not the most pleasant way for Bill Virdon to finish his rookie season as manager of the Pirates, for whom he had starred as a smooth center fielder in the 1950s and 1960s. "I thought we were the best club in baseball that year," he said. "We had good left-handed hitters in Stargell, Oliver, and Hebner, and from the right side we had Clemente. Our pitching was deep, and maybe we lacked some speed, but we really didn't need it.

"Moose threw McRae a couple of breaking pitches. Then he tried to throw a little better one and he bounced it. If we had

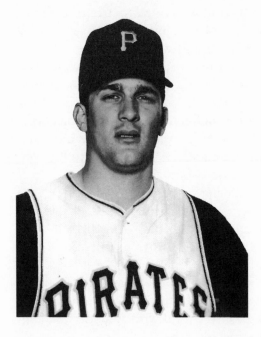

"I was trying to waste the pitch," Moose lamented.

gotten through the ninth, I think we would've had the advantage. I still had all my bench left, and Anderson had nobody left."

In his post-game remarks, Moose said, "I was trying to waste the pitch by throwing a slider outside. When I let it go, I knew it was outside where I wanted it. I didn't think it was that low, but when it started going down, I figured it would bounce up and hit Manny in the stomach. But it took a crazy hop over his head. How many times have you seen a bounce that high?"

Moose was also heard to ask Sanguillen in a soft tone, "Hey, Sangy, couldn't you stop that ball?" He spoke with a sense of disappointment, not antagonism.

"It looked like it hit something," said Sanguillen. "I jumped for the ball and it came up, but it hit me on the hand. It never touched my glove."

Charlie Feeney, a baseball writer for the *Pittsburgh Post-Gazette* who covered the final playoff game, stayed on in Cincinnati for the World Series. "I met so many scouts there," he said, "and they all asked me the same thing: 'What the hell was the matter with Sanguillen backhanding that ball? How could he do that?'"

"A play like that was all that could have beaten us that year," said Willie Stargell. "I didn't know then that game would be the last time Roberto and I would play on the same field together. Had I known, I would have saved some appropriate words for the occasion. I may even have told him I loved him."

While Sanguillen failed to get his body in front of Moose's wild pitch and was not as skillful a defensive catcher as Johnny Bench, he made strong contributions to the Pirates' offense throughout the '72 race. And in game three against the Reds he had driven in two runs in the Pirates' 3–2 decision.

He was known as a bad-ball hitter, and pitchers found it difficult to work the count on him. They could throw him a sharp-breaking curve, down and away, and the next thing they knew there was Sanguillen dusting himself off at second base with an opposite-field double. Earlier in the season, when Sanguillen rapped out five hits in a game against the Cardinals, catcher Ted Simmons complained, "We didn't throw him one pitch in the strike zone."

In fact, Sanguillen that year pretty much typified the Pittsburgh lineup. "Pitching to the Pirates is tough," said Tim McCarver, who was then catching for the Montreal Expos. "You go over each hitter before each game and you really don't know too much. That's because they have so many bad-ball hitters. Some teams have bad-ball hitters and that's good for the other club because they don't get many base hits. The Pirates are a base-hit club."

"It's impossible to throw the ball past Pirate hitters," said left-hander Jerry Koosman, then with the New York Mets. "Even when you pitch them out of the strike zone, they find a way to hit it."

Despite their knack of "hitting balls where they ain't," the Pirates were unable to mount a successful attack against Reds' relievers Pedro Borbon, Tom Hall, and Clay Carroll in the final five innings of the 1972 playoff game, collecting only two singles along the way.

When Moose's pitch skipped away from Sanguillen and Fos-

Pittsburgh Pirates vs. Cincinnati Reds
at Riverfront Stadium, October 11, 1972

Pittsburgh Pirates	AB	R	H	RBI	Cincinnati Reds	AB	R	H	RBI
Rennie Stennett, lf	4	0	1	0	Pete Rose, lf	3	0	1	1
Al Oliver; cf	3	0	0	0	Joe Morgan, 2b	4	0	0	0
Roberto Clemente, rf	3	0	1	0	Bobby Tolan, cf	4	0	0	0
Willie Stargell, 1b	4	0	0	0	Johnny Bench, c	4	1	2	1
Bob Robertson, 1b	0	0	0	0	Tony Perez, 1b	4	0	1	0
Manny Sanguillen, c	4	2	2	0	George Foster, pr (b)	0	1	0	0
Richie Hebner, 3b	4	1	2	0	Denis Menke, 3b	3	0	1	0
Dave Cash, 2b	4	0	2	2	Cesar Geronimo, cf	4	1	1	1
Gene Alley, ss	4	0	0	0	Darrel Chaney, ss	4	1	1	0
Steve Blass, p	3	0	0	0	Don Gullett, p	0	0	0	0
					Ted Uhlaender, ph (a)	1	0	0	0
					Dave Concepcion, pr (c)	0	0	0	0
					Hal McRae, ph (d)	0	0	0	0
Total	**33**	**3**	**8**	**2**		**31**	**4**	**7**	**3**

(a) Pinch-hit for Pedro Borbon in the fifth; (b) Pinch-ran for Perez in the ninth; (c) Pinch-ran for Menke in the ninth; (d) Pinch-hit for Clay Carroll in the ninth.

Pittsburgh	0	2	0	1	0	0	0	0	0 — 3
Cincinnati	0	0	1	0	1	0	0	0	2 — 4

Pittsburgh Pirates	IP	H	R	ER	SO	BB
Steve Blass	7.1	4	2	2	4	2
Ramon Hernandez	0.2	0	0	0	1	0
Dave Giusti (L)	0.0	3	2	2	0	0
Bob Moose	0.2	0	0	0	0	0

Cincinnati Reds	IP	H	R	ER	SO	BB
Don Gullett	3.0	6	3	3	2	0
Pedro Borbon	2.0	1	0	0	1	0
Tom Hall	3.0	1	0	0	4	1
Clay Carroll (W)	1.0	0	0	0	0	0

Errors—Chaney. **DP**—Cincinnati 1. **2B**—Hebner, Rose. **HR**—Geronimo, Bench. **SH**—Gullett, Oliver, Rose. **LOB**—Cincinnati, 5; Pittsburgh, 5. **WP**—Gullett, Moose.
Umpires—Augie Donatelli, John Kibler, Harry Wendelstedt, Ken Burkhart, Doug Harvey, Bill Williams.
Time—2:19. **Attendance**—41,887

ter headed for the plate, Sparky Anderson almost collapsed in the Reds' dugout. He had to be helped by two of his players to the team's dressing room. "I was having trouble catching my breath," said Anderson. "I was just excited."

Anderson was also a gracious winner. "These two teams are still No. 1," he said afterward. "Pittsburgh is just as good as we are. These are the two best."

Pete Rose echoed his manager's sentiments. "That game represented the world's championship," he said. "I know we've got to beat the American League, but the two best teams in baseball played in this playoff."

Rose had to eat those words 11 days later when the Oakland A's beat the Reds in the World Series in seven games, six of which were decided by one run.

In light of Roberto Clemente's death in a plane crash the following December, while he was on a mercy mission to aid earthquake victims in Nicaragua, many of the '72 Pirates look back with sorrow at that last clubhouse gathering after the heartbreaking playoff game with the Reds. One of Clemente's closest friends on the team, Dave Cash, approached Roberto and said goodbye for the winter. "I remember leaving the clubhouse," said Cash, "and we shook hands and hugged each other. We wished each other well and hoped we could come back and win the next season."

Steve Blass and Dave Giusti, who lived in the same community near Pittsburgh, flew home on the team plane accompanied by their wives. The two couples left the Pittsburgh airport in the same car and drove some distance, as Blass recalled, "in stone silence before stopping at a light. At that point I shouted, 'Everybody out for our fire drill! We've got to lighten up!' So we all got out of the car. We were so pissed off that we all started screaming obscenities. When we got done with that outburst, we all felt better, got back in the car, and drove home."

A last note that might be added about the '72 Pirates involves the untimely death of the pitcher who was on the mound when they saw their championship slip away from them.

Bob Moose was killed in an automobile crash in Martin's Ferry, Ohio, while coming home from a birthday party on October 9, 1976, almost four years to the day he unleashed his infamous wild pitch against the Reds. He had just turned 29.

1975

Red Sox Edged by the Reds in a Memorable Classic

"We had 'em, and then we didn't have 'em, but I
can't take anything away from the Cincinnati Reds."
—Dwight Evans

It may not have been the greatest World Series ever
played, but the 1975 classic was unquestionably a most memorable one, pitting the Cincinnati Reds against the Boston Red
Sox.

With rain delays, it took 11 days to complete, ending on October 22 at Fenway Park where the Reds prevailed 4–3 in game
seven on a bloop single to center by Joe Morgan.

"I felt we were playing a poker hand going into the last
game," said Morgan. "We had eight great players out there, and
baseball's best pitcher in Don Gullett in the middle. We had a
full house going for us, and it was going to take four-of-a-kind
to beat us."

Frank Robinson began the 1975 season as the first black
manager in the majors, and not only piloted the Cleveland Indians but also played for the team, primarily as a designated
hitter. In the Indians' Opening Day game he hit a home run in
his initial at-bat as a DH, connecting against George Medich
of the Yankees to help beat New York 5–3.

Nolan Ryan made news on June 1, pitching a 1–0 no-hitter
for the California Angels against the Baltimore Orioles at Ana-

heim. It was Ryan's fourth career no-hitter, tying him with the record set by Sandy Koufax ten years earlier.

Fred Lynn, a prized 23-year-old rookie center fielder for the Red Sox, accomplished something special on June 18 when he collected three home runs, a triple, and a single while driving in ten runs in Boston's 15-1 rout of Detroit at Tiger Stadium. Two days before Lynn demolished Tiger pitching, he had rounded off an impressive 20-game hitting streak.

On August 2, Billy Martin was named to replace Bill Virdon as manager of the Yankees. While the club finished far out of the running in '75, Martin would have the Bronx pinstripers back on top in 1976 and 1977.

In the American League the East Division race was won handily by the Red Sox, managed by Darrell Johnson, a former journeyman catcher who had played for seven major league teams in the 1950s and early 1960s. Boston finished four and a half games in front of second place Baltimore with a 95-65 record. In September the Bosox beat the Orioles in three of four games, taking the measure of Jim Palmer twice, 3-2 and 2-0, and Mike Torrez once, 3-1.

While the Orioles registered the league's best winning record, 49-25, after the All-Star break, they could not overcome Boston's lead. "We did what we had to do in order to win," said their manager Earl Weaver, "but the Red Sox also did what they had to do. Their pitching staff did a great job down the stretch."

Although none of their starters or relievers led the American League in any category, the Red Sox had five pitchers who won 13 or more games. They included Rick Wise, 19-12; Luis Tiant, 18-14; Bill Lee, 17-9; Roger Moret, 14-3; and Reggie Cleveland, 13-9.

Boston also packed a wallop on offense, led by rookies Lynn in center and Jim Rice in left, who with Dwight Evans in right formed one of the club's most highly regarded outfields ever.

A left-handed batter and thrower, Lynn won not only the American League's 1975 Rookie of the Year award, but also its Most Valuable Player award for a season in which he hit .331, collected 21 homers and 105 RBI in addition to leading the league in doubles with 47, runs scored with 103, and slugging percentage, .566.

Rice, 22, hit from the right side with raw power and, like Lynn, made a big impact with 22 homers, 102 RBI, 92 runs, and a .309 batting average. Once he was moved from the DH spot, he worked hard to become a dependable left fielder and in fact did not commit an error in the outfield in 168 chances.

Catcher Tim McCarver, who was with the Red Sox early in 1975 before joining the Phillies, saw both Lynn and Rice break in. "Lynn had a stance that looked like you could never get him out," McCarver said. "I don't think I've ever seen a young hitter look as good as he did in the beginning of the '75 season. And the thing about Rice, he was so strong even at a young age, and you knew he was going to get stronger. He was hitting balls out with regularity in right center field, over the bullpen, in batting practice. So both of them impressed you for different reasons—Lynn with the great stroke, Rice because of his strength."

Johnson's two rookie standouts were augmented by a relatively experienced cast that included future Hall of Famers Carlton Fisk behind the plate and Carl Yastrzemski who moved from left field to first base. Rico Petrocelli was at third; Rick Burleson played short, with Denny Doyle, who had been acquired from the Angels on June 14, and Doug Griffin sharing second-base duties. Cecil Cooper filled an important role as the team's DH, batting .311 with 14 homers, and Bernie Carbo came up with clutch hits as a utility outfielder, producing 15 home runs and 50 RBI.

Carbo had begun his major league career with the Reds and was with them from 1969 until 1972 when he was dealt to the Cardinals. He was traded by St. Louis to the Red Sox along with Rick Wise after the 1973 season for outfielder Reggie Smith. "That 1975 team, I thought at the time," Carbo said of the Red Sox, "was the best team I ever played on. Better than the Big Red Machine. There was a lot of camaraderie. When you left the clubhouse, your belly hurt, your face hurt from laughing so much."

It was not all laughs for the Red Sox, however, as they closed in on their first pennant since 1967. Fisk caught only 71 games because of injuries, including a broken arm in spring training, and on September 21, Rice was lost for the season after his left hand was broken by a fastball thrown by Vern Ruhl of the Tigers.

Born in Bellows Falls, Vermont, in 1947, Fisk had been a natural choice by the Red Sox in the January 1967 amateur draft, even though as a high school basketball player he had been good enough to win a scholarship to the University of New Hampshire. "What I really wanted to be," Fisk said of his younger days, "was a power forward for the Boston Celtics." That notion vanished when the only baseball team he wanted to play for made him its fourth draft pick in the nation. He earned the regular catching job with the Red Sox in 1972, a season in which he was unanimously elected the American League Rookie of the Year.

But he had a hard time staying out of harm's way. Two years later, during spring training of 1974, he took a foul tip in the groin and missed the start of the regular season. Then, in June, he tore knee ligaments while trying to block the plate, and underwent reconstructive surgery. "Doctors gave me no hope of ever coming back," Fisk said. Without the services of their regular catcher, the Red Sox finished third in the East Division race that year.

With intensive rehabilitation, Fisk recovered in time for spring training in 1975, only to suffer a broken right forearm when he was struck by a pitch in the team's second exhibition game in March. When he returned to the lineup on June 23, the Red Sox were off and rolling. They held first place from June 29 on, thanks to uncharacteristically strong pitching and the league's best team batting average, .275, coupled with the most runs scored, 796. In his limited role, Fisk still did his share to help the Boston cause, batting .331 with 52 RBI.

The Red Sox clinched the East Division title six days after Rice was disabled in late September. New England fans were convinced his presence would have altered the outcome of the World Series that year. The loss of Rice nonetheless had little effect on Boston in the American League Championship Series as Darrell Johnson shifted Yaz back to left field and stationed Cecil Cooper at first base during the Red Sox three-game sweep of the Oakland A's by scores of 7–1, 6–3, and 5–3. The sweep ended an Oakland dynasty during which the A's won the World Series in 1972, 1973, and 1974.

In the same span of days that it took the Red Sox to qualify for the Fall Classic, the Reds wiped out the Pirates in the National League playoff series, also in dominating fashion, 8–3, 6–1, and 5–3. It marked the third time Sparky Anderson had guided his team to a World Series in the 1970s. In winning 108 games during the regular season, the Reds were regarded by many Cincinnati fans as the best in the club's long history. They simply ran away from their competition in the West Division, finishing 20 games ahead of the second-place Dodgers.

The Reds led the league in stolen bases, 168, and in fielding, committing the fewest errors, 102. There was no weakness in their lineup with Tony Perez at first, Joe Morgan at second, Dave Concepcion at short, Pete Rose at third, George Foster in left, Cesar Geronimo in center, Ken Griffey in right, and Johnny Bench behind the plate.

Anderson had a deep pitching staff too, including six starters who won in double figures. Don Gullett, Gary Nolan, and Jack Billingham led the way with 15 victories each. And the Reds were fortified in the bullpen with right-handers Clay Carroll, Rawley Eastwick, and Pedro Borbon, and lefty Will McEnaney.

They were favored against the Red Sox in the World Series.

Anderson spoke almost reverently of his team. He once told Cincinnati broadcaster Ken Coleman, "I don't manage this team. The Reds are managed by Johnny Bench, Joe Morgan, Pete Rose, and Tony Perez. I just change the pitchers now and then."

"In the media's eyes," said Dwight Evans, "we weren't even supposed to be in the same ball park with the Big Red Machine. They were going to roll over us—but we easily could have won that World Series. We had 'em, and then we didn't have 'em, but I can't take anything away from the Cincinnati Reds."

The World Series opened at Fenway Park on October 11, with Red Sox starter Luis Tiant's father throwing out the ceremonial first pitch. The elder Tiant, a former outstanding pitcher in Cuba, threw out not only one ball but three—all of them strikes with some zip on them—to Carlton Fisk, before he was escorted from the mound.

The pitching matchup pitted the younger Tiant against Don Gullett, and it remained a scoreless duel until the bottom of the seventh inning when the Red Sox pushed over six runs. Their 6–0 lead held up as Tiant surrendered only five hits.

Known for his pirouette pitching motion and after-game cigars, Tiant led off the seventh-inning rally with a single. His extra contribution to winning was possible because American League designated hitters were not allowed to bat for pitchers in the World Series at that time.

In September, Red Sox pitchers had begun taking batting practice in preparation for the Series, an exercise that almost wiped out Bill Lee's availability. While working out at the plate, the rangy left-hander was jammed by a pitch, swung the bat too hard, and hyperextended his arm, tearing a small tendon in his elbow. Lee was useless for six weeks and missed pitching in the playoffs against the A's. But he was healed in time to face the Reds in game two on October 12. "I was up for the Series," he said. "I liked the idea of competing against the best."

A free spirit with a finely honed sense of the ridiculous, Lee recalled that the scouting report he studied on the Reds amazed him: "Pitch around Rose. Pitch around Morgan. Pitch around Perez. According to our scouts, the best strategy to use against the Reds was start the game with the bases loaded, five runs in, and their pitcher at the plate. Then you had a chance."

The second game at Fenway was played with rain falling throughout much of the contest. Matched against Jack Billingham, Lee made the most of his chance of beating the Reds for eight full innings. He carried a 2–1 lead into the top of the ninth when he gave up a leadoff double to right field by Bench. Johnson summoned Dick Drago from the bullpen. Drago almost closed out the game by retiring the next two batters, Perez and Foster, but Concepcion beat out a high hopper over the pitcher's head to score Bench with the tying run.

"Concepcion broke our hearts with that seeing-eye single up the middle," Lee admitted.

The Reds' speed came into play as Concepcion stole second and then raced home on Griffey's double to the wall in left center, making it 3–2 Cincinnati. The Red Sox went down in order in their half of the ninth, and the Series was even.

Although he was not charged with the loss, following the game Lee was angry. After the Reds had batted in the top of the seventh inning, there was a 27-minute rain delay. During the break, Bench was interviewed on national television in the Reds' clubhouse and told millions of viewers what his strategy would be against Lee when play resumed. Bench said he would try to hit to the opposite field instead of attempting to pull the ball.

"Nobody thought to tell me about Bench's plans," said Lee. "Did that piss me off! In the ninth inning, if I had known what he was trying to do, I wouldn't have thrown him that first pitch, a sinker down and away, where he was able to hammer it to right."

With the Series even and a day off for travel, the next three games were set for Riverfront Stadium in Cincinnati.

Game three ran ten innings and was marked by plate umpire Larry Barnett's controversial call that figured in the Reds' 6–5 decision. The score was tied 5–5 when Geronimo led off the final inning with a single to center. Pinch-hitter Ed Armbrister, then bunted in front of the plate. When Fisk reached for the high-bouncing ball, Armbrister was slow to react and appeared to impede the Red Sox catcher, but Barnett ruled no interference. In trying for a force play on Geronimo at second, Fisk threw the ball wildly into center field, allowing Geronimo to dash to third and Armbrister to second. The Red Sox protested the umpire's noninterference call, but the play stood and Fisk was charged with an error.

Shortly thereafter, with the bases loaded, Joe Morgan drove a fly ball over the head of drawn-in center fielder Fred Lynn to score Geronimo with the winning run.

In game four, Tiant again went the distance in stopping the Reds 5–4, while Gullett took care of game 5 for Cincinnati with a 6–2 victory.

With the Reds up three games to two, a travel day was followed by three days of rainstorms that swept the New England coast. Five days later, game six was destined to be one of the most dramatic games in World Series history.

In a battle the Red Sox had to win to stay alive, Johnson started Tiant, who was approaching 35 years of age and probably could have used another day of rest after toiling 18 innings in games one and four. Anderson went with his 27-year-old right-hander Gary Nolan, who had worked only four innings in game three a week earlier.

As it turned out, neither starter was particularly effective. Nolan lasted only two innings. The Red Sox jumped on him for a 3–0 lead in the first inning on a three-run homer by Fred Lynn into the right-center-field bleachers. The Reds tied the game with three runs against Tiant in the fifth inning and built that lead to 6–3 in the eighth before Boston evened it again at 6–6 on Bernie Carbo's three-run, pinch-hit homer into the center-field bleachers in the bottom half of the inning.

"When he made contact," recalled Lee, "everyone in our dugout went crazy. We all knew the ball was gone when he hit it."

The score remained deadlocked until the 12th inning. Pat Darcy was on the mound for the Reds, and Carlton Fisk was the leadoff hitter.

Before he stepped to the plate, Fisk said he had "one of those feelings." In the on-deck circle he had turned to Lynn and said, "Fred, I'm going to hit one off the wall. Drive me in."

Fisk did better than that. He slammed reliever Pat Darcy's second pitch high and deep down the left-field line. As Fisk headed to first base he watched the ball, jumping up and down and trying to will the ball fair with his hands and body as it sailed into the night. "I was giving it every bit of body English I could muster," he said. The ball caromed off the left-field foul pole to win the game, 7–6.

It was one of baseball's most memorable home runs, and Fisk's antics created a lasting image for fans at the game and watching on television. By the time he jumped joyously on the plate, it was 12:33 in the morning. The tension-packed marathon had lasted four hours and one minute and had whetted the baseball public's appetite for the climactic game seven.

Starting pitchers for the finale were Bill Lee and Don Gullett. Before the game Sparky Anderson said, "I don't know about that fellah for the Red Sox but some time after this game, my boy is going to the Hall of Fame." Lee heard about Anderson's remark and told reporters, "I don't care where Gullett's going,

Carlton Fisk's famous
homer off the left-field
foul pole tied the Series at
three games each.

because after this game I'm going to the Eliot Lounge," a pop-
ular watering hole in Boston.

It was now a one-game World Series. "It's a shame we have
to play it," Lee said. "These teams are so close they should call
the game off, declare us co-champions of the world, and stage
a picnic at old Fenway."

With the cozy, misshapen ball park near Kenmore Square
jammed with 35,305 spectators, and with an estimated 75 million television viewers taking in the proceedings, the Red Sox
appeared early in the game as though they would literally walk
to the championship. In the third inning, Gullett had control
problems. After striking out Lee, the Reds' left-hander walked
Carbo on four pitches, gave up a single to Doyle and another
single to Yastrzemski who drove in Carbo. He then walked Fisk
intentionally to load the bases, but after fanning Lynn he walked
both Petrocelli and Evans to force in two more runs, putting
the Red Sox ahead 3–0.

Bill Lee brought his free
spirit to the Series'
seventh game.
(Clifton Boutelle)

"When we scored those three runs," said Lee, "the crowd went wild, but after we failed to score again, the stands went dead quiet. It was like you were in Carnegie Hall. The fans sat on their hands, worrying, something they do very well at Fenway. It was as if they were thinking, 'How are we going to screw this one up?'"

Anderson later said he was stunned by Gullett's loss of control. "During the entire season he gave up only 56 walks in 160 innings," Anderson said, "but here he gave up three runs, two of them on walks with the bases full. That was a shock. So we had to do our normal thing, come from behind."

Through the first five innings, Lee maintained his 3–0 lead, choking the Reds effectively by not allowing an extra-base hit and by throwing two double-play balls that eliminated potential rallies.

In the top of the sixth inning, a move by one of the Red Sox coaches proved damaging to Lee. Rose started the inning with a single to right, but Lee retired Morgan on a fly before facing Bench. "Before I threw the first pitch to Bench," Lee said, "somebody on the bench moved Denny Doyle away from second base. I got Bench swinging on a fastball, low and away, a perfect double play ball he hit to Burleson at short.

"It was a nice two-hopper. Rick gloved it and was ready to throw, but Doyle had to come a long way to get to the bag. Doyle took the toss as he came flying across the bag to force Rose who was sliding in, but he threw the ball to first before he had a chance to get set. The ball sailed over first for an error, moving Bench to second. I thought Yaz stretched too soon for the throw at first that went over his head. Instead of being out of the inning, now I had Bench on second with two out, and Tony Perez at the plate.

"I had been having good success with Perez, throwing him my slow, arching curveball," reasoned Lee, "so I thought I'd throw it to him again. Wrong move. Perez timed it just right and hit it over the left-field screen."

Lee escaped the inning with a thin 3–2 lead, but disaster was about to strike him in the seventh. "A blister developed on my left thumb," he said, "and when it broke, I couldn't get my pitch down. I had a good sinking fastball that day, but when the thumb was bleeding, I lost my control and walked Griffey on four pitches.

"At that point, I knew my season was over, and Johnson brought in Roger Moret. It was the right move by Johnson, but if our trainer had had a silver nitrate stick, he might've been able to cauterize the thumb and maybe I could've stayed in the game. If I had been able to stay in and been okay, we would've won the World Series."

Lee now sat in the dugout and watched with anguish as Pete Rose drove in Griffey with the tying run before the inning ended.

The score remained 3–3 as the Reds came to bat in the top of the ninth inning, with rookie left-hander Jim Burton on the mound for the Red Sox.

Johnson had summoned Burton because in the eighth inning he had removed his more experienced reliever, Jim Willoughby, for a pinch-hitter, Cecil Cooper. A right-hander, Willoughby had retired four Reds batters in a row—Bench, Perez, Foster, and Concepcion—all of whom batted from the right side. The gamble to mount a rally in the eighth failed when Cooper fouled out to end the inning, and the strategy by the Red Sox manager of removing Willoughby was criticized in some quarters.

Johnson was merely going by the book. He had used Willoughby against right-handed batters; now he wanted Burton matched up against lefty swingers who would be coming up in the ninth, including Griffey, Geronimo, and possibly Dan Driessen as a pinch-hitter.

"It was a tough decision," conceded Lee. "We either had to take our best shot for a possible run [with Cooper] or leave in a guy who had been our best pitcher over the last two months. Maybe Willoughby should have been left in the game."

After the game ended, a reporter asked Johnson why he had called on Moret, who had a history of wildness, to replace Lee, and Burton to come in after Willoughby. "They were the best men at the time for the hitters coming up," Johnson said.

Burton, not yet 24, had pitched only 53 innings during the regular season. He made a mistake that often afflicts young pitchers with little experience in such critical situations, when so much rides on their ability to deny the opposition a gratuitous base-runner. He walked the first batter he faced, Ken Griffey.

Griffey was sacrificed to second by Geronimo and moved to third as Dan Driessen, batting for Reds' reliever Clay Carroll, grounded out to second.

With two outs, Pete Rose then walked on a 3-and-2 pitch, bringing Joe Morgan to the plate. Almost immediately Burton was jolted by bad luck. He had two strikes on Morgan when he delivered a tough pitch to hit, a slider down and away. Morgan was able to fight it off and lob the ball into short center, in front of Lynn, for a single to score Griffey and push the Reds ahead 4–3.

That was the game. The score held as the Red Sox went down in succession in the bottom of the ninth against Cincinnati's fourth pitcher, left-hander Will McEnaney, with Carl Yastrzemski making the final out on a fly to center.

"When I saw Morgan hit that ball off the end of his bat," said Lee, "it was a letdown. And when Yaz made the last out,

The Reds' lead held for the Series victory. *(AP)*

it was like a big catharsis. We had come so far, only to come
up short."

Dwight Evans had a similar reaction. "It was very frustrat-
ing," he said. "We had played well. We had swept the A's three
straight in the playoffs and had the momentum after that sixth
game in the World Series—but if you don't win, you have an
empty feeling. Myself, I was drained emotionally and physically."

Evans said he always regretted he didn't play on a world
championship team in Boston, mentioning the loss to the Yan-

kees in an East Division playoff game in 1978 and the World Series defeat by the Mets in 1986.

"That always bothered me," he said. "I don't know what it was that we couldn't win."

In the 1975 Series he did well at bat, hitting .292 and driving in five runs while handling 24 chances in right field without an error. He also made a spectacular catch that robbed the Reds of a chance of ending the World Series in the sixth game rather than the seventh. In the 11th inning with the score tied 6–6, one out, and Griffey on base, Morgan slammed a long drive to right field for a probable home run off Dick Drago. Evans raced back and made a leaping, one-handed catch of the liner at the low wall. His throw back to the infield easily doubled up Griffey who had rounded second.

"After the game," Evans recalled, "somebody asked me if that was the greatest catch I ever made. I said, 'No, but it was the most important one I ever made.' That ball never curved. It stayed straight. Normally when a left-handed batter like Morgan hits a ball that way, it hooks to the line. This one didn't, and I actually had to make that catch, almost awkwardly, behind my head. If I didn't catch the ball, maybe Fisk wouldn't have had a chance to hit his home run and win the game for us."

In the Red Sox clubhouse after the game, Burton defended his pitch to Morgan. "I'm not going around hanging my head about it," he said. "It's not like I killed a person. It was a very good pitch, a slider low and away, right where I wanted it. Give the man credit for hitting it. I don't think I could've made a better pitch."

Morgan concurred with his young opponent's assessment. "It was a good pitch," he said. "Two years ago I would have struck out on it, but I'm a better hitter now."

What about the off-speed pitch from Lee that Tony Perez hit in the sixth inning for a critical two-run homer that started the Reds' comeback? "He threw me that change-of-pace in the second inning," Perez said. "I guessed it was coming."

As Geronimo settled under Yastrzemski's final fly ball, the Reds began their celebration on the field. Sparky Anderson did not go out to join them. "I realized at last I had a world cham-

"I was drained emotionally and physically," Dwight Evans
remembered. *(Sports Clip / R. A. Schnoor, Jr.)*

pionship," he said. "I trotted to the runway leading to our clubhouse to wait for the guys. I was weak, drained. I couldn't have
run out on the field if my life depended on it."

Later, the 41-year-old Reds' manager proclaimed, "It was the
greatest World Series ever played. I think we're the best team
in baseball, but not by much."

"It took them six games and eight and two-thirds innings
of the last one before they finally beat us," said Carlton Fisk.
"I wouldn't say we were beaten that badly."

Darrell Johnson agreed with his catcher. "It was an even Series," the Red Sox manager said, "and we didn't disgrace our-
selves. The last game was determined by a little flip here and
a little flip there. That's how close it was."

"The thing I remember about that game," said veteran third baseman Rico Petrocelli, "was the ball I hit in the third inning with the bases full off Gullett. It would've been a home run except it was a foot foul. It would've made the score 5–0 right there, but Gullett then walked me to force in a run, and we came out of the inning ahead three to nothing.

"I hit that foul ball on the first pitch Gullett threw me. It was an inside fastball. I jumped on it because they had been working me away during the Series.

"We knew the Reds had a great team, but it was very disappointing for us to lose. We wanted to win that game. I was going on 33, and I had the feeling that was probably going to be my last hurrah, that I'd never get back to the World Series. That's the way it worked out."

When it was all over, the *Boston Globe* editorialized that for two weeks during the World Series, "Nobody cared if the trains ran on time, or if the stocks rose or fell. Busing was buried by baseball. New York faced default, and Henry Kissinger met Mao. But in Boston and Cincinnati, all that was put aside for the time."

Afterward, Carl Yastrzemski tried to assure the club's long-time owner Tom Yawkey. "We'll be back to win it for you in the next two years," Yastrzemski promised.

It was an unfulfilled promise. Yawkey, who had owned the Red Sox for forty-three seasons, suffered from leukemia. At 73, he died in his sleep during the summer of 1976.

Cincinnati Reds vs. Boston Red Sox
at Fenway Park, October 22, 1975

Cincinnati Reds	AB	R	H	RBI	Boston Red Sox	AB	R	H	RBI
Pete Rose, 3b	4	0	2	1	Bernie Carbo, lf	3	1	1	0
Joe Morgan, 2b	4	0	2	1	Rick Miller, lf	0	0	0	0
Johnny Bench, c	4	1	0	0	Juan Beniquez, ph (e)	1	0	0	0
Tony Perez, 1b	5	1	1	2	Denny Doyle, 2b	4	1	1	0
George Foster, lf	4	0	1	0	Bob Montgomery, ph (f)	1	0	0	0
Dave Concepcion, ss	4	0	1	0	Carl Yastrzemski, 1b	5	1	1	1
Ken Griffey, rf	2	2	1	0	Carlton Fisk, c	3	0	0	0
Cesar Geronimo, cf	3	0	0	0	Fred Lynn, cf	2	0	0	0
Don Gullett, p	1	0	1	0	Rico Petrocelli, 3b	3	0	1	1
Merv Rettenmund, ph (a)	1	0	0	0	Dwight Evans, rf	2	0	0	1
Ed Armbrister, ph (b)	0	0	0	0	Rick Burleson, ss	3	0	0	0
Dan Driessen, ph (d)	1	0	0	0	Bill Lee, p	3	0	1	0
					Cecil Cooper, ph (c)	1	0	0	0
Total	**33**	**4**	**9**	**4**		**31**	**3**	**5**	**3**

(a) Hit into a double play for Gullett in fifth inning; (b) Walked for Billingham in the seventh inning; (c) Fouled out for Willoughby in the eighth inning; (d) Grounded out for Carroll in the ninth inning; (e) Flied out for Miller in the ninth inning; (f) Grounded out for Doyle in the ninth inning.

Cincinnati	0	0	0	0	0	2	1	0	1 — 4
Boston	0	0	3	0	0	0	0	0	0 — 3

Cincinnati Reds	IP	H	R	ER	SO	BB
Don Gullett	4.0	4	3	3	5	5
Jack Billingham	2.0	1	0	0	1	2
Clay Carroll (W)	2.0	0	0	0	1	1
Will McEnaney (S)	1.0	0	0	0	0	0

Boston Red Sox	IP	H	R	ER	SO	BB
Bill Lee	6.1	7	3	3	2	1
Roger Moret	0.1	1	0	0	0	2
Jim Willoughby	1.1	0	0	0	0	0
Jim Burton (L)	0.2	1	1	1	0	2
Reggie Cleveland	0.1	0	0	0	0	1

DP—Boston 2, Cincinnati 1. **2B**—Carbo. **HR**—Perez. **SB**—Morgan, Griffey. **SH**—Geronimo. **LOB**—Boston 9, Cincinnati 9. **WP**—Gullett.
Umpires—Art Frantz, Nick Colosi, Larry Barnett, Dick Stello, George Maloney, Satch Davidson.
Time—2:52. **Attendance**—35,205

1977

Royals Flushed by the Yankees

"I thought we had it in our hip pocket. You're supposed to win when you go into the ninth inning with the lead."—Frank White

Almost a year earlier, Chris Chambliss had stood at the plate in Yankee Stadium in the bottom of the ninth inning and lashed Mark Littell's first pitch for a dramatic home run that won the 1976 American League Championship Series for the New York Yankees against the Kansas City Royals.

"Personally," said Chambliss, "that homer was the highlight of my career and remains my favorite memory of Yankee Stadium."

Now it was October 9, 1977, and Chambliss was playing first base at Royals Stadium in Kansas City, again in the bottom of the ninth inning of the season's deciding playoff game between the same rivals.

With the Yankees in front 5–3, and with Darrell Porter, a left-handed batter at the plate, Chambliss was poised for action. He knew this was not the time to mess up defensively. He watched reliever Sparky Lyle retire Porter on an infield popup and then yield a single to center to Frank White.

Fred Patek, at 5–4 the smallest player in the major leagues, was the next batter to face Lyle. Despite his diminutive stature, he represented a "tough out" for the Yankees. He had already collected seven hits in the series, including three doubles, and his threat to spark a rally could not be taken lightly. But Lyle got Patek to ground into a game-ending double play that went from third baseman Graig Nettles to second baseman Willie Randolph to Chambliss. When Chambliss gloved the ball, the Yankees had nailed down their second straight pennant under the leadership of their volatile manager, Billy Martin.

After the game, Martin sneaked up behind club owner George Steinbrenner in the noisy Yankee clubhouse and poured champagne over the head of his boss. "That," said Martin, "is for trying to fire me."

So ended another luckless effort by the Royals to capture their first league championship since the founding of the franchise in 1969.

Baseball developments in 1977 included the expansion of the American League from 12 to 14 teams, with the new franchises located in Seattle and Toronto. The trade of Tom Seaver from the Mets to the Reds on June 15 created a stir in the National League, with the *New York Post* headlining the event, in typical, pungent style: "Mets Trade THE Franchise."

Also in the news early in the season was the offbeat story of Ted Turner, owner of the Atlanta Braves, donning a uniform and taking over the manager's reins after his team had lost 16 straight games. Turner signed himself to a coaching contract, gave his regular manager Dave Bristol a ten-day leave of absence, sat in the dugout, and played acting manager on May 11 as the Braves were beaten by the Pirates in Pittsburgh 2–1 for their 17th loss in a row.

Although he was promptly ordered to cease and desist in such conduct by National League president Charles Feeney, Turner blithely dismissed the complexity of a manager's job. "Managing isn't all that difficult," he claimed. "All you've got to do is score more runs than the other guy."

By the time the books were closed on the season, major league baseball had posted its greatest attendance record— 38,709,781 paying customers, wiping out owners' earlier fears that million-dollar contracts and constant media coverage about players' salaries would alienate fans and damage gate receipts.

In spring, forecasts of the coming pennant races by baseball pundits gave the Kansas City Royals a good chance of repeating as champions of the American League West Division. Their manager, Whitey Herzog, was never one to discourage optimistic observations about his team. "The 1977 Royals were by far the best baseball team I ever managed," he said.

"We had power with George Brett, John Mayberry, and Amos Otis. We had speed with Otis and Frank White. We had good defense at every position, strong starters in Dennis Leonard, Paul Splittorff, Larry Gura, and Jim Colborn, and a solid bullpen. The team had no weaknesses."

Herzog's assessment is hard to refute. The Royals in 1977 won 102 games, most ever in the club's history, and finished eight lengths ahead of the second-place Texas Rangers to capture their second successive West Division title.

At the end of August that year, four teams were bunched at the top of the division, with the Royals in front by half a game. Gene Mauch, manager of the Minnesota Twins who were also in the hunt, declared, "Nobody in our division has the horses to pull away from the pack."

"We had the stud hosses, all right," countered Herzog.

The Royals went on a tear in September, winning 25 of 30 games and making a shambles out of what was once a tight race. From the start of the month, they scored 15 straight victories, then lost a 1–0 game to the Seattle Mariners on September 16 before resuming another string of eight wins. "That September," said Herzog, "we put on one of the greatest stretch drives in baseball history."

The record book reinforces Herzog's comments about the '77 Royals. Shortstop Fred Patek led the American League in stolen bases with 53. He was followed by Frank White and Amos Otis with 23 thefts apiece, Hal McRae with 18, and Al Cowens, 16.

White was the best-fielding second baseman in the league, committing eight errors in 752 chances for a .989 percentage, and earning a Gold Glove in the process. First baseman John Mayberry also topped all league players at his position on defense; he had seven errors in 1,384 chances. In center field the Royals had another skillful defensive player in Amos Otis, who committed only three errors in 339 chances and was credited with ten assists. In right field Al Cowens, who had come up through the club's farm system, was in his second season as a regular and provided the Royals with the entire package of

"We had the stud hosses,"
Royals manager Whitey
Herzog said. *(Ronald L.
Mrowiec)*

speed, defense, and offense. He won a Gold Glove for his fielding and was credited with 14 assists. Among American League
outfielders, only Carl Yastrzemski of the Red Sox had more assists with 16.

"Al complemented Otis in center," said Patek. "He covered
the ground so well out there, he made the job easier for Otis,
especially on balls hit to right center." In addition to his defense, Cowens hit for average, .312, and power, 23 homers,
while leading the Royals in RBI with 112 and collecting 32 doubles and 14 triples. During the playoff series against the Yankees, Herzog said, "If I were to vote for the Most Valuable
Player award this year, I'd vote for Al Cowens." After the season, Cowens finished second in the MVP voting to the Twins'
high-average hitter Rod Carew.

The Royals had a great deal more going for them in '77, including the hitting of Brett, their future Hall of Fame third
baseman, who batted .312 with 22 homers and 88 RBI, along
with Mayberry, 22 HR and 82 RBI; and designated hitter Hal
McRae with a .298 average, 21 HR, and 92 RBI.

"In the off-season," Patek recalled, "we got catcher Darrell
Porter and starter Jim Colborn in a trade with Milwaukee, and
they really gave us a boost. Besides winning 18 games for us,

Royals shortstop Fred Patek, bloodied after being spiked by Reggie Jackson in a play at second base, refused to leave the game. *(Ronald L. Mrowiec)*

Colborn pitched a no-hitter against the Rangers in May, and toward the end of the season I think he won six of his last eight decisions. Darrell did a great job handling the pitching staff. He was a hard-nosed player. He knew how to win. With his hits and walks, he got on base a lot."

For most of the season Herzog platooned Tom Poquette and rookie Joe Zdeb in left field, and defensively they committed only three errors between them while hitting .292 and .297 respectively.

The Royals' manager also relied heavily on a well-stocked bullpen, especially Doug Bird and Mark Littell, who together accounted for 19 wins and 26 saves.

Clearly the Royals had the talent to redeem themselves after suffering a heart-stopping loss to the Yankees in the 1976 playoffs. This time around their formidable opponents from the Bronx had to run for their lives to win a close East Division race, finishing two and a half games ahead of the second-place Orioles and Red Sox.

It would take considerable nitpicking to choose between the Royals and Yankees in 1977. They had split their ten games with each other during the regular season. Their team batting and slugging averages were close. So were their runs scored, the number of runs they allowed opponents, their fielding averages, total errors committed, and shutouts pitched.

Kansas City held a big edge in stolen bases, 170 to 93; in doubles, 299 to 267; in triples, 77 to 47; and had a better earned run average in pitching, 3.52 to 3.61, while New York produced more home runs, 184 to 146.

The biggest advantage the Yankees held, however, could not be reduced to a mere statistic. It was represented in the person of left-handed reliever Sparky Lyle, who had command of one of the best sliders in baseball. Lyle did a yeoman's job during the season, pitching in 72 games, saving 26, and finishing with a 13–5 record. For his work, the mustachioed Yankee bullpen leader earned the American League Cy Young award for pitching excellence.

He was one of six Yankee moundsmen who notched 11 or more winning decisions. The staff included Ron Guidry, 16–7; Ed Figueroa, 16–11; Mike Torrez, 14–12; Don Gullett, 14–4; and Dick Tidrow, 11–4. Future Hall of Famer Catfish Hunter finished at 9–9, but he was plagued with arm miseries and generally used as a fifth starter.

Gullett was one of two high-priced free agents that George Steinbrenner signed after his club was wiped out in the 1976 World Series by the Reds on the heels of beating the Royals in the league playoffs. Right fielder Reggie Jackson, who had played for the Orioles, also signed on for heavy money with New York as a free agent.

The Yankee front office made two significant trades in April to strengthen the team. Shortstop Bucky Dent was acquired from the White Sox, and veteran right-handed starter Mike Torrez from the Oakland A's.

So manager Billy Martin was knee-deep in talent, including five regulars who had been with the '76 championship team: Chambliss at first, Willie Randolph at second, Graig Nettles at third, Roy White in left, Mickey Rivers in center, and Thurman

Munson behind the plate. Dent replaced Fred Stanley at short, and Jackson took over in right for the departed Oscar Gamble.

Four players formed the heart of the team's offense: Jackson with 32 homers and 110 RBI; Nettles, 37 and 107; Munson, 18 and 100; and Chambliss, 17 and 90.

Despite all their ability, the Yankees weren't much better than a .500 team by the end of May, with a 25–21 record. They hit a low point on June 18 when Martin pulled Jackson off the field in a game against the Red Sox for what the manager thought was a lack of hustle. In an ugly confrontation in the dugout, the two nearly came to blows in full view of fans watching the game on national television. Martin was livid, and his explosive temper almost cost him his job—one of five times during the season he claimed Steinbrenner was ready to fire him. The incident occurred in the middle of a three-game sweep by the Red Sox; by June 24 the Yankees were trailing Boston by five games.

Not until August 7 did the team finally find its way, winning 22 out of 29 games during the month, and staying hot through September with a 19–9 record to retain its East Division title by nosing out Boston and Baltimore. The Yankees might have started coming together on August 18 when Martin finally installed Jackson as the cleanup hitter to stay.

The best-of-five League Championship Series opened at Yankee Stadium on October 5, with left-handers Paul Splittorff and Don Gullett drawing the starting assignments. Herzog's crew jumped off to an early 6–0 lead and cruised to a 7–2 victory behind the pitching of Splittorff, who worked all the way into the ninth inning before being relieved by Doug Bird. The only runs Splittorff allowed came on a homer he yielded to Thurman Munson with Mickey Rivers on base in the bottom of the third inning.

Gullett came out of the game after the second inning, complaining of a sore shoulder, an ailment that had bothered him through the season. "I couldn't get loose, even in the bullpen before the game," he said. "When you can't get loose, you don't have control of the ball, and I didn't have any velocity." Martin was afraid he might lose his left-hander for the rest of the playoff series.

If the Yankees were distressed after getting beaten so emphatically in the opener, they showed no signs of it in game two which they won easily 6–2, behind the three-hit pitching of Ron Guidry. They were energized in the sixth inning when Hal McRae broke up a double play by throwing a vicious body block on Willie Randolph at second base. "There was no hate between these two clubs, at least before this game," said George Brett, "but I think there is now."

The remainder of the series was played at Royals Stadium in Kansas City where Dennis Leonard, like Guidry, pitched the full nine innings in fashioning a 6–2 decision while allowing only four hits in game three.

Now the Royals were just one victory away from their first league pennant with two games to play at home, where the Yankees had beaten them only once in five tries during the regular season.

Herzog started left-hander Larry Gura in game four against the Yankees' Ed Figueroa. Gura was primarily a reliever, having appeared in 52 games, only six of them as a starter. Years later, Herzog explained his decision to go with Gura. "The Yankees were such a good left-handed hitting club," he said. "They had power guys like Nettles, Chambliss, and Jackson who hit from the left side. I thought Gura, with his little screwgie, would do better against them than a right-hander like Jim Colborn."

Critics questioned Herzog's choice, but not Martin, who had discarded Gura while managing the Texas Rangers in 1974 and the Yankees as well in 1976. Herzog, however, figured Gura would have strong motivation to beat Martin because he had been dumped by him twice in trades.

Martin employed a little psychology to agitate Gura. "The only worry I have," he said before the game, "is that Gura doesn't get hurt on the way to the ball park, I mean, in an accident or anything. Maybe I ought to send a bodyguard to his home."

Martin told that story to any newsmen who would listen. He wanted Gura to read or hear what he said. "The more he wants to beat us," said Martin, "the more fine he will try to make his pitches. And when he gets too fine, that's when he can't get anything over."

It can't be proven that Martin's psychology worked, but Gura pitched only into the third inning, yielding six hits and a walk before being relieved. By the time the Royals came to bat in the bottom of the third, they were behind 4–0.

Figueroa didn't do much better for the Yankees, lasting into the fourth inning. Kansas City closed the gap to 5–4 and had White on third base and McRae on first with two out when Martin summoned Lyle from the bullpen to replace Tidrow who had relieved Figueroa. It was a critical moment for Lyle. Standing in the batter's box was the ever-dangerous George Brett, perhaps the Royals' best clutch hitter. Lyle retired him on a fly to left field to end the threat, stayed in the game, and allowed only two hits in the remaining five innings to preserve a 6–4 decision for the Yankees.

"That was the game where we should've won it all," said Paul Splittorff. "Mayberry didn't do too well in that game. He struck out a couple of times and misplayed a foul pop-up. Whitey benched him for game five. I don't know to this day what happened to him."

An amiable, gregarious character who was known for his prodigious home runs into the right-field bleachers of Royals Stadium, Mayberry made an ill-timed personal mistake before the Saturday afternoon game. Two of his brothers had come to Kansas City from Detroit to see the series, and on Friday night Mayberry joined them in some serious and lengthy partying. As a result, he was late to the Royals' clubhouse on Saturday, which was unusual for him. It was apparent he was not in the best condition to play.

"He struck out in his first two times up, and he screwed up a bunt play," Herzog recalled. When the Royals manager lifted Mayberry from the game and replaced him with John Wathan, it was an ominous portent of what was about to befall Kansas City's baseball fortunes.

Splittorff and Guidry were matched as starters in the fifth and final game of the series on Sunday night. Recalling the occasion, Splittorff said, "It had been an overcast day with dark clouds in Kansas City. In retrospect, that pretty much described our feelings after it was all over."

Guidry, a rookie who had pitched 211 innings during the season and nine innings in beating the Royals on Thursday night, was not ecstatic about being called on to work with only two days' rest. He normally started every fifth or sixth day. "Usually I feel stiff for two days after I pitch," he said, "and it eases up the third day."

"He's a wiry 160-pounder," said Martin. "I don't say he's the best man I've got. I say he's my hottest pitcher now."

Splittorff, on the other hand, was a veteran of seven seasons with the Royals. He had turned 31 the day before and was ready for the challenge, even though he had just three days' rest since winning the series opener. "That didn't bother me," he said, "because during the season there were a number of times I'd pitch with only three days' rest. We didn't have many complete games. You'd go six, seven, or eight innings and then turn it over to the bullpen. My arm was good, never had any trouble with it."

For game five, Herzog sat Mayberry on the bench and replaced him again with Wathan, a right-handed batter. Word went around that Mayberry was idled because of a tooth problem, but that was not the real story. In any event, the absence of Mayberry could not be considered a major setback because he had slumped in the series, collecting only two hits in 12 at-bats for a .167 average.

In the Yankee camp, Billy Martin also created a stir by sitting Reggie Jackson and starting Paul Blair in right field. Jackson, like Mayberry, was having a terrible series at the plate. In the first four games he had managed only a single in 14 at-bats for a .071 average. "If Jackson were hitting," said Martin, "I'd put him at DH. But he hasn't been swinging well, and this guy [Splittorff] has always bothered him."

So Cliff Johnson became the DH in the Yankee lineup. Jackson would be available as a pinch-hitter if a right-handed pitcher came in to relieve Splittorff.

After McRae's crunching body block on Randolph in the second game, the threat of physical violence hovered over the series. It finally erupted in the bottom half of the first inning of game five when the Royals scored their first run against Guidry. With one out, McRae reached first on an infield single and scored on a triple to right center field by Brett. As Brett roared into third, just beating the relay throw, he came up from his slide in one continuous motion. As he did, his right hand struck Graig Nettles in the chest.

The Yankee third baseman did not wait to ask Brett if he had hit him intentionally or not. He kicked Brett in the chest and, as Brett was falling, again with his left foot. Brett jumped to his feet and swung at Nettles, high enough on the head to knock his cap off. Nettles tried to strike back, but by that time Chuck Hiller, the Royals' third base coach, had grabbed Nettles, and Guidry restrained Brett. Players from both sides burst out of their dugouts, pushing and shoving before order was restored on the field.

The Royals quickly boosted their lead to 2–0 against Guidry when Brett scored on a grounder by Al Cowens. The Yankees picked up a run off Splittorff in the third, but in the bottom of the inning an RBI single by Cowens put Kansas City in front 3–1.

Guidry had been lifted with one out in the third inning, and Mike Torrez came in to pitch shutout ball against the Royals for the next five and a third innings before being relieved by Lyle in the eighth.

Meanwhile, Splittorff held the Yankees at bay. Going into the top of the eighth inning, he was in front 3–1.

"I was getting a little bit tired in the seventh," Splittorff admitted. "At the start of the eighth, Randolph got to me for a bloop single on a curve over the outer half of the plate. The next batter was Munson, in our mind the toughest guy in their lineup, their most accomplished hitter. He was the guts of their team. He had homered off me to score their only two runs in the first game. So Whitey figured it was time for a change.

"In that game at Yankee Stadium, I had thrown Munson a fastball inside. It was my first pitch to him in the third inning. As soon as I let go of the ball, I saw his hips open up as he adjusted to the pitch. He pulled it over the fence in left field."

Splittorff had already yielded a run-scoring single to Munson in the third inning of game five. Herzog figured the percentages called for the removal of his left-handed starter. He signaled for Doug Bird, who came in and struck out Munson.

"Paul was beginning to tire there," said Herzog. "And he was running out of tricks with Munson. He had pitched him in and out all night, and I didn't know if he could get him out again. We didn't want to take any chances."

But the Royals were not yet out of trouble. After Munson fanned, Yankee left fielder Lou Piniella lined a single to center.

Now, up to the plate strode pinch-hitter Reggie Jackson, who had been saved by Billy Martin for just such an occasion: one out, the tying runs on base, and a right-hander on the mound. Jackson had been sitting because he was only two for 15 against Splittorff during the season and was considered a defensive liability on the Royals Stadium carpet. "I'm not a very good pinch-hitter," he conceded—but he proved himself wrong when he drilled a single to center in front of Otis, scoring Randolph and shaving the Royals' lead to 3–2.

That was all for Bird. Left-hander Steve Mingori was summoned from the bullpen to confront Graig Nettles, who lined to left field for the second out, leaving Piniella on second and Jackson on first.

Chambliss then lined a one-hopper to the right of second baseman Frank White, who speared the ball, fell, uprighted himself, and threw just in time to shortstop Fred Patek for the force on Jackson to end the Yankee rally.

"I thought that was it," said White. "I thought we had it in our hip pocket. You're supposed to win when you go into the ninth inning with the lead.

"That was one of the best plays I ever made. I dove up the middle and was able to get the ball to second to force Jackson who spiked Fred in the leg as he was sliding in. I thought we'd seize the momentum after that play and keep the lead."

Patek's leg was bleeding from the spike wound and had to be taped. "No way was I coming out of a game like that," Patek said. "After I was taped, I put a couple of socks on and was ready to go."

The Royals threatened to add to their lead in the bottom of the eighth when Torrez weakened and walked Amos Otis and Pete Lacock with two out. But Martin brought in Lyle, who struck out Cookie Rojas to end the threat.

Dennis Leonard, the hardest thrower among Royals starters and the winner of game three, took the mound in the ninth inning. "Whitey had asked me if I could pitch in the final game on short rest, which amounted to about a day and a half," Leonard said. "I'm resilient, and I said yes. I went out to the bullpen in the seventh inning and had been warming up since the eighth inning. My adrenaline was pumping.

"I felt fine. I never had any problems with my arm. Buck Martinez was catching me in the bullpen, and I said to him, 'Tell me if I'm throwing good.' That was different for me. I never used to ask for a second opinion. I'd just say, 'Give me the ball and I'll get 'em out.'"

A relief appearance was a new experience for Leonard. "It was something he hadn't done before," said White.

The first batter to face the big redheaded right-hander was Paul Blair, who ran the count three balls and two strikes. "He must've fouled off seven pitches," Leonard said of Blair. "Then I threw him a fastball inside and he got a broken-bat single, a blooper over first base."

With the tying run on first, the next batter, pinch-hitter Roy White, also dueled Leonard to a three-and-two count, then fouled off two pitches before walking.

"That was it for me," said Leonard. "When I came out of that game it was my low point. It was kind of weird because I had just enjoyed my highest point of the season by winning game three."

Now it was Larry Gura's turn on the mound. Mickey Rivers was at the plate. "First they wanted me to bunt," said Rivers. "Then the infield came in and they called it off. When that happened, I just tried to chop the ball."

On a two-and-two pitch, Rivers slapped a game-tying single through the right side of the infield, past Frank White, scoring Blair with the tying run and moving Roy White to third.

Once again Herzog made a pitching change, bringing in right-handed Mark Littell to face the right-handed Willie Randolph. "I wanted to make good contact," said Randolph. "I knew he'd be coming at me. I took a few pitches because I had to get my pitch." On a three-and-one count he did, lofting a long fly to Amos Otis in center that allowed Roy White to score easily from third base after the catch to give the Yankees a 4–3 lead.

Left-hander Paul Splittorff (left) was Herzog's choice to start the deciding game against the Yankees. The hard-throwing Dennis Leonard relieved in the ninth and put the tying and winning runs on base. *(Clifton Boutelle, Ed Mailliard)*

Before they were retired, the Yankees added one more run on George Brett's throwing error to make it 5–3.

It was a run they would not need. Sparky Lyle saw to that. In the bottom of the ninth he erased Darrell Porter on a pop-up to short, yielded a single to Frank White, and then closed out the game by getting Patek to hit into a double play.

Patek had played inspired ball for the Royals during the series, hitting .389 and driving in five runs. He took the loss hard. For 15 minutes after the game ended he sat in the Royals dugout, crying while the Yankees celebrated in their champagne-soaked clubhouse.

The final pitch from Lyle was a slider, Patek recalled. "Eight out of ten of his pitches were sliders, the others wasted fastballs. I hit the ball too hard. Just before the pitch I looked at third base and noticed that Nettles had moved closer to the bag. If Nettles doesn't move and the ball gets by him, it goes into the corner, and I'd be on second base and I know Frank would've scored from first. That would've made it 5–4, and with

New York Yankees vs. Kansas City Royals
at Royals Stadium, October 9, 1977

New York Yankees	AB	R	H	RBI	Kansas City Royals	AB	R	H	RBI
Mickey Rivers, cf	5	2	2	1	Fred Patek, ss	5	0	0	0
Willie Randolph, 2b	3	1	1	1	Hal McRae, lf	4	2	3	0
Thurman Munson, c	5	0	1	1	George Brett, 3b	3	1	1	1
Lou Piniella, lf	5	0	2	0	Al Cowens, rf	4	0	2	2
Cliff Johnson, dh	2	0	1	0	Amos Otis, cf	3	0	1	0
Reggie Jackson, ph/dh (a)	2	0	1	1	John Wathan, 1b	2	0	0	0
Graig Nettles, 3b	4	0	0	0	Pete Lacock, ph/1b (c)	1	0	0	0
Chris Chambliss, 1b	4	0	0	0	Cookie Rojas, dh	4	0	1	0
Paul Blair, rf	4	1	1	0	Darrell Porter, c	4	0	1	0
Bucky Dent, ss	3	0	1	0	Frank White, 2b	4	0	1	0
Roy White, ph (b)	0	1	0	0					
Fred Stanley, ss	0	0	0	0					
Total	**37**	**5**	**10**	**4**		**34**	**3**	**10**	**3**

(a) Singled for Johnson in the eighth inning; (b) Walked for Dent in the ninth inning; (c) Struck out for Wathan in the sixth inning.

New York	0	0	1	0	0	0	0	1	3	—	5
Kansas City	2	0	1	0	0	0	0	0	0	—	3

New York Yankees	IP	H	R	ER	SO	BB
Ron Guidry	2.1	6	3	3	1	0
Mike Torrez	5.1	3	0	0	4	3
Sparky Lyle (W)	1.1	1	0	0	1	0

Kansas City Royals	IP	H	R	ER	SO	BB
Paul Splittorff +	7.0	6	2	2	2	2
Doug Bird	0.1	2	0	0	1	0
Steve Mingori	0.2	0	0	0	0	0
Dennis Leonard ++ (L)	0.0	1	2	2	0	1
Larry Gura +++	0.0	1	1	0	0	0
Mark Littell	1.0	0	0	0	0	0

+ Pitched to one batter in the eighth inning; ++ Pitched to two batters in the ninth inning; +++ Pitched to one batter in the ninth inning.

E—Brett. **DP**—New York 1. **2B**—Piniella, McRae, Johnson. **3B**—Brett. **SB**—Rivers, Rojas, Otis. **SF**—Randolph. **LOB**—New York 9, Kansas City 7.
Umpires—Nick Bremigan, Bill Deegan, Jerry Neudecker, Marty Springstead, Russ Goetz and Jim McKean.
Time—3:04. **Attendance**—41,133

two good hitters behind me [McRae and Brett], who knows how that game would've ended up?

"Even though I hit the ball hard, it took a bang-bang play at first to get me for the final out. When I came back from first base I looked up in the stands, and all I saw were the backs of fans going out the exits. It was eerie. I sat on the bench for a long time afterward.

"When I got to the clubhouse there was dead silence. In my heart and mind I felt we were the best team in baseball that year. That's what was so disappointing. We were really good, and we didn't get to play in the World Series.

"We had a great combination—consistency, no bad slumps, guys who could help off the bench. At three o'clock on any given afternoon, I thought nobody could beat us. That's how we felt.

"I always had that boyhood dream of getting to a World Series, but I never made it. That ball I hit to Nettles—I dreamed it got by him and rattled around in the left-field corner for a double. But that was a long time ago."

"In all aspects of the game that was the best team I ever played on," said Frank White. "We had timely hitting, guys who knew how to play the game. We had come off that playoff experience in '76 and were ready to blossom.

"After we lost again in '77, the guys were stunned. We had battled so hard and went all the way to the ninth inning only to fall short. Otis, Porter, and myself, we were so devastated we went over to the Holiday Inn and cried in our beer. We closed the bar there at three or four in the morning."

When Splittorff left the game he went into the Royals clubhouse to change into a dry shirt and put on a jacket. He then returned to the bench to watch the rest of the action. "When we lost," he said, "it was the lowest point in my career and for our organization. I felt numb. I was in a vacuum. I didn't want to see anybody. I didn't want to eat, didn't want to drink. I've often thought how I would have pitched to Munson if I had stayed in the game, and if I had gotten him out, whether I would have been able to finish the job."

"If you lose when it counts," said Leonard, "obviously you aren't the best. But in '77 I don't think anybody was better than we were. Our balloon got popped. In '76 we were happy to be in the playoffs. In '77 we deserved to be there and we had a good opportunity to win, but it wasn't to be. We had a few 'cocktails' after the game. A few tears were shed, but some of the guys said 'Get over it, get refocused, get ready for next year.'"

The Royals did get refocused and made it back to the American League Championship Series in 1978, only to be beaten by the Yankees once more, this time in four games. They would not play in the World Series until the 1980s.

1978

Bucky "Dents" the Red Sox with a Borrowed Bat

"Dent's home run was part of it, but what really
beat us were Piniella's two plays in right field."
—Fred Lynn

How does one explain the 1978 Boston Red Sox? They
were a team that during the season resembled a bouncing ball,
first up, then down, up again and down again, and finally up
once more to finish in a dead heat in the American League
East Division race with their archrivals, the New York Yankees.

At one point, on the morning of July 19, the Red Sox, with
a crisp record of 61–28, led the second-place Milwaukee Brewers by eight games and had left the fourth-place Yankees in
their dust, 14-1/2 games behind them as they threatened to turn
the chase for glory into a runaway.

But the threat never became a reality. The Yankees, under
their new manager Bob Lemon, who replaced Billy Martin in
July, staged a strong finish to force a one-game playoff with
the Red Sox for the division crown at Fenway Park on October 2.

"It was an unbelievable season from start to finish," said
Carl Yastrzemski, Boston's future Hall of Famer. "We had such
a big lead because we played .700 ball at a time the Yankees
were hurting. Then, while we were having problems, they were
playing .700 ball, and they caught us."

The end result produced only the second playoff game in

American League history—the other one, ironically, also involving the Red Sox at Fenway 30 years earlier. While the 1978 game would determine the winner of the East Division title, the 1948 playoff between Boston and Cleveland had offered the victor a greater prize—the American League pennant. (Largely through the efforts of Lou Boudreau, the Indians had won it.)

A constantly repeated slogan—"Baseball fever, catch it!"— was introduced to promote the game in 1978, and perhaps the message helped boost major league attendance to an all-time high of 40,636,886.

That year, in his final season with the Reds at age 37, Pete Rose twice created a big splash in the news. On May 9 he singled off Montreal's Steve Rogers for the three thousandth hit of his career, and on June 14 he embarked on a 44-game hitting streak that tied a National League record set by Wee Willie Keeler in 1897.

Tom Seaver, also with the Reds, pitched a 4–0 no-hitter against the Cardinals on June 16, adding another Hall of Fame credential to his career.

During or after the season, nine major league clubs changed managers, including the Padres, who bounced Alvin Dark three weeks into spring training, and the Reds, who said goodbye to Sparky Anderson in November. The managerial change that aroused the most interest in the news media, however, involved the resignation of Billy Martin, whose tenure as Yankee field boss was filled with controversy, temper tantrums, incendiary remarks, a feud with Reggie Jackson, and a personal failure to control his drinking.

Two incidents triggered Martin's departure in 1978. One centered on Jackson disobeying a sign to swing away, rather than bunt, in a game the Yankees lost at home to the Kansas City Royals, 9–7, in 11 innings on July 17. In the tenth inning, with the score tied 5–5 and Thurman Munson on first base, Jackson twice disregarded the sign to take his normal cut at the ball and popped out on a bunt attempt. His flagrant defiance of authority infuriated Martin and made the defeat all the more bitter to swallow.

It was the Yankees' ninth loss in their last 12 games. Afterward an angered Martin stormed into his clubhouse office, smashed a beer bottle on the floor, and threw a clock radio against the wall. After consulting with owner George Steinbrenner and other Yankee officials, Martin announced, "Reggie Jackson is suspended without pay, effective this moment."

The suspension lasted five days, and without Jackson the Yankees suddenly came alive and won their next five games, two at Minnesota and three in Chicago.

The second incident occurred after Jackson returned to the club in Chicago on July 23. Defending himself, he told reporters that Martin had not talked to him since spring training. The remark incensed Martin. When he and the team were at O'Hare International Airport in Chicago, waiting for a flight to Kansas City, he was still seething. With his speech slurred by drink, Martin told two New York writers that Jackson and Steinbrenner "deserve each other. One's a born liar, the other's convicted." (He referred to Steinbrenner's conviction for making illegal contributions to Nixon's presidential campaign in 1972.)

When his remarks became public, Martin anticipated his firing. On July 24 he made a tearful statement of resignation at the Crown Center Hotel in Kansas City. He was replaced by Bob Lemon, who a month earlier had been fired as manager by the White Sox.

Lemon was cut from different cloth than Martin. He once declared that he never took a loss home with him but always left it at a local bar. When he assumed the manager's job on July 25, the change in the club's fortunes was dramatic under his easygoing leadership—even though Martin had directed the team to five straight victories before his departure.

At the time the Yankees were languishing in fourth place, ten and a half games behind Boston. With Lemon at the helm, they won 47 of their remaining 67 games, a .701 pace, to pull even with the Red Sox at the end of the season. One playoff game would resolve the tie.

It was the greatest comeback in American League history. Only the National League's 1914 "Miracle (Boston) Braves," who were 14 games out on July 4, regained so much lost ground to win a championship.

The Yankees could scarcely be called a "miracle" team because they were not an assembly of untested or mediocre players. They were better than good. They had an infield of proven performers in Chris Chambliss at first, Willie Randolph at second, Bucky Dent at short, and Graig Nettles at third. They had veteran outfielders in Reggie Jackson, Mickey Rivers, Roy White, and Lou Piniella. Thurman Munson remained a steadying force with his work behind the plate.

Most important, however, they had two dominant pitchers: starter Ron Guidry, 25–3 with an eye-popping 1.75 ERA, and reliever Goose Gossage, who saved 27 games and won ten with his blazing fastball. Their performances on the mound were complemented by starters Ed Figueroa, 20–9, and Catfish Hunter, 12–6, as well as by reliever Sparky Lyle who finished at 9–3 with nine saves. The staff ERA was 3.18, best in the American League.

The Red Sox were also flush with exceptional talent, including Jim Rice, who in 1978 emerged as the most dangerous power threat in the game, leading the league in home runs with 46, in RBI with 139, and in hits with 213 while scoring 121 runs and producing a .315 batting average that included 24 doubles and 13 triples. The numbers earned Rice the league's Most Valuable Player award.

During much of the season, unless player injuries dictated otherwise, manager Don Zimmer used a set lineup, with George Scott at first, Jerry Remy at second, Rick Burleson at short, Butch Hobson at third, Rice in left, Fred Lynn in center, Dwight Evans in right, and Carlton Fisk behind the plate. Carl Yastrzemski turned 39 during the season and played 71 games in the outfield, 50 at first base, and 27 as a designated hitter.

The cast featured additional long-ball punch besides that generated by Rice. Evans hit 24 home runs; Lynn, 22; Fisk, 20; and Hobson and Yaz, 17 apiece.

Remy was one of two key acquisitions by the Red Sox in the off-season. He came in a December trade with the California Angels to solve Boston's second-base problem and provide much-needed speed at the top of the lineup. And in November the club had shored up its pitching by signing free agent Mike Torrez, a 17-game winner for the A's and Yankees in 1977.

One other transaction, completed just before the end of spring training, also figured in the Red Sox improvement: they

Carl Yastrzemski, at age 39, appeared in the outfield, at first base, and as a DH for the Red Sox in 1978. *(Ronald L. Mrowiec)*

obtained Dennis Eckersley, a promising 23-year-old right-handed pitcher, in a trade with the Indians. When the final figures were entered in the 1978 record book, Eckersley led Boston starters with 20 wins, followed by Torrez with 14, Luis Tiant, 13, and Bill Lee, ten. Reliever Bob Stanley compiled a 15–2 mark in addition to posting ten saves.

In spring training Don Zimmer said, "We might win 100 games, but it won't mean anything if the Yankees win 101." In retrospect he was clairvoyant.

In the first half of the season the Red Sox were almost unbeatable in Fenway Park and were romping through American League opponents. After a so-so start in April, Zimmer had his troops flying. The Red Sox were 23–7 in May and 18–7 in June, and were 10–5 through their first 15 games in July when their pace began to slow.

Then the Yankees, who had been hampered by injuries as well as dissension, began their move upward under new manager Bob Lemon. As New York started to win, the Red Sox started to lose, and by July 31 their 14-game lead had been shaved to six and a half games.

They stopped their slide at that point and lost no more

ground in August, but fell apart once more when they lost 13 of their first 16 games in September, including a crushing four-game sweep by the Yankees at Fenway Park in a series that became known as the "Boston Massacre." Before that series the Yankees had won only two games at Fenway in two years, but now they took the Red Sox apart by scores of 15–3, 13–2, 7–0, and 7–4. They left town tied for the division lead with Boston.

The Red Sox were plunging at a dizzying rate and by September 15 were three and a half games out of first. But again they bounced back. They won 12 of their last 14 games, including their last eight in a row, to finish in a tie for the division leadership with the Yankees on the last day of the season. The records of the two clubs were identical at 99–63.

In their final game the Yankees could have clinched the division title if they had won, but they were bombed by the Indians 9–2 while the Red Sox pulled even as Luis Tiant pitched a two-hit, 5–0 shutout against the Blue Jays.

So the stage was set for another chapter in one of baseball's most heated rivalries, at Fenway Park on Monday, October 2.

It had been a wild, roller-coaster ride for Zimmer and the Red Sox on the way to the 163rd game of their schedule. Their season had been marred by injuries. Carlton Fisk played with a broken rib while bone chips in Butch Hobson's right elbow made every throw an adventure. In all, Hobson made 43 errors at third base and begged Zimmer to take him out of the lineup because of his poor throws. "I'm killing this team," he lamented. Zimmer used Hobson in 33 games as a designated hitter.

Physical problems beset other key players. Shortstop Rick Burleson suffered a torn ankle ligament on July 9 and was disabled for seventeen games. Second baseman Jerry Remy was hit by a pitch that cracked a bone in his wrist on August 26, knocking him out of the lineup for more than two weeks. And right fielder Dwight Evans, beaned by Seattle pitcher Mike Parrot on August 29, continued to suffer dizzy spells that hampered his effectiveness.

The pitching matchup for the playoff game added further drama to the occasion: for Boston, Mike Torrez, an ex-Yankee, against New York's Ron Guidry, whose 24–3 record before his final start made him a virtual cinch to win the American League

Cy Young award. Guidry would be working on three days' rest; he was accustomed to four. There was a question whether the slender left-hander would be as sharp as usual. He had already pitched 267 innings.

Torrez also was going on three days' rest. But in contrast to Guidry he was a big 6–5, 220-pound, hard-throwing right-hander who had pitched fewer innings, 243, to that point.

A week earlier, a coin flip determined that if the two teams ended the season tied, Fenway would be the site of the one-game playoff.

"After all that's happened to both teams," said Yastrzemski, "this is probably the only way this should be settled. These are the two best teams in baseball. There should be no loser."

The last comment by Yaz could have been left unsaid. Base-ball, like the sea, can be cruel. Its delineation between winners and losers has always remained impervious to wishful think-ing, especially among Red Sox fans who, as one writer put it, "have always felt deserving of victory, but deep down expect only heartbreak and loss."

For their classic showdown both teams fielded their regu-lar lineups with only a few exceptions. The Red Sox played Jack Brohamer at third base in place of Hobson, and Jim Rice in right field instead of Dwight Evans. The Yankees started rookie Brian Doyle at second as a replacement for the injured Willie Randolph, and Reggie Jackson was penciled in as their DH, though he thought he should be playing right field. That job went to 35-year-old Lou Piniella, who did not cover much ground defensively.

The playoff game started on a sunny, early autumn day in Boston, with both pitchers retiring the opposition in order in the first inning. In the second inning, Guidry, on his second pitch, left a fastball up to Yastrzemski, the leadoff hitter, who pulled a hard drive down the right-field line for a homer that barely wrapped itself around the foul pole to give Boston a 1–0 lead.

The Red Sox threatened to score again in the third when Scott led off with a double and advanced to third on Brohamer's sacrifice bunt. Scott was stranded, however, as Burleson was retired on a grounder and Remy flied out.

Meanwhile Torrez held the Yankees off the board despite allowing the leadoff batter to reach base in both the fourth and fifth innings.

By the time they came to bat in the bottom of the sixth inning, with the score still 1–0, the Red Sox knew Guidry was showing signs of fatigue. His fastball was a foot or two short, his slider did not have its usual sharpness, and his control was slightly off.

Through the season it was a mystery to many batters how the Yankees' 5–10, 160-pound lefty could throw a 98-mile-an-hour fastball as well as an exceptionally hard slider. They made it difficult for a hitter to tell which pitch was coming at him. Now his pitches appeared less intimidating.

In the sixth, Burleson reached Guidry for a double down the left-field line. Remy sacrificed Burleson to third, and Rice brought him home with a single to center to put Boston up 2–0. After retiring Yastrzemski on a grounder that advanced Rice to second, Guidry elected to walk Fisk and face Lynn, a left-handed hitter. What happened next was one of two critical plays that affected the outcome of the game.

"With two out and two runners on, I hooked one of Guidry's sliders into the right-field corner," Lynn recalled. "Guidry did not have his best stuff. When Yaz hit his home run and when I lined out in my first time at bat, I knew that. Maybe that's why Piniella was playing way over toward the right-field line. If Reggie was out there, I would've had a double. It would've been 4–0 and we'd have broken their backs." Lynn's drive, however, was stabbed by Piniella for the third out.

After the game Piniella was asked why he was playing Lynn as a dead pull hitter, and he admitted he really didn't know.

"Later on," Lynn laughed, "I asked Lou why he was so far out of position on that play.

"He tells me, 'I had a hunch.'

"I told him, 'You're full of shit.'"

Lynn's response was made in jest, but Piniella never denied he was taking a big risk in moving so far to his left when Lynn was batting. It just happened that luck was on his side.

Although he had been getting behind in the count on bat-

Mike Torrez had allowed
the Yankees just two hits
going into the seventh
inning. *(Chuck Solomon)*

ters through the first six innings, Torrez had allowed only two
hits going into the seventh. He was pitching in the classic Fenway Park pattern: up and in to lefties, down and away to right-
ies to keep them from zeroing in on the close left-field wall,
long known as the "Green Monster." He had already struck out
Thurman Munson, one of the Yankees' toughest clutch hitters,
three times. Torrez's good fortune was about to change with
shocking swiftness.

After retiring Graig Nettles to start the seventh inning, the
Red Sox right-hander threw an outside pitch to Chris Chambliss, who dribbled the ball between third and short for a single—only the third Yankee hit of the afternoon. Roy White then
punched another single to center. Torrez set down pinch-hitter
Jim Spencer on a fly to left for the second out. He then faced

Bucky Dent, a low-average hitter who was 0-for-2 in the game so far. Dent was not known for smacking the long ball. He had four home runs during the season.

After Torrez's first pitch, Dent swung at an inside fastball, fouling it off his left ankle. He dropped to the ground in pain, scrambled up, and hobbled around trying to shake off the ache. While he was doing this, Mickey Rivers, who was in the on-deck circle, noticed that Dent's bat had a chip in it. He handed a new, lighter bat to the batboy and told him to bring it to Dent. It was a Roy White model.

"Give this to Bucky," Rivers said. "Tell him there are lots of hits in it. He'll get a home run."

Dent accepted the replacement bat and choked up on it two inches. Torrez then threw a fastball, inside and up. Dent jerked back slightly from the plate and sent the ball soaring to left.

"I thought it was a routine fly ball, ending the inning," said Torrez. "I looked over my shoulder on the way to the dugout and couldn't believe it. Yaz is back to the wall, popping his glove, looking up. I said, 'What's this? What the . . .'

"'Goddamn,' I was saying to myself. 'Goddamn, how could that happen?'"

As Dent was running to first, he did not think the ball would clear the fence either, but it did, settling into the screen by the barest of margins to give the Yankees the lead, 3–2.

An unlikely source of power, Dent stood 5–9, weighed 170 pounds, and had been bothered by a leg injury during the season. But the number nine hitter in the Yankee lineup had changed the course of the game. The home run was so unexpected that it ravaged the hopes of Red Sox fans, who had begun to believe at long last that a most special victory would be fashioned over the despised Yankees.

Torrez was shaken by the dramatic turn of events. He walked Rivers, who stole second. With Munson coming up, Zimmer decided it was time for a pitching change, and he pulled Torrez for sinkerball reliever Bob Stanley.

In his three previous trips to the plate Munson had fanned, but this time he doubled off the wall in left center to score Rivers easily, increasing the Yankee edge to 4–2. Stanley escaped further damage by retiring Piniella to end the rally.

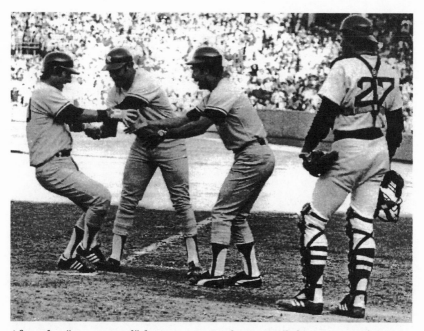

After the "unexpected" home run, Bucky Dent (left) gets a welcome
at home plate from Chris Chambliss and Roy White as Boston
catcher Carlton Fisk looks on.

In the bottom of the seventh, Guidry, who had been struggling to compensate for his diminished fastball, retired Hobson but yielded a single to George Scott and was finally lifted
by Bob Lemon. Goose Gossage, the most intimidating reliever
in the majors, was summoned from the bullpen.

Years later the Goose recalled his feelings before entering
the game. "With the whole season on the line, there was a helluva lot of pressure," he said. "My legs were shaking when I
was warming up in the bullpen. Walking out to the mound at
Fenway, I just thought I could be back home in Colorado instead of pitching in the big game. That thought really took a
lot of pressure off me."

The heavy-set right-hander threw a fearsome fastball. He
put everything he had into each pitch, rocking back, flipping
his left foot out, and firing the ball to the plate without trying
to spot it.

Gossage struck out pinch-hitter Bob Bailey on three pitches

and retired Burleson to end the inning. The Yankees were six outs away from the division title.

In the top of the eighth, Reggie Jackson crunched a belt-high fastball from Stanley for a 430-foot homer into the right-center-field bleachers, fattening New York's lead to 5–2.

The Red Sox, however, were not going easily. They got to Gossage in the bottom of the eighth, closing the gap to 5–4 on a double by Remy and singles by Yastrzemski, Fisk, and Lynn. Fenway Park partisans came alive. The next two batters were Hobson and Scott, both free-swinging fastball hitters. If either connected for a home run, the playoff encounter might have a happy ending after all. Gossage had other ideas. Hobson popped up on a high fastball, and Scott went down swinging on a similar pitch.

The Yankees were shut down in the top of the ninth but now needed only three outs to assure themselves of a trip to Kansas City for another American League Championship Series against the Royals.

Dwight Evans was the first batter in the ninth, hitting for third baseman Frank Duffy who had replaced Brohamer in the eighth. Evans was still suffering periodic dizzy spells caused by the beaning he had received in late August, and Gossage got him to fly out. Next came Burleson, who laid off Gossage's high fastballs and walked on four pitches. Then followed another play that proved crucial in the Yankees' ultimate triumph.

With Burleson on first with the tying run, Jerry Remy lined a Gossage pitch to right field where Piniella once again had positioned himself perfectly. Late in the afternoon in autumn, the sun hangs low over the grandstand behind third base at Fenway. The right fielder, facing almost due west, looks directly into the sun and can easily lose sight of a ball driven toward him. That is what happened to Piniella on Remy's hit. He took a step to his left, stopped, drifted back another step, and threw up his arms in despair. He had lost track of the ball.

"I knew from the bench," said Lynn, "that he didn't see the ball. The sun was brutal out there."

Burleson broke for second but had to hold up in case the ball was caught. Piniella had guessed right again. As he stepped to his left the ball appeared ten feet in front of him. He stabbed it on one hop with his glove hand, limiting Remy to a single.

Lynn found no fault in Burleson's decision not to run. "Lou stuck up his hand like a decoy. It was a tough decision for Rick. He couldn't assume a decoy. Piniella looked like a scarecrow out there. Luckily the ball came down right in front of him."

Burleson explained his action in not running all out on the hit. "It wasn't a low line drive but a high line drive that might've been catchable," he said. "When Piniella threw up his arms, I knew he had lost it in the sun, but I had to see if the ball would fall in or not. If he catches it, I'm doubled up, but the ball bounced up to his glove and as I rounded second, I had to shut it down. If the ball had got by Piniella, I would've scored easily."

With the tying and winning runs on base for the Red Sox, it now became a test of strength between one formidable pitcher and two formidable hitters, matching Gossage first against Rice and then against Yastrzemski.

Rice worked the count to 1-and-1 against Gossage, then hit a long fly ball to right field that was caught by Piniella. Burleson advanced to third after the catch while Remy held first. Had Burleson been on third, he would have scored the tying run after the catch.

Now the outcome of the game rested on the strong arm of Gossage and the strong shoulders and wrists of Yastrzemski, who had already driven in two runs with a homer and a single.

"I don't think the Red Sox would have wanted anybody else but Yaz at the plate at that time," said Burleson. "We couldn't have picked a better guy." As Yastrzemski stepped to the plate he was greeted by a resounding roar from Red Sox fans. He took a pitch low for a ball, and then Gossage threw what Yaz was looking for, an inside fastball.

Yastrzemski wanted to pull the ball through the hole between first and second to score Burleson, but he did not get the head of his bat out quickly enough. The pitch beat him.

"The pitch came in on the inside, just at the knees," Yaz ex-

New York Yankees vs. Boston Red Sox
at Fenway Park, October 2, 1978

New York Yankees	AB	R	H	RBI	Boston Red Sox	AB	R	H	RBI
Mickey Rivers, cf	2	1	1	0	Rick Burleson, ss	4	1	1	0
Paul Blair, ph/cf (c)	1	0	1	0	Jerry Remy, 2b	4	1	2	0
Thurman Munson, c	5	0	1	1	Jim Rice, rf	5	0	1	1
Lou Piniella, rf	4	0	1	0	Carl Yastrzemski, lf	5	2	2	2
Reggie Jackson, dh	4	1	1	1	Carlton Fisk, c	3	0	1	0
Graig Nettles, 3b	4	0	0	0	Fred Lynn, cf	4	0	1	1
Chris Chambliss, 1b	4	1	1	0	Butch Hobson, dh	4	0	1	0
Roy White, lf	3	1	1	0	George Scott, 1b	4	0	2	0
Gary Thomasson, lf	0	0	0	0	Jack Brohamer, 3b	1	0	0	0
Brian Doyle, 2b	2	0	0	0	Bob Bailey, ph (b)	1	0	0	0
Jim Spencer, ph (a)	1	0	0	0	Frank Duffy, 3b	0	0	0	0
Fred Stanley, 2b	1	0	0	0	Dwight Evans, ph (d)	1	0	0	0
Bucky Dent, ss	4	1	1	3					
Total	**35**	**5**	**8**	**5**		**36**	**4**	**11**	**4**

(a) Flied out for Doyle in the seventh inning; (b) Struck out for Brohamer in the seventh inning; (c) Singled for Rivers in the ninth inning; (d) Popped out for Duffy in the ninth inning.

New York	0	0	0	0	0	0	4	1	0	—	5
Boston	0	1	0	0	0	1	0	2	0	—	4

New York Yankees	IP	H	R	ER	SO	BB
Ron Guidry (W)	6.1	6	2	2	5	1
Goose Gossage (Save)	2.2	5	2	2	2	1

Boston Red Sox	IP	H	R	ER	SO	BB
Mike Torrez (L)	6.2	5	4	4	4	3
Bob Stanley +	0.1	2	1	1	0	0
Andy Hassler	1.2	1	0	0	2	0
Dick Drago	0.1	0	0	0	0	0

+ Pitched to one batter in the eighth inning.

2B—Rivers, Scott, Burleson, Munson, Remy. **HR**—Yastrzemski, Dent, Jackson.
SB—Rivers (2). **SH**—Brohamer, Remy. **PB**—Munson. **LOB**—New York 6, Boston 9.
Umpires—Don Denkinger, Jim Evans, Al Clark, Steve Palermo.
Time—2:52. **Attendance**—32,925

plained later. "My pitch. I swung, but just as I got the bat out, the ball exploded on me, coming in quicker than I had thought. I tried to turn on it, but I got underneath the ball."

Even catcher Thurman Munson was surprised by the velocity of the pitch. After the game he asked Gossage, "Where'd that extra foot come from?"

Yastrzemski hit a high pop foul that Graig Nettles caught just beyond third base to end the game. "I was hoping," said Carlton Fisk, "that ball would never come down."

Thus ended another failed quest by the Red Sox.

"In the clubhouse afterward," said Lynn, "there wasn't much talking. Everybody felt terrible. Carl probably felt the worst since he was one of the older guys. It was so discouraging because we had played so well in the first half of the season, then struggled, and finally bounced back at the end when we had to win every game to finish in a tie. We thought the chances of winning would lean toward us because of the home-field edge, but they had the big guy in the pen. Gossage was the difference."

Lynn thought for a moment and then added, "Dent's home run was part of it," he said, "but what really beat us were Piniella's two plays in right field. Lou was not known as a great defensive player. Call it luck, a rub of the green, but there's some luck in winning.

"I still think we were a superior team, but both of us felt that whoever won the playoff would go on to win the World Series. And that's what the Yankees did to the Dodgers. Beat them in six games."

When the Yankees lost to Cleveland in the final game of the regular season, Reggie Jackson had played right field and Piniella had been the DH. Their roles were reversed for the playoff against the Red Sox. "There were actually two turning points to our game," said Jim Rice. "Dent's home run and their decision to play Piniella in right field."

Looking back, Burleson admitted the loss tore at his emotions. "I lockered next to Remy, and after the game he was shook up, breaking down. I was upset about it myself. Even though we lost, the thing I'm proud about is that we never quit.

The Yankees had a three-game lead in September, and we came on strong to tie them. We gave it everything we had."

Resurrecting his ninth-inning matchup against Yastrzemski, Gossage praised his adversary as one of the greatest batters he ever faced. "I wasn't going to get beaten by anything but my best," he recalled. "Forget the breaking ball. I just wound up and threw as hard as I could."

The player who received the most condolences in the Boston clubhouse was Yastrzemski. "My stomach is a bunch of knots now," he said. "I don't have words to express how I feel." As his son, Michael, consoled him, he broke down and went into the trainer's room to compose himself.

A reporter asked Carlton Fisk if the playoff loss was as hard on him emotionally as the defeat the Red Sox suffered against the Reds in the seventh game of the 1975 World Series. "I don't think the Series was comparable to today," he said. "This is much more disappointing."

Fisk was asked about the critical line drive Jerry Remy hit in the ninth inning. "It's strange," he said. "Piniella didn't ever see the ball, and it landed right in front of him and bounced into his glove. If it lands four or five feet on either side of him . . ."

"It's a triple," a reporter said, finishing the sentence.

"Easy," said Fisk.

The conversation reinforced one of baseball's oldest maxims: it's a game of inches. Mike Torrez agrees. Recalling his pitch to Bucky Dent, he said, "I can still see Carlton calling for the fastball, inside. It wasn't exactly where I wanted it, but Bucky hit it just hard enough to get it out of the park with that breeze.

"I would have loved to have won that game, beating my ex-mates. I would have loved it, but, hey, you can't put every pitch exactly where you want it. I'm sorry we didn't win it. In my heart I know I gave it all I had, but I can't keep going over that homer, that pitch. It's not too good a memory."

1984

Cubs' Lofty Intentions Are Grounded by the Padres

"It was pretty devastating to fall one game short of the World Series, but I prefer to remember how well our fans and the city reacted to us."

—Bob Dernier

In 1984 the Cubs posted the best record in the National League, but a long-established scheduling format prevented them from enjoying a home-field advantage in the five-game playoff series for the pennant against the San Diego Padres.

Since 1969, the National League arrangement had dictated that in even years, the team winning the East Division would play at home in the first two games of the best-of-five championship series. So it was ordained that Chicago would be the site of the first two playoff matches in 1984, with the remaining games played in San Diego.

"We were close to being unbeatable at Wrigley Field that season," recalled Bob Dernier, who played center field and was the leadoff hitter for the 1984 Cubs. "I'm not using that as an excuse for us losing to the Padres, but if we had played three games at home the result might have been different."

The Cubs that year were indeed tough playing on the slow, natural grass of the "friendly confines" of Wrigley Field, where they won 51 of 80 games for an impressive .638 winning percentage. They completed the season with a 96–65 record under manager Jim Frey to capture the East Division title and send their fans in Chicago and in many parts of the Midwest into a state of euphoria.

Could it be that the Cubs, after 39 years of deprivation, were actually headed for another World Series? The question would be answered the first week in October when they were scheduled to meet the Padres, who had run away from mediocre competition in the West Division to finish with a 92–70 mark under manager Dick Williams.

Although the Cubs were favored in the league championship playoffs, it was hard to overlook the fact the two teams had played evenly during the season, splitting their 12 games against each other. The Cubs had won three and lost three games at Wrigley, while the Padres fashioned a similar record at Jack Murphy Stadium in San Diego. And the parity between the two clubs was highlighted by one other note: seven of the 12 games had been decided by one run.

As happens so often in baseball, reality vaporized the dreams that Cubs fans entertained in 1984.

During the year, Peter Ueberroth, who had headed the Los Angeles Olympic Organizing Committee, was named new baseball commissioner to succeed Bowie Kuhn. Jack Morris of the Tigers was among several players who were acclaimed for special individual achievements during the season. He pitched a 4–0 no-hitter against the White Sox at Comiskey Park on April 7, helping Detroit to burst out of the gate with nine straight wins. The following week Pete Rose collected the four thousandth hit of his career in a game at Montreal, and in September, Reggie Jackson slammed his five hundredth lifetime home run in a game against the Royals at Anaheim Stadium.

Morris's no-hitter was only part of the Tigers' amazing start. By May 24 Sparky Anderson's club had notched a 35–5 record and never looked back. The Tigers finished at 104–58 and swept the Royals in the American League playoffs, on the way to their first World Series appearance since 1968.

In the National League, both the Cubs and Padres had made significant moves to strengthen themselves for a run at their respective division titles. General manager Dallas Green, a big, 6–5 forthright front-office man, put the right pieces together for the Cubs. When he came over from the Phillies' organization in October 1981, he set out to rid the Cubs of their losing image. "I knew what I had here," he said when asked for an assessment of the team he inherited, "and I didn't have crap."

One writer suggested Green had undertaken "a task that would have given Hercules a hernia." "I'm not here to win friends," he said bluntly. "I'm here to win ball games."

The winning did not come right away, but Green wasted little time in rebuilding the Cubs. In January 1982 he dealt shortstop Ivan De Jesus to the Phillies in exchange for another shortstop, Larry Bowa, and a throw-in, young Ryne Sandberg, who was at first penciled in at third base but soon became one of the great second basemen in the club's history.

With the exception of catcher Jody Davis and reliever Lee Smith, who came to the Cubs directly from the minors, virtually the entire 1984 team was formed through Green's trades. Among the regulars, the lone exceptions were first baseman Leon Durham, obtained in an earlier deal with the Cardinals in 1980, and right fielder Keith Moreland, acquired in a 1981 transaction with the Phillies.

Otherwise Green might have been compared to a frenetic chemist, mixing all sorts of potions until he found a winning formula. In 1983 he acquired via trades veteran third baseman Ron Cey from the Dodgers, and pitchers Steve Trout (from the White Sox), Dick Ruthven (from the Phillies), and Scott Sanderson (from the Expos).

Heading into the 1984 season, Green knew more work had to be done to turn the Cubs around from their losing ways in 1982 and 1983 when they finished with records of 73–89 and 71–91 respectively.

In spring training the team looked terrible. First-year manager Jim Frey described the training period as "horrendous." It included the release of veteran pitcher and future Hall of Famer Fergie Jenkins, two intrasquad brawls, and a 7–20 exhibition record.

But Green was busy in his chemistry lab. On March 26 he obtained reliever Tim Stoddard from the Oakland A's, and on March 27 he once again swung a crucial deal with his old club, the Phillies. He acquired a talented and speedy young center fielder in Bob Dernier and a left fielder and proven leader in Gary Matthews. The Cubs now had an entire outfield and half an infield of former Phillies, but Green wasn't finished.

After injuries struck Ruthven and Sanderson, the general manager on May 25 dealt away first baseman Bill Buckner, who had been sitting on the bench, to the Red Sox in exchange for starter Dennis Eckersley. And, in his biggest trade of all, he acquired Rick Sutcliffe from the Indians on June 13 for outfielders Mel Hall and Joe Carter, a promising power hitter who was highly regarded by the Cubs organization.

Sutcliffe went on to win 16 games for the Cubs and lose only one while recording a 2.69 earned run average. Eckersley posted ten victories with a 3.03 ERA.

"When we got Dernier and Matthews," said Frey, "I felt we had become a .500 team. Getting Eckersley and Sutcliffe made us contenders."

At the time of the Sutcliffe trade, the Cubs were 34–25 and in first place. Following the arrival of the big right-hander, who at one point won 14 straight games, they went 62–40 and took control of the division race. After the season ended, Sutcliffe was the unanimous selection of baseball writers for the Cy Young award in the National League, while Ryne Sandberg was an overwhelming choice for the Most Valuable Player award.

While there were critics of Frey's tactics during the '84 season, the Cubs manager deserved credit on several counts. He switched Leon Durham from the outfield to first base, his normal position. He encouraged Ryne Sandberg to use his strength in driving the ball rather than just meeting it, with the result that Sandberg doubled his home-run output to 19 from nine in 1983, and increased his RBI total to 84 from 48 the previous year.

Frey also knew that Mel Hall was not the answer to the Cubs' long-standing problem in center field, and Green responded to his request for help in filling the position by trading for the speedy Dernier, who also gave the team a genuine base-stealing threat.

And in Gary Matthews, Frey had the "never-say-die" type of leader the Cubs needed to contend over the long pennant chase. Speaking of Matthews, Pete Rose said, "His statistics don't really

Manager Jim Frey's outlook improved as general manager Dallas Green built the Cubs into contenders. *(Dennis Mock / Focus West)*

reflect the contributions he's made over the years. He's a very take-charge guy. That's why I named him Sarge."

After Green had completed all his maneuvering with the Cubs' roster, Frey was asked what he thought of the team's chemistry. "I'm not much of a chemistry guy," he said. "Chemistry to me is a pinch-hit double with the bases loaded."

When the Cubs led the East Division by eight and a half games with only 12 left to play, writers wanted to hear his assessment of the team's title possibilities. "Gentlemen," said Frey, "I think we've got a chance."

Although Sutcliffe and Sandberg individually enjoyed highly productive seasons, the Cubs in '84 led their National League competitors in only three statistical categories. They scored the most runs, 762, received the most bases on balls, 567, and their pitchers allowed the fewest walks, 442.

Otherwise they were good but not dominant. They ranked fourth in team hitting, second in home runs, fourth in stolen bases, second in fielding, and tenth in pitching ERA. Yet they rang the bell with more wins than any other team in the majors except for Detroit, and finished six and a half games ahead of the second-place New York Mets in the East Division.

Sandberg, who batted second, was the only member of the regular starting lineup who hit over .300, finishing at .314. He also led all major league second basemen in fielding with a .993 average, committing only six errors in 864 chances. After the season, when a writer asked Frey about Sandberg's defensive prowess, the manager remarked, "They say he made six errors, but I can't remember any of them."

It was Sandberg who performed heroically in a game that seemed to indicate 1984 would be the Cubs' year of redemption. On June 23, a Saturday afternoon, he led off the bottom of the ninth inning against the Cardinals at Wrigley Field and hit a home run off the tough reliever Bruce Sutter to tie the score at 9–9. In the last half of the 11th inning, Sandberg came to the plate to face Sutter again. Now the Cubs were behind 11–9, with two outs and Bob Dernier on first with a walk. Once more Sandberg delivered, hitting a game-tying home run, giving him a total of five hits in six at-bats and seven RBI. The Cubs finally won the game in the 12th inning, 12–11. The victory did a great deal to energize them for the rest of the season.

With Dernier batting in front of him and Gary Matthews hitting behind him, Sandberg was the centerpiece of a dangerous trio of run producers. Dernier hit .278 with 26 doubles and 45 stolen bases. Matthews led the league in walks with 103 while averaging .291 with 21 doubles, 14 homers, 101 runs scored, and 82 RBI. Combined, the trio had a robust .377 on-base percentage.

Others in the lineup helped manufacture important runs. Leon Durham, who made only seven errors at first base, hit .279 with 23 homers and 96 RBI. Third baseman Ron Cey, though bothered by an injured wrist, connected for 25 homers and drove in 97 runs. Catcher Jody Davis had 19 HR and 94 RBI, with right fielder Keith Moreland adding 16 home runs and 80 RBI.

So the Cubs' offensive ability was spread out evenly, with the exception of shortstop Larry Bowa who at 38 was nearing the end of his career and batted only .223.

With Sutcliffe leading the way, the pitching staff received strong support from reliever Lee Smith, a big, hard-throwing right-hander who amassed 33 saves. Tim Stoddard, another bullpen specialist, won ten games and saved seven. Left-handed starter Steve Trout, under the tutelage of pitching coach Billy Connors, turned in his best season ever with a 13–7 record and a 3.41 ERA. Dennis Eckersley finished 10–8 and Scott Sanderson, 8–5, despite back problems.

If the Cubs made a significant turnaround in 1984, so did the Padres who for two seasons had been a break-even, fourth-place team in the West Division. They made two moves before the start of the '84 season that made them into contenders. They signed free-agent relief pitcher Goose Gossage and traded for third baseman Graig Nettles, both of whom had been Yankee stalwarts the year before. Nettles solidified the Padres' infield and added power with 20 home runs. Gossage chalked up 25 saves and a 10–6 record working out of the bullpen.

With former Dodger Steve Garvey set at first base and the veteran Garry Templeton at short, manager Dick Williams rounded out the infield by shifting outfielder Alan Wiggins to second base. In their outfield the Padres had three 24-year-olds: Carmelo Martinez in left, Kevin McReynolds in center, and Tony Gwynn in right. McReynolds added punch to the lineup with 20 homers, and Gwynn won his first league batting title with a .351 average.

Williams had concerns about Garvey who was coming back from a thumb injury that caused him to miss the last two months of the 1983 season, and catcher Terry Kennedy who had undergone arthroscopic knee surgery in February. He also had questions about his rotation of starting pitchers, including Eric Show, Mark Thurmond, Andy Hawkins, Ed Whitson, and Tim Lollar, who had a combined 105–113 lifetime record in the majors going into the '84 season.

Williams' concerns gradually receded as the Padres won ten of their first 12 games and finished April at 15–8. By June 9 the club had taken command in the West Division and never relinquished first place, finishing 12 games ahead of the Braves and Astros, who tied for the runner-up spot.

The Padres ended the season in Atlanta, then went to

Chicago, where Cubs partisans were going slightly mad over the forthcoming playoffs and the possibility of a World Series in Wrigley Field. Some members of the press stoked the embers of this nuttiness. Columnist Mike Royko of the *Chicago Tribune,* which was part of the company that owned the Cubs, busily stirred up appropriate animosity against the Padres and their followers. "Because we have fairness, equity, truth, and justice and the American way on our side," he wrote, "we are going to slaughter those lousy wimps."

It looked as though that was exactly what would happen after the Cubs demolished the Padres 13–0 in the opening game of the League Championship Series at Wrigley Field on a sunny Tuesday afternoon, then came back to win the next day, 4–2.

In the first game the Cubs simply dominated the Padres behind the pitching of Rick Sutcliffe, who yielded only two hits over seven innings while his teammates clobbered the opposition for 16, including five home runs, two by Gary Matthews, and one each by Dernier, Cey, and Sutcliffe.

"Before the game," recalled Dernier, "I asked Larry Bowa when the butterflies went away. He said after the first pitch."

When Dernier came to bat as the Cubs leadoff hitter in the bottom half of the first inning, he showed no uneasiness. He hit Eric Show's second pitch for a home run. That proved to be enough offense against the muzzled Padres, who collected only a bunt single by Garvey and a bloop single by Templeton off Sutcliffe.

It was a stunning victory for the Cubs, and when Steve Trout defeated the Padres in game two, the odds of a pennant being hoisted at Wrigley Field rose sharply.

Royko once more expressed the emotions of many Cubs fans. "All of a sudden, it hit me," he wrote. "These are the Cubs—the Chicago Cubs—beating the hell out of people. Bullies, that's what we've become. Big, bad, mean bullies. And, oh boy, does it feel great. Why didn't we think of this years ago?"

Before the two teams boarded planes for the trip to San Diego to complete the series, Tony Gwynn poked fun at the overwhelming media attention being focused on the Cubs. He joked, "It's like we're in 'the National League playoffs, starring the Chicago Cubs. Also with the San Diego Padres.'"

On the way to the West Coast, some of the Cub players showed signs of a dangerous overconfidence. After all, they had beaten up the Padres twice and needed only one more win in three chances to bring home the big prize.

Larry Bowa was particularly upset when he heard talk that the team had the pennant all but wrapped up. He and Gary Matthews and Keith Moreland knew better than to think that way. They knew from their years with the Phillies that a team might win a few battles in baseball but still lose the war. Which is precisely what happened.

Why it happened may be found in the way the Cubs used their best starting pitchers, Sutcliffe, Trout, and Eckersley, in the final three playoff games. Eckersley lost game three in San Diego, 7–1, on Thursday night, October 4. With Friday being an off day, manager Jim Frey had a choice of starting Sutcliffe or Scott Sanderson in Saturday night's game. He chose Sanderson, figuring he had Sutcliffe available, if needed, for the clincher on Sunday afternoon.

"Originally I was going to pitch game four," said Sutcliffe. "I got taken out of the first game and saved some innings so I could do that. Then Frey changed his mind and started Sanderson."

In making his decision, Frey in effect eliminated Trout, his second-best pitcher, from starting another game.

"The biggest reason we're not bringing Sutcliffe back on three days' rest," Frey said at the time, "is we're not yet in position where we have to do that. If we do get down to the one game that is the most important game for the Cubs in almost 40 years, then we've got the right man at the right place."

About Sanderson, Frey said, "Scott has pitched very well lately. We told him last week to prepare himself for Saturday the way he would any other start. I'm confident we have the right man going out there."

What Frey failed to mention was that Sanderson, who had been disabled with back spasms in May and had pitched in pain during most of the second half of the season, had won only two of his last ten starts. But the Cubs' manager defended his pitching strategy. "I don't want to move Rick out of his normal routine," he added. "I want to give him his full rest so he'll have the best chance to do his best. I want all the conditions right for him."

Dissenters maintained that Sutcliffe, an imposing, 6–7 competitor nicknamed the "Red Baron," would have fared better pitching in the cooler air on Saturday night instead of in the Sunday afternoon heat. Frey, they said, should have gone for the kill right away, and if the Cubs failed to win behind their ace right-hander, he would still have a highly motivated and rested Steve Trout ready for game five.

As it unfolded, Sanderson worked into the fifth inning of game four before being relieved with the score tied 3–3. In a dramatic, seesaw skirmish, the Padres won 7–5 on Steve Garvey's two-run homer off Lee Smith in the bottom of the ninth inning.

Garvey virtually beat the Cubs by himself, driving in five runs on four hits, including two singles, a double, and the home run that soared into the bleachers in right center field as though it had been shot out of an Army field piece.

"As soon as the ball went toward the fence," Garvey said, "everything froze in time. It was as if all sound stopped."

"I threw him my best fastball," said Smith. "If the same situation came up again, I would've done the same thing. I'm not second-guessing myself."

So the National League pennant race came down to one game, and 58,359 fans packed Jack Murphy Stadium on Sunday to watch the showdown, pitting Sutcliffe against the Padres' Eric Show.

When the Cubs had last appeared in a World Series in 1945, the Tigers had been their opponent. Now there was speculation that with Sutcliffe on the mound, they once again would be taking on Detroit in a Fall Classic. Sutcliffe was the top pitcher in the National League, having fashioned a combined record of 20–6 with the Indians and Cubs as well as a decisive victory over the Padres in game one.

The Cubs quickly appeared to be on the way to fulfilling the hopes of their legions of supporters. In the first inning Matthews walked and stole second. Then Durham belted a two-run homer to right field off Show to give the Cubs a 2–0 lead.

It became 3–0 in the second inning when Jody Davis hit a solo home run to left. Show then retired Bowa but yielded a single to Sutcliffe and was relieved by Andy Hawkins.

From that point on, the Padres' bullpen, including Hawkins, Dave Dravecky, Craig Lefferts, and Goose Gossage pitched seven and two-thirds innings of shutout relief, allowing the Cubs only two hits.

Sutcliffe, meanwhile, was rolling along and had checked the Padres on two hits through five innings. "I must admit," Frey said later, "I felt pretty confident at that point."

Steve Trout, who was in the bullpen from the start of the game, had similar feelings. "I started warming up in the sixth inning," he recalled. "Johnny Oates [bullpen coach] was out there with me. My stuff was great, but maybe I had jinxed us because I had been asking guys in the bullpen if they had extra tickets for the games in Detroit. It was like the kiss of death. We were up 3–0, and then all of a sudden we're down."

In the sixth inning the Padres closed their deficit to 3–2 on a pair of singles by Wiggins and Gwynn, a walk to Garvey, and sacrifice flies by Nettles and Kennedy.

"The first five innings, Sutcliffe threw pitches you couldn't hit," said Gwynn. "Then it looked like he was starting to get tired." Garvey added, "In the sixth inning, Rick's ball began to straighten out, lose some of its movement. And his location wasn't as good as it had been earlier. It was a hot day, and you could tell he was losing it. I thought they were going to lift him then, but they left him in. They shouldn't have."

Disaster struck Sutcliffe and the Cubs in the seventh inning when the Padres pushed across four runs to take a 6–3 lead. Carmelo Martinez, a former Cub, opened the inning by drawing a walk from Sutcliffe on four pitches. He moved to second on a sacrifice by Templeton, and then scored the tying run when a sharp grounder by pinch-hitter Tim Flannery went through first baseman Leon Durham's legs for an error.

Alan Wiggins, the next batter, punched a checked-swing single into short left field. What followed merely proved how arbitrary fate can be in a critical game. Tony Gwynn hit a hard smash that took a bad hop over second baseman Ryne Sand-

Rick Sutcliffe (left) tired as the deciding game went into the seventh inning. Steve Trout, after warming up in the bullpen, faced only two batters in relieving Sutcliffe. *(Chicago Cubs, Ed Mailliard)*

berg's shoulder and bounded into right center field for a double that scored both Flannery and Wiggins to put San Diego up 5–3.

Gwynn took third on the throw home, and scored the Padres' sixth run on Garvey's line single to center. That was all for Sutcliffe, and Trout was finally waved in from the bullpen.

The left-hander quickly ended the uprising, retiring Nettles on an infield grounder and Kennedy on a strikeout. Because Frey had sat on his hands too long, that was Trout's only contribution to the Cubs' most important game of the season.

In the eighth inning, with Gossage on the mound to protect the Padres' three-run lead, Richie Hebner, batting for Trout, reached first base with two outs after being hit by a pitch. Sandberg singled to left center, moving Hebner to third. Sandberg then stole second, putting two runners in scoring position. That brought Matthews, representing the tying run, to the plate, but Gossage struck him out to end the Cubs' threat. He then closed them out in the ninth inning to send Padre fans at Jack Murphy Stadium into a condition of mass delirium.

Matthews said he remembers his final at-bat against Gossage "as though it happened yesterday. I told Ryno before he went to the plate to give me a shot at tying the game up. He got his hit and stole second, so now I'm up there with two runners on.

"I had had problems with Gossage in the past, and had asked some people how to hit him. They told me to go after him on the first pitch. Well, he hung a slider to me on the first pitch, and I missed it. Maybe I was trying too hard to hit the ball out of sight. He had the edge on me, and he finally struck me out on a high fastball. I didn't perform, and that still burns me when I think about it."

In the somber Cub clubhouse after the game, Durham was dejected as reporters asked him about Flannery's grounder that went through his legs for a critical error that opened the floodgates for the Padres in the seventh inning. In anticipating the ball, Durham did not lower his glove to the ground. He was expecting the ball to take a bounce before it reached him.

"It stayed down," he sighed. "It was about a five-hopper. You know it's going to come up somewhere, but it just stayed flat all the way through. It had a little bit behind it, but it was nothing like a hot shot."

Durham was obviously stunned by the Cubs' downfall. "I've got to let it go, man," he said. "Somebody has to win, and somebody has to lose. I make that play two hundred times in a row. I'll remember it, for sure. It hurts a lot. We had a chance to go to the World Series, and now it's out the window. I still don't believe the season's over."

His interviews completed, Durham excused himself and walked to a corner of the clubhouse to talk to Reggie Jackson, who was among the playoff broadcasters. "Don't feel bad, Bull," said Jackson as he put his arm around Durham. "It happens to everybody."

Jim Frey was questioned about his reluctance to relieve Sutcliffe when he started to get into trouble in the seventh inning. "He was pitching a four-hitter," said Frey. "They weren't exactly

"It stayed down," Leon
Durham explained about
the ground ball that went
through his legs in the
crucial seventh inning.
(George Gojkovich)

beatin' on the ball. I thought he was still throwing the ball
well."

"I should've been able to hold that [3–0] lead," Sutcliffe said
quietly.

A reporter asked the Cubs pitcher, "Is there any one pitch
you'd like back?"

"Four," he answered quickly. "Those four I threw to Martinez."

Sutcliffe was referring the four straight balls he threw to
Carmelo Martinez to open the Padres' half of the seventh inning. "The key wasn't Durham's error," he said. "It was the four
pitches to Martinez. That walk set the stage for the whole inning. It was my loss, and I don't know quite how to describe
the hurt."

"Sut seems to think it was all his fault," said Sandberg. "No,
us getting only five hits, that was the key to the game."

"Without Durham," added Larry Bowa, "we don't get here.
Without Sutcliffe, we don't get here."

Bowa's sentiments pretty much reflected the team's attitude then as well as years later when players were asked for their recollections of the comeback triumph by the Padres.

"We won as a team, we lost as a team," said Dernier.

"You can't put the blame on any one individual," said Matthews. "In that seventh inning it seemed like we got one bad bounce after another, and we just couldn't get out of the inning."

Matthews dismissed the notion that overconfidence was a factor in the Cubs' three straight losses in San Diego, but he and Steve Trout both agree to this day on what really brought about the Cubs' defeat. It was the decision not to pitch Sutcliffe in game four and use Trout to start game five if necessary.

"It didn't make sense at all," said Matthews, "to change the three-man pitching rotation of Sutcliffe, Trout, and Eckersley, our three best starters, in a short series. Once we got to San Diego, things changed because they were trying to set the rotation for the World Series in Detroit. They were putting all their eggs in one basket by holding Sutcliffe back. And I was wondering, 'What if we don't get to the World Series?'

"Some time later I met Steve Garvey at a golf outing, and he said to me, 'I'm glad you guys didn't start Trout against us again.' Trout deserved another start. He had pitched well for us all year. There was just no logic in not going with our three best starters."

Trout's father, Paul "Dizzy" Trout, had been a successful pitcher for the Tigers in the 1940s and had won a game against the Cubs in the 1945 World Series. Steve was eager to link with his father's past by also pitching in a Fall Classic involving the Cubs and Tigers. Like Matthews, he felt the Cubs messed up their rotation for the games in San Diego.

"I think when we left Chicago, they were debating and deciding what was going to happen with the pitching rotation and especially who would start game four," he recalled. "They could have changed it at any time, but they would never change it on the day of the game. So most everyone realized that Sanderson was going to pitch Saturday, but a lot of the guys thought that wasn't necessary in view of the amount of time

Sutcliffe and myself had to recuperate from our starts in Chicago. Sanderson pitched and didn't do that badly, but he didn't do that good either."

"We're always smarter in hindsight," said Trout, "but in truth probably the right way to go would have been, in a best-of-five series, to rotate your three best pitchers, who were Sutcliffe, myself, and Eckersley. By going with Sanderson and then Sutcliffe, they don't start me on the weekend in San Diego. Here I am, maybe their second- or third-best pitcher, and they don't fully utilize my pitching. I faced only two batters in relief on Sunday.

"You have to wonder what management was thinking. What was done with the rotation doesn't make any sense."

Before the final game Frey told Trout he would be the first man out of the bullpen if Sutcliffe got in trouble. "Well, yeah," Trout said, "if they had done it the right way, and if Sutcliffe got beat on Saturday, I should've been the first guy starting the game on Sunday, not the first guy out of the bullpen."

"In the clubhouse after the game," he said, "it was like we were attending a funeral. Frey went around shaking hands, but nobody really wanted to shake hands. It was such a comedown. That week in Chicago and San Diego was like what Dickens wrote in *A Tale of Two Cities*, 'It was the best of times and the worst of times.' It was the highest, most glorious ride one could ever fathom, and then it was as if our plane had lost its gas and plunged straight to earth. That's exactly the way it went.

"We felt it was completely over after their runs came in during the seventh inning.

"It was a horrible flight home. When we won the division in Pittsburgh and flew back to O'Hare Airport, there was a huge crowd waiting for us. When we landed after our trip from San Diego, I remember Dennis Eckersley saying, 'Where are all the fans now?'"

After the game Dallas Green said, "Give the Padres credit. We had them by the throat and let them get away. They were flat and dead in our ball park, but were electrified by their fans in their own park."

Frey took the loss hard. He was near tears later and admitted he felt sorry for young players like Sandberg and Durham

Jody Davis and Dave Johnstone wonder what happened. *(Phil Velasquez)*

not being able to go to a World Series. "Jim had his hands on his knees," said Matthews, "and he was starting to cry. I had to turn away from him to keep from crying myself."

"It was pretty devastating to fall one game short of the World Series," said Dernier, "but I prefer to remember how well our fans and the city reacted to us. Despite the disappointment, it was a magical season in a lot of respects. We were a tightly knit team, and there were a lot of true friendships among us. There were a lot of hugs after game five. We all knew it wasn't just that one error by Leon that decided our season."

Padres catcher Terry Kennedy noted another positive—if dubious—aspect to the Cubs' crash landing. "I know one thing," he said. "We took the '69 Cubs off the hook."

A final, ironic touch should be added to the story of the 1984 Cubs. In the last two games in San Diego, Padres' manager Dick Williams shuttled in a steady stream of relievers who held down the Cubs. "The bullpen did an outstanding job," said Williams.

One of those unsung Padre relievers, left-hander Craig Lefferts, received credit as the winning pitcher in games four and five. He was the same Craig Lefferts who toiled for the Cubs in 1983 before being dealt to San Diego as part of a three-team transaction that brought Scott Sanderson to Chicago. For anguished Cub fans, that fact was just one more stab in the heart.

Chicago Cubs vs. San Diego Padres
at Jack Murphy Stadium, October 7, 1984

Chicago Cubs	AB	R	H	RBI	San Diego Padres	AB	R	H	RBI
Bob Dernier, cf	4	0	0	0	Alan Wiggins, 2b	3	2	2	0
Ryne Sandberg, 2b	4	0	1	0	Tony Gwynn, rf	4	2	2	2
Gary Matthews, lf	2	1	0	0	Steve Garvey, 1b	3	0	1	1
Leon Durham, 1b	4	1	1	2	Graig Nettles, 3b	3	0	0	1
Keith Moreland, rf	3	0	1	0	Terry Kennedy, c	3	0	1	1
Ron Cey, 3b	4	0	0	0	Bobby Brown, cf	3	0	0	0
Jody Davis, c	4	1	1	1	Luis Salazar, cf	1	0	1	0
Larry Bowa, ss	2	0	0	0	Carmelo Martinez, lf	3	1	0	0
Thad Bosley, ph (d)	1	0	0	0	Garry Templeton, ss	3	0	1	0
Tom Veryzer, ss	0	0	0	0	Eric Show, p	0	0	0	0
Rick Sutcliffe, p	2	0	1	0	Andy Hawkins, p	0	0	0	0
Richie Hebner, ph (e)	0	0	0	0	Mario Ramirez, ph (a)	1	0	0	0
					Kurt Bevacqua, ph (b)	1	0	0	0
					Tim Flannery, ph (c)	1	1	0	0
Total	**30**	**3**	**5**	**3**		**29**	**6**	**8**	**5**

(a) Fouled out to catcher for Hawkins in the third inning; (b) Flied out to center for Dave Dravecky in the fifth inning; (c) Reached base on an error for Lefferts in the seventh inning; (d) Struck out for Bowa in the eighth inning; (e) Hit by a pitch for Steve Trout in eighth inning.

Chicago		2	1	0	0	0	0	0	0	0	—	3
San Diego		0	0	0	0	0	2	4	0	x	—	6

Chicago Cubs	IP	H	R	ER	SO	BB
Rick Sutcliffe (L)	6.1	7	6	5	2	3
Steve Trout	0.2	0	0	0	1	0
Warren Brusstar	1.0	1	0	0	1	0

San Diego Padres	IP	H	R	ER	SO	BB
Eric Show	1.1	3	3	3	0	2
Andy Hawkins	1.2	0	0	0	1	1
Dave Dravecky	2.0	0	0	0	2	0
Craig Lefferts (W)	2.0	0	0	0	1	0
Goose Gossage (S)	2.0	2	0	0	2	0

E—Durham. DP—San Diego. 2B—Gwynn. 3B—Salazar. HR—Durham, Davis. SB—Matthews, Sandberg. SH—Templeton. SF—Nettles, Kennedy. **Hit by pitch**—by Gossage (Hebner).
Umpires—John Kibler, Paul Runge, John McSherry, Doug Harvey.
Time—2:41. **Attendance**—58,359

1986

Angels' Wings Are Clipped by the Red Sox

"I don't think Donnie Moore ever got over losing that fifth game."—Doug DeCinces

It would require a great stretch of the imagination to think that the major leagues will ever again produce as many agonizing defeats in three separate and critical post-season actions as those suffered by losing teams in 1986. The victims were the California Angels and Houston Astros, who failed in their bids to win pennants in the American and National League Championship Series, and the Boston Red Sox, who came within one strike of beating the New York Mets in the World Series.

The fate of all three teams was determined in dramatic extra-inning games.

"If ever there was a year that broke the hearts of fans devoted to so many different teams, it had to be 1986," said Jerome Holtzman, the official major league historian. Within a two-week span in October, crucial games that lasted 11, 16, and ten innings, respectively, figured in the outcome of the 1986 league playoffs and the World Series, spreading disappointment among fans in California, Texas, and New England.

On Sunday afternoon, October 12, at Anaheim Stadium, the Angels were one strike away from winning the first pennant in their 26 years of existence, only to see victory snatched away from them by the Red Sox in game five of the American League Championship Series. The game lasted 11 innings.

On Wednesday, October 15, the Astros, also seeking their first-ever pennant, fought valiantly for 16 innings in the Houston Astrodome before dropping the deciding game six of the National League Championship Series to the Mets.

Finally, on Saturday night, October 25, at Shea Stadium, the Red Sox had a World Series title within their grasp but were humbled by the Mets in an astonishing tenth-inning finish of game six.

The 1986 baseball season provided its faithful followers in the United States and Canada a pleasant form of diversion from personal and worldly troubles, despite the fact all four division races were settled without photo finishes.

In the National League East, the Mets ran away from the crowd, winning 108 games under manager Davey Johnson and finishing 20-1/2 lengths ahead of the second-place Phillies.

In the West Division, the Astros hit the wire ten full games ahead of their closest challenger, the Cincinnati Reds.

The Red Sox won the American League East with a five-and-a-half-game bulge over the Yankees, while the Angels, directed by manager Gene Mauch, took the West Division title by a margin of five games over the second-place Rangers.

Despite the absence of pulse-quickening division races, major league baseball recorded an all-time-high attendance of 47,506,203 customers during the regular season. It also featured some unusual episodes that attracted the attention of local partisans in a number of cities.

Fans in Baltimore, for instance, had a chance to see President Ronald Reagan throw out the ceremonial first ball to open the season on April 7 and then catch a glimpse of him watching the game against the Indians for two innings from the Orioles' dugout.

A game in San Diego on May 3 was delayed for seven minutes when a skunk wandered onto the field and had to be carefully escorted from the premises by groundskeepers.

Fog ended a May 27 game in Cleveland with the Red Sox leading 2–0 with two outs in the bottom of the sixth inning.

"First, I couldn't see the scoreboard," said Boston pitcher Mike Brown, "and then the center fielder [Tony Armas] disappeared. When second base grew dim, I knew we were in trouble."

Oakland's designated hitter, Dave Kingman, a creative but crude chauvinist, was slapped with a $3,500 fine by A's officials after he arranged for a rat to be delivered in a box to a female baseball writer named Susan in the Kansas City press box on June 23. A note attached to the rat's tail read: "My name is Susan."

And the Cubs fired their 28-year-old ball girl on July 22 when club officials learned that she was featured in an eight-page *Playboy* magazine spread entitled "Belle of the Ball Club."

In more substantial achievements, Roger Clemens, in only his third year with the Red Sox, set a record on April 29 by striking out 20 Mariners as he defeated Seattle 3–1 in nine innings at Fenway Park. His dominating performance came only eight months after surgery on his right shoulder and was an early highlight of a season in which he unanimously won the American League's Cy Young award with a 24–4 record, a lean ERA of 2.48, and 238 strikeouts.

One of two no-hitters in 1986 was especially important in that its author, Mike Scott of the Astros, pitched it on September 25 in a game that clinched the National League West Division title for Houston. Scott shut down the San Francisco Giants 2–0 in the Astrodome, striking out 13 batters as he notched his 18th victory of the season. The Astros' right-hander, like Clemens, received his league's Cy Young award.

Bob Horner of the Braves hit four home runs in a nine-inning game against the Montreal Expos in Atlanta on July 6. And Reggie Jackson, at age 40, showed he still had some of his old power by slamming three home runs for the Angels in a home game against the Kansas City Royals on September 18. By season's end Jackson owned 548 career homers, placing him sixth on the all-time list.

In 1985 the format for the league championship playoffs had been changed from a best-of-five to a best-of-seven series. In 1986 that format produced some of the most dramatic postseason play in history.

In the case of both the Red Sox and the Angels, there was a longing for a soul-satisfying triumph that had gone unfulfilled so many times in the past. Boston had been denied a World Series crown in 1946, 1967, and 1975, had come close to a pennant in 1948, 1949, and 1972, and had lost a one-game playoff to the Yankees for a division title in 1978.

Meanwhile Angels owner Gene Autry and manager Gene Mauch were still seeking their first league pennant.

Baseball insiders had a certain amount of fraternal feeling for Autry, 79, a congenial, likable figure nicknamed the "Cowboy," who had poured millions of dollars into his club since its inception in 1961 in an effort to savor a league championship.

Mauch, 60, was completing his 25th year of managing. Only three men in major league history had managed more seasons: Connie Mack, John McGraw, and Bucky Harris, all of whom had taken teams to the World Series. When it came to winning a pennant, however, Mauch had come up short.

Nicknamed the "Little General" and described by Pete Rose as "the thinking man's manager," Mauch had almost won a National League pennant with the Phillies in 1964, and in 1982 had guided the Angels within reach of an American League flag, extending a strong Milwaukee Brewers team to the limit before losing the final battle of the five-game playoff.

Before the 1986 season, Mauch told his players what it would take to finish on top in the West Division. "Give me 90 victories," he said. "Ninety will get the job done."

When the Angels finally clinched the division title on September 26, trouncing the Rangers 8–3 at Anaheim for their 90th victory, Autry entered the clubhouse after the game and put his arm around Mauch. "He said if we could win 90 games," Autry remarked in reference to Mauch, "we would win the West. And, he had it right on the nose!"

The Angels coasted the rest of the way, losing seven of their remaining nine games to finish at 92–70 as they prepared to meet the Red Sox, a team they had not played since July. The Angels had won seven of their 12 meetings that year.

In becoming division champions, the Angels dispelled the notion they were too old to outlast younger rivals in the de-

Gene Mauch, "the thinking man's manager," was still seeking his first pennant. *(Mitchell Layton)*

manding grind that stretched from April through early October. The core of the team was made up of aging veterans who were called the "Last Hurrah Gang."

Besides Sutton and Jackson, they included catcher Bob Boone, 38; second basemen Bobby Grich, 37, and Rob Wilfong, 33; third baseman Doug DeCinces, 36; outfielders Brian Downing, 35, George Hendrick, 37, and Ruppert Jones, 31; utility infielder and DH Rick Burleson, 35; starting pitcher John Candelaria, 32; and reliever Donnie Moore, 32.

On the younger side were rookie first baseman Wally Joyner, 24; shortstop Dick Schofield, 23; center fielder Gary Pettis, 28; and starting pitchers Mike Witt, 26, and Kirk McCaskill, 25.

It was a mixture of talent that took the team a long way, but in the end, Angel players and manager alike were burdened with memories of what might have been. Years after the loss to the Red Sox in the playoffs, Mauch was asked if he still thought about the heartbreaking defeat in pivotal game five. "Only in the morning when I first wake up," he responded.

In marching over their West Division competition, the Angels received a big lift from their young first baseman Wally Joyner, whose hospitalization during the playoffs diminished the Angels' chances against the Red Sox. Joyner was especially effective in the first half of the season, and even though he later cooled off, he produced 22 homers, 100 runs batted in, and 14 game-winning hits.

Other players who added power to the team's offense were DeCinces with 26 homers and 96 runs batted in, and Downing with 20 round-trippers and 95 RBI.

As a DH, rounding out his fifth and final season with the Angels, Reggie Jackson contributed 18 home runs.

The Angels' Don Sutton finished the season with a 15–11 record and a career total of 310 victories. Other leading winners on the pitching staff were Witt, a 6–7 right-hander who finished with an 18–10 record; McCaskell, who was 17–10; and Candelaria, 10–2. The bullpen was anchored by Moore, who collected 21 saves despite an ailing right shoulder.

In catcher Bob Boone and center fielder Gary Pettis, who made more putouts, 462, than any other player at his position in the majors, the Angels also had two Gold Glove winners on defense.

Yet as a team they did not dominate the league in any significant hitting, pitching, fielding, or stolen-base category, though their batters did receive the most walks, 671, and produce the most sacrifice hits and sacrifice flies.

Their playoff opponent was not much better in that respect, but the Red Sox did amass the league's most doubles, 320, and Boston pitchers yielded the fewest walks, 474, during the season.

Perhaps the biggest difference between the two division champions was represented in the Red Sox' two exceptional individual performers, power pitcher Roger Clemens and third baseman Wade Boggs. Clemens won his first 14 decisions in 1986 and did not suffer a defeat until July 2 on his way to not only a Cy Young award but the American League's Most Valuable Player award as well. Boggs hit .357 to win his third league batting title in four years.

Outside of catcher Rich Gedman and first baseman Bill Buckner, who both swung from the left side, and shortstop Spike Owen, a switch-hitter, the Red Sox featured a varied array of right-handed batters, including Boggs; second baseman

Marty Barrett; outfielders Jim Rice, Dwight Evans, Tony Armas, and Dave Henderson; and DH Don Baylor.

The long ball was provided by Baylor with 31 homers; Evans with 26; Rice, 20; Buckner, 18; and Gedman, 16. Henderson had 15 home runs, but he hit 14 of them with the Mariners before Seattle traded him and Spike Owen to the Red Sox on August 19.

With Clemens setting the pace, manager John McNamara also called on such starters as Oil Can Boyd, 16–10; left-hander Bruce Hurst, 13–8; and Al Nipper, 10–12. Boston's relievers included Bob Stanley, Joe Sambito, and Calvin Schiraldi, whose composite totals included 12 wins and 37 saves. McNamara had managed the Angels in 1983 and 1984. In the playoff series, he would be directing strategy against many of his former players. McNamara had replaced Mauch, who had resigned as manager of the Angels after the 1982 season. Appointed director of the club's playing personnel, Mauch had stayed out of the dugout for two years, a personally painful time in which his wife, Nina Lee, died of cancer, before he returned as field manager of the Angels in 1985.

Despite the skepticism of pre-season "experts" in 1986, Mauch knew he had a good shot at winning another division title and perhaps the pennant that had eluded him and Autry for what seemed like a lifetime. While he had his critics, Mauch was regarded as a keen tactician and "a walking rules book," and he had the knack of creating matchups advantageous to his players.

Through June his team was playing at a 40–35 pace. By July 7, at the halfway mark of the season, the Angels had moved into first place in the West Division with a 44–37 record, on the heels of a 16-inning, 3–1 decision over the Brewers in Milwaukee. They remained atop the division from that point to the end of the season.

Twelve Angel players were in the last year of their contract, and they knew they might not be together as a team much longer. The veterans wanted their potential "last hurrah" to be a good one, not only for themselves but for Autry and Mauch.

"If we could've won that playoff series," said Bob Boone, "all of us, the players, would've wanted the spotlight on Autry and Gene Mauch. There was no 'I' or 'me' in that clubhouse. We wanted to win it for them. We owed it to the Cowboy and Gene."

Boone was especially grateful to Angels management, including former general manager Buzzie Bavasi. "They resurrected my career when they bought me from the Phillies after the '81 season," he said. "Everybody was saying I was an over-the-hill player, that I couldn't throw like I used to. But the Angels gave me the chance. Autry treated me great."

The first two games of the 1986 American League Championship Series were held in Fenway Park. In the opener, Tuesday night, October 7, an anticipated pitchers duel between Clemens and Witt never materialized as the Angels pounded Clemens for ten hits in routing the Red Sox 8–1. Witt pitched superbly, retiring 16 batters in succession and not allowing a hit until two were out in the sixth inning. He went the distance, yielding only five hits.

Boston bounced back the next day to win 9–2 behind Bruce Hurst, who was a tough adversary even though the close left-field wall at Fenway demanded that left-handed pitchers avoid throwing into the power of right-handed batters. Both teams kicked the ball around that day, committing a combined five errors, three by the Angels in the seventh inning when three unearned runs were charged against Angel starter Kirk Mc-Caskill. The errors allowed the Red Sox to take a commanding 6–2 lead.

"I haven't seen a game like that since I played in the Little Leagues," said McCaskill, who absorbed the loss.

The next three games in Anaheim each drew crowds of more than 64,200 fans, virtually double the average attendance for the first two contests in less spacious Fenway Park.

After an off day, game three was played on Friday night, October 10, with Candelaria going against Oil Can Boyd. The game was tied at 1–1 in the bottom of the seventh inning when the Angels reached Boyd for three runs. With two outs, Schofield hit Boyd's first pitch for a home run over the left-field fence. Boone singled, and Gary Pettis drove a two-and-one offering by Boyd into the right-field seats.

The Angels held on to win 5–3, though Donnie Moore was

not particularly effective over the last two innings in relief of Candelaria, surrendering a walk, four hits, and two runs while committing a costly balk.

They now held a two-to-one edge in the series, but the Angels suffered a serious setback when their prized rookie, Wally Joyner, was hospitalized before game four. Abrasions on the lower portion of Joyner's right leg, the result of the young first baseman being hit on the shin by foul balls off his bat, had become infected. The bacterial infection came from the sweat in his socks. Joyner had beat up on Red Sox pitching in the first three games, averaging .455 with two singles, two doubles, a home run, and two RBI in 18 at-bats while hitting in the number two spot in the lineup. He was sidelined for the rest of the series.

"That was a huge loss for us," said Boone.

With Joyner bedridden, Mauch moved George Hendrick to first base for game four, then switched second baseman Bobby Grich to the position for the remainder of the playoffs.

In the fourth game Clemens came back on three days' rest for the first time in his career to face veteran Don Sutton. In a swift turn of events, the Boston right-hander faltered in the bottom of the ninth inning when he had a 3–0 lead and was working on a five-hit shutout. He gave up a towering leadoff home run to DeCinces and successive one-out singles to Schofield and Boone before McNamara brought in reliever Calvin Schiraldi.

Schiraldi gave up a double off the left-field wall by Gary Pettis, scoring Schofield and sending Devon White, running for Boone, to third base with the tying run. Ruppert Jones was then walked intentionally to fill the bases. After Grich struck out, Schiraldi hit Brian Downing with a pitch that forced in White to tie the score at 3–3 as the crowd went wild.

The Angels capitalized on their ninth-inning comeback and won the game 4–3 in the 11th inning on a run-scoring single by Grich.

Schiraldi was disconsolate after the game, particularly because he had hit Downing. "It was the stupidest pitch I ever made in my life," he murmured. "I screwed up. What else can I say?"

Now the Angels were one game away from winning their first pennant and were poised to resume their quest on Sunday afternoon, October 12, in their home park. Mauch felt comfortable with the pitching matchup—Witt versus Hurst. His lineup card featured a few changes. He penciled in Rick Burleson at second base and as the leadoff hitter, Grich at first base, and Hendrick in right field. Otherwise he was going with the regulars who had brought the team this far.

Before the game the Angels manager was on the phone in his clubhouse office talking to Joyner, who said the swelling in his infected leg had gone down but not enough for him to get out of bed.

Mauch felt confident that Grich could handle the fielding intricacies of first base because Grich had played the position 71 times during his career with the Orioles and Angels. He also was confident that Witt, with four full days of rest, would be strong and near peak efficiency.

"That was one thing about Mauch," said Boone. "He was always prepared for any eventuality. He had a terrific memory. He used his players properly so they could perform to the best of their ability. He was the best and smartest manager I ever played for."

Boone made that assessment of Mauch long after he ended his 19-year career as catcher with the Phillies, Angels, and Royals from 1972 through 1990, a stretch during which he caught a staggering 2,225 games. His assessment merits consideration by second-guessers who scoffed at Mauch for never winning a pennant.

Mauch was able to take the sniping of his critics in stride. He had mastered the nuances of managing, planning ahead, anticipating an opponent's moves and countermoves. So he could shrug off the barbs, sometimes with a touch of dry humor. "If you're supposed to learn more from losing than winning," he once cracked, "I must be one smart SOB."

In dominating the Red Sox in the first game, Witt had allowed only one extra-base hit, a double by Don Baylor. With a 93-mile-an-hour fastball and knee-buckling curve, he was ready to exercise the same command of Red Sox batters as he had five days earlier. But no two baseball games are ever the same.

Boston jumped off to a 2–0 lead in the second inning when Gedman pulled a Witt pitch over the right-field fence for a two-run homer.

In the bottom of the second inning, DeCinces hit a drive to deep center where Tony Armas gave chase and slammed into the wall in a futile attempt to make the catch. DeCinces pulled into second with a double, but Armas came up limping. He had sprained his left ankle.

Favoring his sore ankle, Armas asked to be taken out of the game after popping up during his time at-bat in the fourth inning. He told McNamara, "I better come out." McNamara then ordered Dave Henderson to get ready to take Armas's place in center. The substitution led to Henderson's appointment with playoff destiny.

Meanwhile the Angels had come to life in their half of the third inning when Boone homered against Hurst to trim their deficit to 2–1.

While Witt held the Red Sox in check, the Angels scored two runs in the sixth inning and two in the seventh to move ahead 5–2. Their runs in the sixth were the result of DeCinces's double and Grich's home run to center that glanced off Henderson's glove and over the padded green wall.

DeCinces was leading off second when the freakish play put the Angels ahead 3–2. "I went up for the ball and it hit the heel of my glove," explained Henderson. "When my wrist hit the top of the wall, the ball got away."

Grich leaped jubilantly in the air as he was rounding the bases after seeing his drive squirt out of Henderson's glove and disappear into a bank of cameramen on the far side of the wall.

"When I hit my home run," he said later, "I thought that was it for us."

Henderson was grim. Before Grich's homer he had lost DeCinces's routine fly in the sun, pulled up short, and let the ball drop for a two-base hit between him and right fielder Dwight Evans.

His moment of redemption, however, was coming.

The Angels needed six more outs before they could savor the champagne awaiting them in their clubhouse. Witt stopped the Red Sox in the eighth inning and was still sitting on a 5–2 lead at the start of the ninth inning. The tall right-hander was about to be reminded that baseball can be a humbling game.

Leadoff hitter Bill Buckner slapped a broken-bat grounder up the middle, just out of the reach of Schofield, for a single. Witt then fanned Jim Rice with a curve, and needed only two more outs.

Next up was DH Don Baylor. He worked the count to 3-and-2 before he reached out and drove one of Witt's curveballs to left center for a two-run homer that made the score 5–4.

Despite the home run, Witt remained absorbed in the job he still had to do. He threw two strikes to Dwight Evans, the next batter, then got him to pop out to DeCinces on the left side of the infield.

With one out to go, fans at Anaheim Stadium were ready to celebrate.

"After Evans popped to me at third," DeCinces recalled, "Mike came over, and when I flipped the ball to him I could see in his eyes that he was totally focused. In my mind he was one of the best right-handers in the game. I sensed it was over, that we'd win."

The next batter was Gedman, who had hit the ball hard off Witt all afternoon, reaching him for a homer in the second inning, a double in the fifth, and a single in the seventh. He was swinging a hot bat, and Mauch wasted no time in making his move. The Angels manager sent pitching coach Marcel Lachemann to the mound to relieve Witt.

DeCinces re-created the scene. "When the pitching coach came to the mound to talk," he said, "and waved his left arm for Gary Lucas to come in, I was thinking, 'What are we doing?' Lucas had made only five or six warmup tosses and here we're asking him to get the biggest out in Angels history.

"Boone was there on the mound with me. Lachemann said, 'It's not my decision. Gene says to take him out.' Witt gave the ball to Lachemann and then looked at me and said, 'Just get the last out.'"

Mauch had his reasons for bringing in Lucas. "It wasn't so much to get a lefty-against-lefty advantage," he said. "Lucas had struck out Gedman both times he faced him, once during the regular season and once in the fourth game of the playoffs."

But with his first pitch, Lucas threw a split-finger change-up that slipped from his hand and struck Gedman on the forearm, putting the tying run on base.

"I've never faulted Gene for going with Lucas," Boone said. "Witt was pitching great except against Gedman, who was crushing the ball. Gedman was the only one in their lineup who was eating us up.

"It was a tough managerial decision for Mauch, but knowing him, I'm sure he considered all the variables of the situation and figured Lucas had the better chance in that spot.

"When Gary hit Gedman, that really hurt. He was a good control pitcher. I don't think he had hit a batter in three years."

Now, with Henderson coming to the plate, it was time for another decision by Mauch. He told Lachemann to lift Lucas and wave Moore in from the bullpen.

"When they called in Donnie Moore," recalled DeCinces, "I was thinking, 'Oh, my gosh, what now?' Donnie had taken a cortisone shot the night before, and it takes about 48 hours to get over the discomfort from the injection. It weakens you out. He had been bothered by a chronic bad shoulder all year, but much to his credit he never refused the ball."

"Moore," added Boone, "was a journeyman pitcher until he learned the split-finger fastball. Then he became a dominant closer. That year he struggled with a bad back. We used the split-finger a lot, but a good split-finger is made by quick arm action."

Moore went to work on Henderson. If the cortisone was affecting his arm action, he would be the last man to admit it.

His first pitch was low for ball one. He threw a fastball past Henderson for a strike. He threw another strike that Henderson swung at and missed. Then he fired a fastball low, for a ball.

With the count 2-and-2, Henderson fouled Moore's next two pitches. The first one he barely tapped foul down the third-base line; the second he fouled straight back.

One more strike and the Angels would have their pennant.

Figuring Henderson had the fastball timed, Boone called for a split-finger, a pitch that came into Henderson like a change-up.

"He pushed it," said Boone about Moore's pitch. "It was readable. If he had thrown it hard like hundreds of others he had thrown, we would've won the thing right there."

Instead Henderson slammed the ball over the wall in left center for a home run, scoring Gedman and giving Boston a 6–5 lead.

Boone admitted, "Gene was mad at me for my pitch selection, but I didn't want to come back with another fastball." Moore's fatal pitch, according to Boone, "had batting practice speed, was down and over the plate."

"It was a forkball," said Henderson. "When I hit it, I knew it was gone. That's when my emotions took over." As Henderson leaped in the air before going into his home run trot, there was some question whether the Angels would be able to recover from what must have felt like a hard punch to the stomach.

They did—momentarily.

In the bottom of the ninth, Boone led off with a single against reliever Bob Stanley. Then pinch-runner Ruppert Jones was sacrificed to second by Pettis. Joe Sambito replaced Stanley on the mound for the Red Sox, and Rob Wilfong followed with a line single to right, scoring Jones and tying the game at 7–7.

McNamara made another pitching change, summoning Steve Crawford from the bullpen. A big right-hander, Crawford threw in the low 90s. Besides his fastball, he employed a slider and a good forkball.

Schofield now singled to right, moving Wilfong to third and setting up an intentional pass to Downing. The bases were jammed, there was only one out, and again the pennant was waiting to be grasped by the Angels.

DeCinces was the next batter. He had been a strong run-producer for the Angels during the season. All he needed to score the winning run was a sacrifice fly.

"I remember Gene and Reggie Jackson telling me on the bench, 'You can do it. Just nice and easy. Hit the fly ball,'" said

"He pushed it . . . it was readable," said Angels catcher Bob Boone
(left) of Donnie Moore's split-finger pitch to Dave Henderson. *(Jeff
Carlick)*

DeCinces. He hit Crawford's first pitch, and to his dismay the
ball was a high, harmless fly, caught by Dwight Evans in shallow right field, preventing Wilfong from scoring.

"That at-bat remains a vivid memory with me," said
DeCinces. "It comes back to me so many times. I think of all
the runs that I drove in that year, and I couldn't get that one
home.

"I was trying to be a little too fine. I should've been more
aggressive. I should've been swinging for a hit so that I'd drive
the ball. He threw me a fastball out over the plate, but I didn't
get the meat of the bat on the ball.

"All during my career I was confident on certain pitches
that I could hit a sacrifice fly, but this time it didn't work out.
And, besides that, I hit the ball to the wrong guy—Dwight
Evans, who had a great arm."

Crawford needed another out, and he got it when Grich hit
a soft liner back to him to end the inning.

The game remained tied until the top of the 11th inning
when the Red Sox pushed over a run against Moore, who hit

Baylor with a pitch, yielded a single to Evans, a bunt single to Gedman, and a sacrifice fly to Henderson that fashioned Boston's final 7–6 triumph.

The Angels went down in order in the bottom of the inning. They had come as close to winning a pennant as they would that season. They were routed in the two remaining playoff games in Boston, 10–4, and 8–1.

It was game five, though, that stuck with many of the Angels long after the series had ended.

"It was a disappointment, but it wasn't a death knell," said Mauch. "We still had two games to play and only had to win one."

"That ninth-inning comeback by the Red Sox didn't beat us," he said. "What beat us was that we couldn't score a run in the bottom of the ninth with the bases loaded and only one out."

"I don't think Donnie Moore ever got over losing that fifth game," DeCinces said. "Some people say it could have led to his suicide. The next year his whole personality changed."

"It's not true that Moore committed suicide because of that fifth game," countered Boone. "That wasn't the reason. He had a lot of personal problems."

There was no question that Moore was a troubled man. On July 18, 1989, he shot and seriously wounded his wife, then killed himself with the last bullet in his gun.

Boone said he did not dwell on the pitch that Henderson hit for a home run. "Those things never bothered me," he said. "As a catcher, I never spent two seconds thinking, 'Aw, damn, I should've called another pitch.' What I'm thinking is, 'All right, let's get the next guy.'

"When I left the clubhouse, I was over it. It was a tough loss though. I can't deny that."

After the playoff series ended in Boston, Grich announced his retirement. "That was my last game in a baseball uniform," he said. "I hate to go out this way. It's a bitter ending."

Mauch kept the clubhouse door closed for 35 minutes after the seventh game. When he did open it, he said to reporters, "No use discussing a game like that. When you get beat that badly [8–1], there's nothing to talk about.

"Eight months of hard work, and this is how it ends."

"I knew it was gone,"
Henderson said of his
home run in game five.
(Mike Valeri)

Don Sutton was among the players who expressed regret
that Mauch had once again been deprived of a pennant.

"Gene did a heckuva job," he said. "He put the nine best
people on the field every chance he got."

During the winter the pitch he had thrown to Henderson
weighed heavily on Moore, whose sense of failure was com-
pounded the next season when fans at Anaheim Stadium booed
him every time they saw him walk out to the bullpen.

It was the same sort of delayed disrespect Red Sox fans
showered on Bill Buckner a year after he had made a critical
error in the 1986 World Series against the Mets.

Some things never change in baseball.

Losers are seldom favored with cheers.

Boston Red Sox vs. California Angels
at Anaheim Stadium, October 12, 1986

Boston Red Sox	AB	R	H	RBI	California Angels	AB	R	H	RBI
Wade Boggs, 3b	5	0	1	0	Rick Burleson, 2b	2	0	0	0
Marty Barrett, 2b	5	0	0	0	Rob Wilfong, ph/2b (b)	3	0	2	2
Bill Buckner, 1b	4	0	1	0	Dick Schofield, ss	5	0	1	0
Dave Stapleton, pr/1b (e)	1	1	1	0	Brian Downing, lf	3	0	0	1
Jim Rice, lf	5	1	1	0	Doug DeCinces, 3b	5	1	2	0
Don Baylor, dh	4	2	1	2	Bobby Grich, 1b	5	1	1	2
Dwight Evans, rf	5	0	1	0	Reggie Jackson, dh	5	0	1	0
Rich Gedman, c	4	2	4	2	George Hendrick, rf	3	0	1	0
Tony Armas, cf	2	0	0	0	Devon White, pr/rf (a)	2	1	1	0
Dave Henderson, cf	2	1	1	3	Bob Boone, c	3	1	3	1
Spike Owen, ss	2	0	0	0	Ruppert Jones, pr (f)	0	1	0	0
Mike Greenwell, ph (c)	1	0	1	0	Jerry Narron, c	0	0	0	0
Ed Romero, pr/ss (d)	2	0	0	0	Gary Pettis, cf	3	1	1	0
Total	**42**	**7**	**12**	**7**		**39**	**6**	**13**	**6**

(a) Pinch-ran for Hendrick in the seventh inning; (b) Doubled for Burleson in the seventh inning; (c) Singled for Owen in the eighth inning; (d) Pinch-ran for Greenwell in the eighth inning; (e) Pinch-ran for Buckner in the ninth inning; (f) Pinch-ran for Boone in the ninth inning.

Boston	0	2	0	0	0	0	0	0	4	0	1 — 7
California	0	0	1	0	0	2	2	0	1	0	0 — 6

Boston Red Sox	IP	H	R	ER	SO	BB
Bruce Hurst	6.0	7	3	3	4	1
Bob Stanley	2.1	4	3	3	1	2
Joe Sambito	0.0+	1	0	0	0	0
Steve Crawford (W)	1.2	1	0	0	1	2
Calvin Schiraldi (Save)	1.0	0	0	0	2	0

California Angels	IP	H	R	ER	SO	BB
Mike Witt	8.2	8	4	4	5	0
Gary Lucas	0.0+	0	1	1	0	0
Donnie Moore (L)	2.0	4	2	2	0	1
Chuck Finley	0.1	0	0	0	0	0

+ Pitched to one batter in the ninth.

DP—California 2. **LOB**—Boston 6, California 9. **2B**—DeCinces (2), Gedman, Wilfong. **HR**—Gedman, Boone, Grich, Baylor, Henderson. **CS**—Downing, White. **SH**—Burleson, Boone, Pettis. **SF**—Downing, Henderson. **Hit by pitch**—by Lucas (Gedman), by Moore (Baylor).
Umpires—Rocky Roe, Rich Garcia, Larry Barnett, Larry McCoy, Terry Cooney, Nick Bremigan.
Time—3:54. **Attendance**—64,223.

1986

Astros Fall to the Mets
in a 16-Inning Marathon

"There has never been a game I wanted so bad."
—Bob Knepper

Former Astros catcher Alan Ashby wasted little time getting to the core of the subject: Houston's 16-inning loss to the New York Mets in game six of the 1986 National League Championship Series.

"I think that last game revolved around one pitch, the pitch to Lenny Dykstra in the ninth inning," he said.

Ashby was behind the plate when Astros starter Bob Knepper delivered the pitch to Dykstra, who was leading off the inning as a pinch-hitter, with the Mets trailing 3–0 before a crowd of 45,718 fans at the Astrodome.

The Astros were down three games to two in the series. If they lost again, their season would be over with merely a West Division title to show for their efforts. If they won, they would enter game seven with a great chance to capture the club's first-ever pennant—because Mike Scott was scheduled to be their starting pitcher. Scott had already mastered the Mets twice in the playoffs, 1–0 on five hits in game one, and 3–1 on three hits in game four. He had struck out 14 batters and issued only one walk in the opener. All eight of the hits he gave up in the two games were singles. The Mets did not care to face Scott and his almost-unhittable split-finger fastball one more time if there was a final, seventh game.

Knepper had been working brilliantly, shutting down the Mets with an assortment of off-speed pitches, breaking balls, and precise control. He had given up only two, up-the-middle hits to shortstop Rafael Santana and second baseman Tim Teufel.

Now he had one ball and two strikes on Dykstra, a tough-as-nails competitor who was appropriately nicknamed "Nails."

Knepper's next pitch was a slider that came in a little high. Dykstra hit it to right center field where the ball outdistanced speedy Billy Hatcher and bounced away for a triple.

"I thought that ball would be caught," recalled Ashby.

Astros manager Hal Lanier said, "I'm not sure Hatcher picked up on the ball. Dykstra wasn't known for the long ball, and we didn't play him deep."

Dykstra's triple signaled the beginning of a Mets comeback that led to the longest and perhaps most exciting league championship game ever played.

Lanier was rounding out his first year as manager of the Astros, who got off to a fast start in the West Division race, winning 14 of their first 20 games through the end of April.

On May 2, Knepper scored his fifth straight victory without a loss. Through the season, along with rookie Jim Deshaies, he formed an effective left-handed complement to Houston's two top right-handed starters, Scott and Nolan Ryan. Scott finished at 18–10; Knepper at 17–12; Ryan, 12–8; and Deshaies, 12–5. The bullpen included closer Dave Smith, who set a club record with 33 saves. Rookie setup man Charlie Kerfeld won 11 games, lost only two, and saved seven. Aurelio Lopez was signed as a free agent in June and collected seven saves.

Before the season began, Houston was regarded only as a long-shot contender in the West Division, where the Dodgers and Reds were expected to lead the way. Although the Astros could not be considered a big power team, they were resilient and stubborn, especially when they were trailing late in a game. They scored 39 come-from-behind wins in 1986 and posted 24 victories in their final at-bat.

"On offense we were an opportunistic ball club," said Ashby. "We took advantage of breaks. We were well disciplined, played small ball, and relied on our pitching and defense."

Lanier had developed his managing style over a five-year period in the minors with the St. Louis Cardinals organization, and then as a member of Whitey Herzog's coaching staff with the Cardinals from 1981 through 1985. In spring training he let his players know in no uncertain terms that fundamental mistakes by fielders, hitters, and pitchers would not be tolerated. "I'm sure they got tired of hearing it," he said, "but that's the only way I know to play this game. If you continue to make mistakes, you won't be a winning club."

He also pushed for more team speed. Under his run-and-gun style of play, the Astros increased their stolen base total in 1986 to 163, compared to 96 thefts the preceding year. Second baseman Bill Doran almost doubled his 1985 output, stealing 42 bases. Billy Hatcher swiped 38, and Kevin Bass, 22.

First baseman Glenn Davis provided the team with a much-needed boost in power, hitting 31 homers and driving in 101 runs. Four times he hit a home run to win a game in the Astros' final at-bat. Next in line in offensive production was Bass with 20 homers, 79 RBI, and a .311 batting average.

Although the Astros were not noted for the long ball, one aspect to their lineup caused recurring problems for opposing pitchers: three of their regulars—Bass, Doran, and Ashby—were switch-hitters. Doran was especially effective at bat, collecting 152 hits and 81 walks for an on-base percentage of .378.

Besides Ashby, Davis, and Doran, the lineup most frequently used by Lanier included Bass in right field, Billy Hatcher in center, Jose Cruz in left, Dickie Thon or Craig Reynolds at short, and Phil Garner or Denny Walling at third.

From July 18 through July 24 the Astros put together a seven-game winning streak and took command of their division race. But outside the state of Texas they did not seem to gain much attention or, for that matter, respect. One writer described them as "the Rodney Dangerfields of baseball." Some hardened observers waited for them to stumble.

In early August, however, Tony Gwynn of the Padres acknowledged their pennant potential. "They don't have many household names," he said, "but they can play. Doran is a great leadoff man. They've got contact hitters after that, and power

Mike Scott, the Astros'
pitching ace. Did he scuff
the ball? *(Mitchell Layton)*

in the middle of their lineup in Davis and Bass." Gwynn also
expressed high regard for Mike Scott. "He's the nastiest pitcher
in the league," said the Padres' batting leader. "He just wore
me out."

Scott mixed a cut fastball with his split-finger pitch, which
usually darted down and in on right-handed batters and was
extremely tough to hit. He was so dominating in his first two
starts in the playoffs that Mets accused him of scuffing the ball,
perhaps with a hidden piece of sandpaper, causing the ball to
drop sharply.

In game one, however, the league's senior umpire, Doug Harvey, who was working behind the plate, came to Scott's defense.
"I've checked him 65 times this year," Harvey said, "and in my
heart all I know is the man is clean. Are the Mets trying to get
into his mind? They say they have 17 baseballs he scuffed. I'd
say 100 percent of them had been in play and hit the back-
stop, and then were picked up by the batboy."

When Scott stymied the Mets in game four, plate umpire Dutch Rennert said he spotted no scuffed balls, but the Mets persisted in their claim that the Astros' starter was cheating.

Scott, as might be expected, ignored the accusations. As long as the umpires never found evidence that he had defaced the ball, he figured it was to his advantage to keep the batters guessing whether he was doing something illegal.

In September the Astros had come on strong to wrap up the division title, winning 18 and losing nine games that month. Scott's 2–0 no-hitter against the San Francisco Giants at the Astrodome on September 25 clinched first place.

"I really didn't think I'd get the no-hitter until there were two outs in the ninth," Scott recalled. "When Will Clark tapped out to first base for the final out, that's a scene, a thrill that will stay with me forever. The crowd just went wild, and I can't describe the feeling I had when my teammates swarmed around me, and we had clinched the division.

"I remember calling home after the game, and when I talked to my little daughter, Kimmy, she said, 'Daddy, I didn't know you could jump that high.'"

From September 23 until the end of the season on October 5, the Astros won ten of their final 12 games, six of them by shutouts, so Lanier was comforted by the fact his pitching staff was peaking at the right time and would be ready for the showdown with the Mets in the League Championship Series.

The Mets, managed by Davey Johnson since 1984, finished their season with the best record in the majors: 108 wins against 54 losses. Their 21-1/2 game lead over the second-place Phillies at the end was exceeded by only one other team since 1900. The 1902 Pirates finished 27-1/2 games ahead of the runner-up Brooklyn Dodgers.

Several pre-season moves helped the Mets. In November 1985 general manager Frank Cashen obtained left-handed starter Bob Ojeda in a trade with the Red Sox. Ojeda responded by leading the Mets staff with an 18–5 record and a 2.57 earned run average, lowest among the club's starters.

In spring training, Johnson argued for the retention of veteran Ray Knight at third base and won his case. Knight, 33, rewarded his manager's faith in him by hitting .298, a mark 80 points higher than his 1985 average. He also drove in 76 runs and played 132 games at third.

The other smart decision made by Johnson before the season started was to give the full-time center-field job to 23-year-old Lenny Dykstra, replacing Mookie Wilson who was coming off two shoulder operations and had been sidelined by an eye injury in spring training.

Dykstra, like Knight, responded to the confidence Johnson showed in him by hitting .295, scoring 77 runs, and stealing 31 bases. He and second baseman Wally Backman were the "table setters" for the Mets' offense. Dykstra generally led off, with Backman hitting behind him when Backman was not being platooned at second base with Tim Teufel.

Other aggressive batters in the Mets' lineup were catcher Gary Carter, who hit 24 homers and drove in 105 runs; first baseman Keith Hernandez with a .310 batting average and 83 RBI; and right fielder Darryl Strawberry with 27 home runs and 83 RBI. The only weak spot in the batting order was shortstop Rafael Santana, who hit a feeble .218 but had improved his fielding over the previous season.

By the end of July, when the Mets had built a 15-1/2 game first-place lead in the East Division, Johnson was also platooning Mookie Wilson and rookie Kevin Mitchell in left field. The pair finished with a combined 21 homers and 88 RBI.

When the final numbers were added, the Mets led all National League teams in runs scored with 783 and in batting average at .263. Perhaps their most important statistics, however, belonged to the pitching staff which posted the league's lowest earned run average, 3.11. In addition to Ojeda, the Mets had five other pitchers who recorded wins in double figures: Dwight Gooden, 17–6; Sid Fernandez, 16–6; Ron Darling, 15–7; Roger McDowell, 14–9; and Rick Aguilera, 10–7. McDowell joined Jesse Orosco to give the Mets a righty-lefty bullpen combination that accounted for 43 saves.

Before the regular season began, Davey Johnson set a high standard for his team. "We don't just want to win," he said. "We want to dominate."

The Mets accommodated him and never faltered from start to finish. They went 13–3 in April, 18–9 in May, 19–9 in June,

16–11 in July, 21–11 in August, and 16–11 in September. They never had a losing streak of more than four games, and won nine of their last ten regular-season contests, including five straight in October. If they were headed for an astonishing conclusion to their long climb, they had the talent to get the job done.

But strange turns of fate can destroy dreams when it comes to playoff time. The Mets would need every bit of their talent plus a little luck and a controversial umpiring call to beat the Astros.

In the opening game of the playoffs, Scott had the Mets swinging futilely at his split-finger fastball. He struck out Gary Carter and Keith Hernandez three times each, Ray Knight and Dwight Gooden, his opposing pitcher, twice. After Darryl Strawberry fanned to lead off the top of the second inning, he returned to the Mets bench shaking his head. "The guy's unhittable," he said of Scott who, ironically, had pitched for the Mets for two full seasons and parts of two others before being traded to Houston for outfielder Danny Heep in December 1982.

And there was one other touch of irony to the Scott-versus-Mets story. The Astros right-hander was a mediocre pitcher until 1985 when he began using the split-finger, a pitch he learned from Roger Craig, who was one of the original 1962 Mets.

Many fans in the crowd of 44,131 at the Astrodome loudly booed Gary Carter when the Mets catcher, after swinging and missing a Scott pitch, asked plate umpire Doug Harvey to check the ball. "Scott threw me a fastball that seemed to vanish," said Carter. "I couldn't believe my eyes, and I made a mistake in asking Harvey to examine the ball."

Harvey took the ball out of Alan Ashby's mitt, rolled it around in his hands, let Carter take a quick look at it, and then threw it back to Scott. The umpire found no scuff marks on the ball. When Carter missed strike three, the crowd let out a roar of pleasure.

The Astros scored the only run of the game in the second inning when Glenn Davis homered over the center-field wall. Scott protected the 1–0 lead the rest of the way.

After the opener, Davey Johnson simplified the end result. "Mike Scott pitched a great game," he said. "Dwight pitched a good game."

The next night, again at the Astrodome, the Mets drove Nolan Ryan from the mound in the fifth inning and went on to win 5–1 behind Bob Ojeda, who scattered ten hits and pitched the distance.

Ryan was 39, but he still threw a 95-mile-an-hour fastball. In the fifth inning he unleashed a purpose pitch that whizzed past Lenny Dykstra's head after Dykstra had pulled a long foul down the right-field line. The scrappy center fielder answered Ryan's "message" and promptly singled as part of the Mets' three-run outburst that put the visitors ahead 5–0.

"I think it kind of woke us up," Dykstra said of Ryan's attempt to intimidate him. "I know it woke me up."

With the series even, the two teams traveled to New York for game three at Shea Stadium on Saturday afternoon, October 11.

The Astros held a 5–4 lead in the bottom of the ninth when Dykstra hit a two-run homer off reliever Dave Smith to win the game 6–5. His drive carried over the right-field wall into the Mets' bullpen.

On Sunday night the Mets again had to face Scott, who was pitching this time on three days' rest. Although not as overpowering as he had been in game one, Scott was still masterful, and with the help of home runs by Ashby and Thon, he walked away with a 3–1 decision over the Mets' Fernandez.

Rain hit New York on Monday, so game five was postponed until Tuesday afternoon, October 14, when Ryan and Gooden were matched against each other.

Ryan worked nine innings, yielding only two hits and one run while striking out 12 Mets. Gooden lasted ten innings and gave up nine hits but also was charged with only one run. The outcome was decided by relievers. Jesse Orosco became the winner and Charlie Kerfeld the loser when Carter drove in the deciding run in the 12th inning on a single up the middle to make the final score 2–1. The Mets were one victory away from going to the World Series.

The game might have turned out differently if not for a bad

call by first-base umpire Fred Brocklander in the second inning. With one out and Astro runners on first and third, Brocklander called Craig Reynolds out at first to complete a double play. Television replays clearly showed that Reynolds had beaten Santana's relay throw to Hernandez. Had Brocklander ruled correctly, the Astros would have led 1–0, and after they scored another run in the fifth inning, the way Ryan was pitching the game might never have gone into extra innings.

Years later Phil Garner recalled the play. "That blown call cost us a run," he agreed, "and you don't know what else, but those things happen in baseball. An umpire's job can be difficult. I've umpired in Little League games and often asked myself, 'Why did I make that call?'"

Now the drama between two star-laden casts moved back to the Astrodome, where great theater would be offered in game six on Wednesday, October 15. The pitching matchup featured left-handers Knepper and Ojeda. The umpire behind the plate was Brocklander, whose judgment once more would be open to criticism, this time on his ball-and-strike calls.

The Astros quickly jumped on Ojeda, taking a 3–0 lead in the bottom of the first inning. Doran led off with a single but was forced at second by Hatcher on a play that went from Hernandez to Santana. Hatcher scored on a double by Garner to left center, and Garner scored on a single by Davis through the middle. Ojeda then walked Bass on four pitches, and Cruz followed with a single over first base, driving in Davis.

With the score 3–0 and only one out, the Astros had a chance to break the game open. Bass was on third when Ashby missed his pitch on a suicide squeeze. Bass was hung up between third and home and thrown out in a rundown, Carter to Knight. Ashby lined out to short to end the inning.

"I was a little edgy," Ojeda admitted later, talking about his first-inning performance, "but it wasn't that I was out there with nothing. They got a couple of grounders and a broken bat. I wasn't shell-shocked."

Ojeda might not have lost his composure, but the Mets batters were growing uneasy. Knepper retired the first seven hitters to face him before giving up a single and a walk in the

Phil Garner thought an umpire's call in game five might have hurt the Astros' chances of winning. *(Ed Mailliard)*

third inning. Then he set down the next 14 batters before yielding a one-out single to Teufel in the eighth inning.

Still leading 3–0 at the top of the ninth, the Astros were three outs away from pushing the series to a seventh game when Knepper suddenly lost his touch.

Dykstra led off with a triple and scored when Mookie Wilson hit a soft liner over Doran's head at second. "That ball Wilson hit glanced off my glove," Doran said. "It proved again that baseball is a game of inches."

Wilson moved up a base after Mitchell grounded out to third. Hernandez then battled Knepper and on a 2-and-1 pitch slammed the ball to deep center field for a double, scoring Wilson and slicing the Met's deficit to 3–2.

That was all for Knepper, and Lanier called for Dave Smith from the bullpen. Smith walked Carter and Strawberry, both on full counts, to load the bases.

Bob Knepper lost his
touch in the ninth inning.
(George Gojkovich)

With the tying run on third and the game on the line, Smith
wanted desperately to keep the next batter, Ray Knight, from
hitting a long ball that would bring in Hernandez from third.
On a 1-and-2 pitch to Knight, Brocklander called Smith's fastball near the corner of the plate a ball. Ashby protested the call
by slapping his knee in disgust. Smith thought he had struck
out Knight.

"You gear yourself to pitch to certain umpires," Smith said
after the game. "They have zones, but this guy [Brocklander]
doesn't have a zone. It floats. Two pitches before, I threw one
four inches farther out and it's a strike, although it could have
been a ball. Then I bring it in four inches, and it's a ball. An
umpire has to be consistent. If he's not, it screws the pitchers
up and it screws the hitters up. I needed to make a perfect
pitch, which I thought I did. I didn't get it, and it hurt."

With a 2-and-2 count, Knight drove Smith's next pitch to a
deep right field, a sacrifice fly that brought Hernandez home
with the run that tied the game at 3–3.

The score remained that way until the 14th inning. Smith

had pitched in relief through the tenth inning when he was spelled by Larry Andersen, who worked the 11th, 12th, and 13th. Rick Aguilera had succeeded Ojeda on the mound for the Mets in the sixth inning and was followed by Roger McDowell, who worked from the ninth to the 13th inning. In the 14th inning each team was playing behind its fourth relief pitcher, Aurelio Lopez for the Astros and Jesse Orosco for the Mets.

The Mets scored in the top half of the inning on a single by Carter, a walk to Strawberry, and a single by Backman to surge ahead 4–3. In the bottom half of the 14th, with one out, Hatcher delivered a stirring, game-tying home run off Orosco.

"Doran was batting ahead of me, and if he got on I was going to bunt him over," Hatcher recalled. "But Billy struck out, and Hal Lanier told me to go for it. I went up to the plate looking for a fastball. I felt comfortable hitting against left-handers, and Orosco threw a lot of fastballs.

"The count was 2-and-0 when Carter put down the fastball sign. I hit the ball like a rocket down the left-field line. It had home-run distance but it went foul. The count went to 3-and-2, and I got another fastball. I hit it and was hoping this time it would stay fair. It did. It barely hit the net on the fair side of the left-field foul pole."

The noise in the Astrodome was ear-splitting after Hatcher's home run tied the ballgame. The score remained 4–4 until the final act of the drama played out in the 16th inning.

Astros reliever Aurelio Lopez was 38, had pitched many years in the Mexican League, and was nicknamed "Señor Smoke" when he wore a Tigers uniform from 1979 to 1985 before joining the Astros. His "smoke" was not as challenging as it once had been, but his repertoire also included an effective screwball.

Lopez got into trouble right away in the top of the 16th inning. Strawberry led off by hitting a fly to short center that fell in front of Hatcher for a double. A single to right by Knight scored Strawberry with the go-ahead run. Knight advanced to second on the throw home.

Lanier then brought in left-hander Jeff Calhoun, who had been sparsely used during the regular season. Calhoun made a wild pitch, allowing Knight to move to third. The Astros lefty

Billy Hatcher's dramatic
home run tied the game
in the 14th inning.
(Mitchell Layton)

then walked Backman and threw another wild pitch that per-
mitted Knight to score, putting the Mets in front 6–4. A single
by Dykstra sent Backman home. It was 7–4 by the time Calhoun got the third out.

It seemed as though the Astros were finished, but they were
not about to go quietly. In their half of the 16th inning they
scored two runs on a walk to Davey Lopes and singles by Doran,
Hatcher, and Davis. After forcing Hatcher, Denny Walling was
on second with the tying run and Davis on first with the winning run when Kevin Bass struck out against Orosco to end
the game.

Gary Carter recalled the pitch selection against Bass. "Nothing but sliders," the Mets catcher said. "Orosco's fastball was
dragging, and we had to live or die by the slider.

"The slider was darting toward Bass. We ran the count to
3-and-2. Orosco threw one more slider, a pretty good one, sink-

ing down and in—probably ball four, but Bass chased it, swinging at air. Strike three! We were going to the World Series."

Orosco threw his glove in the air. Bass threw his bat to the ground. The Mets had won 7–6 and would head back to New York to play the Boston Red Sox in the World Series.

The Astros were going home.

In their clubhouse after the game, players expressed their regrets. "There has never been a game I wanted so bad," said Knepper. "Normally, when I get charged up, I try to hold it in and not be too emotional. But today I let it go. I wanted Mike Scott to have another chance because the Mets would really have been hurting. I wanted to have the best game of my career in the most important game of my career. It's going to be a long winter."

Bass talked about his final strikeout. "I swung out of control," he said. "I was looking for a mistake and he [Orosco] didn't make one. He made a good pitch. It was a battle. He won and I lost.

"I'm very teed off. It couldn't have been a better situation. I felt great up there. I had the vision of getting a hit. I was gearing up for just one fastball, but I never saw one. I saw nothing but breaking balls. He beat me."

Hatcher was spent. He wanted to be alone, far from the media mob surrounding him. "You get high, then you get down," he sighed. "It starts taking its toll.

"I was dragging. My whole body was hurting. Right now I'm just dead. I don't know how long it will take to recover. I'm exhausted. Mental, physical, any way you want to call it. I feel like going in a room by myself, shut the door, drink two or three beers, and pass out."

Although the Astros lost, Scott was named the Most Valuable Player of the National League Championship Series. He had mixed feelings about the honor. "It's kind of bittersweet," he said. "I guess I'll enjoy the award more in a couple of years or a couple of months. It's hard to celebrate right now."

"Little things went wrong out there," Ashby said, summing up the game. "There was a lot of scratching going on out there. We just came up one scratch short."

The Astros catcher was asked about his missed bunt attempt

in the first inning, forcing Bass into a rundown. "I batted right through a fastball and missed it," Ashby said. "It was a good call. We were trying to score runs. We could have scored another if I had put it down."

The Astros' somber comments capped one of baseball's most nerve-racking post-season conflicts. Years later, some of the players were asked for their remembrances of that series with the Mets.

"It was heartbreaking," said Dickie Thon, "but we played well, so we didn't feel that bad. We didn't lose because of errors or bad pitching. The Mets had great pitching too. Still, it was devastating to lose. There was a lot of tension in that series."

Thon was 28 at the time of the playoffs. He was coming back from a severe head injury suffered in 1984 when he was struck by a pitch thrown by Mike Torrez of the Mets in the first week of the season. It fractured the orbital rim above his left eye and put him out of action for the rest of the season.

Regarded as one of the best young shortstops in the game at the time of his injury, Thon made a comeback in 1985 but still had to deal with occasional headaches and blurred vision. He was limited to 84 games that year; in 1986 he played in 104 games, splitting shortstop chores with Craig Reynolds.

The loss to the Mets in the playoffs resides in the recesses of Thon's memory bank. "It still hurts when I think about it," he said, "because it kept me from playing in a World Series. That was the biggest disappointment of my career.

"I know after the last game that Jose Cruz was upset too, because he figured at his age [39] it was his last chance to get into a World Series. That's how it turned out for him. He retired after the '88 season."

"I was down," Cruz said. "Everybody was down. I was almost at the end of my career, and that was the last chance I had to go to a World Series.

"The Mets, they had better luck. We had good pitching. We had a better team. After the last game, I went to my home in Houston—I still live there—and tried to forget."

When he was interviewed in 2000, Cruz was serving as a coach for the Astros and spoke fondly of his son, Jose Jr., who was developing his potential as a young outfielder with the Toronto Blue Jays.

"My goal as a player," said Cruz, "was to get in a World Series. That was my dream. I hope my son can play in a World Series some day."

Bill Doran had been appointed to the coaching staff of the Cincinnati Reds when he was interviewed in 2000.

"What I remember most about that last game," he said, "is the great pitching performance by Knepper, and Hatcher's home run in the 14th inning that tied the game."

Doran gave credit to the Mets. "They were a competitive group," he said. "They never quit.

"After the game, our clubhouse was pretty quiet. Everybody was drained. I don't know if we were better than the Mets. We had a good club, a great year, but we came up short."

Phil Garner was completing his first year as manager of the Detroit Tigers when he resurrected a few thoughts about the 16-inning marathon in the Astrodome.

"A special memory I have of that game," he said, "is the way Knepper pitched. We both came with the team in '81, and when I was in the infield I was always telling him not to nit-pick too much with his pitches, and that he didn't pitch inside enough. In that game against the Mets, he used both sides of the plate beautifully and was challenging the hitters. He pitched the game of his life, but unfortunately they tied it up in the ninth.

"The other memory I have is when Hatcher hit that home run in the 14th inning. I had been taken out of the game in the eighth inning when Walling pinch-hit for me, and I was in the dugout. Walling stayed in to play third in my place. The Astros dugout had a low roof, and when Hatcher hit the home run I did a body flip over the top of the dugout. That's how emotionally charged a game it was.

"After the game there was nothing but dejection. I lived in Houston and drove home. I had been on such an emotional high, and now there was flat-out depression. I was out of gas, and for four or five days I felt lethargic, even to the point where I could hardly get out of bed. That's what a game like that can do to you."

Billy Hatcher recalled his role in two critical plays that resulted in runs for the Mets: the triple hit by Dykstra to start the ninth inning and the leadoff double by Strawberry in the 16th. "Knepper got ahead of Dykstra on the count, and I moved over toward left field a few steps," Hatcher said. "The ball was hit away from me, and I couldn't get it.

"On Strawberry I was playing a little deeper. I usually played shallow, and they had hit a couple of balls over my head. I got a little timid and moved back on Strawberry. Aurelio [Lopez] was getting tired, and I knew Strawberry was going for the home run. Aurelio threw him a screwball, and he hit it off the end of the bat. He popped up to short center. I busted my behind to get the ball but didn't make it.

"That was one of the best playoff games ever. It could have gone either way. In fact, the whole series could have gone either way."

Alan Ashby, who broadcast Houston Astro games in 2000, caught three no-hitters during his 17-year major league career, including those pitched by Ken Forsch in 1979, Nolan Ryan in 1981, and Mike Scott in the 1986 division clincher.

"That last game against the Mets occasionally comes back to me," he said, "but it's not a recurring dream. All in all, they were the best team, but we had the best pitching. Scott and Ryan were like Koufax and Drysdale.

"In the ninth inning I thought Knepper was still throwing well. Sometimes a pitcher can have his best stuff and still get beat. The Mets were a tough team to hold down.

"We were stunned when it was over. The only thing you can do after a game like that is to put it out of your mind. I remember I sat in my chair for a long time in the clubhouse and tried to forget as best I could. I think the Mets carried a horseshoe in their back pocket that year."

New York Mets vs. Houston Astros
at Houston Astrodome, October 15, 1986

New York Mets	AB	R	H	RBI	Houston Astros	AB	R	H	RBI
Mookie Wilson, cf-lf	7	1	1	1	Bill Doran, 2b	7	1	2	0
Kevin Mitchell, lf	4	0	0	0	Billy Hatcher, cf	7	2	3	2
Kevin Elster, ss	3	0	0	0	Phil Garner, 3b	3	1	1	1
Keith Hernandez, 1b	7	1	1	1	Denny Walling, ph-3b (b)	4	0	0	0
Gary Carter, c	5	0	2	0	Glenn Davis, 1b	7	1	3	2
Darryl Strawberry, rf	5	2	1	0	Kevin Bass, rf	6	0	1	0
Ray Knight, 3b	6	1	1	2	Jose Cruz, lf	6	0	1	1
Tim Teufel, 2b	3	0	1	0	Alan Ashby, c	6	0	0	0
Wally Backman, ph-2b (c)	2	1	1	1	Dickie Thon, ss	3	0	0	0
Rafael Santana, ss	3	0	1	0	Craig Reynolds, ph-ss (f)	3	0	0	0
Danny Heep, ph (d)	1	0	0	0	Bob Knepper, p	2	0	0	0
Roger McDowell, p	1	0	0	0	Terry Puhl, ph (g)	1	0	0	0
Howard Johnson, ph	1	0	0	0	Jim Pankovits, ph (h)	1	0	0	0
Bob Ojeda, p	1	0	0	0	Davey Lopes, ph (i)	0	1	0	0
Lee Mazzilli, ph (a)	1	0	0	0					
Lenny Dykstra, ph-cf (e)	4	1	2	1					
Total	**54**	**7**	**11**	**6**		**56**	**6**	**11**	**6**

(a) Struck out for Ojeda in the sixth inning; (b) Grounded out to second for Garner in the eighth inning; (c) Walked intentionally for Teufel in the ninth inning; (d) Struck out for Santana in the ninth inning; (e) Tripled for Aguilera in the ninth inning; (f) Struck out for Thon in the 10th inning; (g) Grounded out to pitcher for Dave Smith in the 10th inning; (h) Grounded out to third for Larry Andersen in the 13th inning; (i) Walked for Jeff Calhoun in the 16th inning.

New York	0	0	0	0	0	0	0	0	3	0	0	0	0	1	0	3	—	7
Houston	3	0	0	0	0	0	0	0	0	0	0	0	0	1	0	2	—	6

New York Mets	IP	H	R	ER	SO	BB
Bob Ojeda	5.0	5	3	3	1	2
Rick Aguilera	3.0	1	0	0	1	0
Roger McDowell	5.0	1	0	0	2	0
Jesse Orosco (W)	3.0	4	3	3	5	1

Houston Astros	IP	H	R	ER	SO	BB
Bob Knepper	8.1	5	3	3	6	1
Dave Smith	1.2	0	0	0	2	3
Larry Andersen	3.0	0	0	0	1	1
Aurelio Lopez (L) +	2.0	5	3	3	2	2
Jeff Calhoun	1.0	1	1	1	0	1

+ Pitched to two batters in the 16th inning

E—Bass. **DP**—Houston 2. **LOB**—New York 9, Houston 5. **2B**—Garner, Davis, Hernandez, Strawberry. **3B**—Dykstra. **HR**—Hatcher. **SB**—Doran. **CS**—Bass (2). **SH**—Orosco. **SF**—Knight. **Wild pitch**—Calhoun 2.
Umpires—Fred Brocklander, Doug Harvey, Lee Weyer, Frank Pulli, Dutch Rennert, Joe West. **Time**—4:42. **Attendance**—45,718.

1986

Red Sox Denied a World Series Title Once More

"I can't remember the last time I missed a ball like that."—Bill Buckner

It was the third of three breathtaking post-season games involving separate sets of opponents in 1986 and, like the other two games, it was destined to gain legendary status. It was played between the Red Sox and the Mets at Shea Stadium on Saturday night, October 25.

For Boston it was an opportunity to win the club's first World Series championship since 1918, a year in which the fabled Babe Ruth had starred as a Red Sox pitcher.

Boston had won three of five games in the '86 Series so far. Now, holding a 5–3 lead in the bottom of the tenth inning of game six, they were within one out of grasping baseball's most coveted prize. In a surprising turn of events, they failed to complete their mission.

The two teams had survived serious challenges during the league playoff games and were elated to reach the World Series after prevailing in critical extra-inning games against the Angels and Astros. The Mets were so jubilant after beating Houston in 16 innings in game six of the National League playoffs that they caused $7,500 worth of damage to the interior of their chartered plane during an uninhibited celebration on the flight back to New York.

The Red Sox had narrowly escaped a season-ending defeat against the Angels in game five of the American League play-offs at Anaheim, an 11-inning heart-stopper. With few exceptions, the players were getting their first chance to play in a Fall Classic. Bill Buckner had played in a World Series with the Dodgers in 1974, and Dwight Evans with the Red Sox in 1975, a year in which teammate Jim Rice had missed the championship showdown with the Reds because of an injury. Veteran pitcher Tom Seaver had joined the club in a June trade with the White Sox but was disabled after suffering torn cartilage in his right knee in a game against Toronto in September. He would not play in the '86 World Series, though he would watch the games from the bench. Otherwise the Series would be a new experience for the rest of the Red Sox.

While expectations were high on both sides, many Boston fans, per custom, found it difficult to control pessimistic feelings that something dreadful, sooner or later, would unravel their Red Sox during the run for a world championship.

The Mets, on the other hand, approached the Series opener on October 18 with an attitude that, one way or another, they would win. "We weren't an arrogant or cocky ball club," said catcher Gary Carter. "We were just a confident ball club."

While the Mets' confidence was tested almost to the breaking point during the Series, their grittiness remained intact. They simply refused to surrender.

One of the reasons the Mets were favored to win the Fall Classic was their home-field advantage for games six and seven if the Series went that far. But the home-field advantage was nonexistent in games one and two at Shea Stadium, where the Red Sox won 1–0 behind the brilliant pitching of Bruce Hurst in the opener, then came right back the next night and pounded the Mets and Dwight Gooden 9–3 in the second game.

In the first game, Ron Darling pitched well for the Mets, allowing only three hits in seven innings and one unearned run. The Red Sox scored the game's lone run in the top of the seventh inning. After walking Jim Rice, Darling threw a wild pitch to Dwight Evans, with Rice advancing to second base as the ball bounced away from Gary Carter. The Mets' right-hander retired Evans and then faced Rich Gedman, who hit a lazy ground ball that skipped through Tim Teufel's legs at second base for an error, permitting Rice to race home.

"What happened," Teufel said afterward, "is every infielder's nightmare. No excuses. My job is to field that ball and I didn't field the thing, and it cost the game."

Darling declined to suggest or even hint that Teufel was to blame for the Mets' loss. "What beat us," he said, "was Hurst's pitching." His observation was on target: Hurst did baffle the Mets over eight innings with an assortment of curves, fastballs, and off-speed pitches, striking out eight batters, including Lenny Dykstra and Darryl Strawberry twice each. Calvin Schiraldi closed out the game for Hurst in the ninth inning, retiring the side without damage, allowing only one Met to reach base.

An interesting aspect of the game unfolded in the bottom of the eighth inning when Red Sox manager John McNamara sent in Dave Stapleton as a defensive replacement for a hobbling Bill Buckner at first base.

Buckner had injured his ankle in game seven of the playoffs against the Angels and was wearing high-top shoes for extra support, but he could barely run. With only a one-run lead, McNamara wanted a tighter defensive alignment in the infield.

McNamara failed to make a similar switch in game six of the Series, a failure that would become a source of severe criticism for the Red Sox manager.

Little drama was attached to the rout of the Mets in game two, as Boston pounded out 18 hits against Gooden and several relievers. Both starting pitchers failed to work beyond the fifth inning. Gooden was excused after five innings. Roger Clemens, his counterpart, was relieved after four and a third innings.

"We were worried," Carter admitted later, "not so much that we got beat by a lopsided score, but that they had a two-game lead."

After the game the Red Sox left for Boston, where talk of a sweep was gaining momentum. The Mets departed New York the next morning, and on the bus ride from Shea Stadium to La Guardia Field for their flight to Boston, manager Davey

Red Sox manager John McNamara decided not to send in a defensive replacement for Bill Buckner at first base in the tenth inning of game six. *(Mitchell Layton)*

Johnson decided to cancel the team's workout at Fenway Park later that day.

The players agreed they needed the rest more than a workout, but Johnson's decision was ravaged by some members of the press who considered it one more example of the Mets' overbearing arrogance.

Even though they had won 108 games in the regular season and had outlasted a stubborn Houston team in the National League Championship Series, the Mets did not deserve being labeled arrogant just because they skipped an afternoon batting practice. The charge against them seemed to be based either on a dislike of everything New York or on the partisan emotion of Boston fans.

The Mets were an extremely buoyant team, and they would prove it within a span of eight days.

They won game three on Tuesday night, October 21, at Fenway, 7–1, behind the five-hit pitching of Bob Ojeda and some strong hitting of their own against Oil Can Boyd. On Wednesday night they went to work on starter Al Nipper and reliever Steve Crawford, and came away with a 6–2 victory to even the Series. The winning pitcher was Ron Darling.

In game three the Mets wasted little time in displaying their comeback talent. In the first inning Dykstra, batting in the lead-off spot, stroked a one-and-one pitch from Boyd into the right-field seats for a home run. The blast evidently upset Boyd, who gave up singles to Wally Backman and Keith Hernandez, and then threw an 0-and-2 fastball down the pipe to Carter who slammed the pitch to deep center field for a double, scoring Backman and putting the Mets up 2–0.

One of the strangest plays of the Series followed, helping set up a quick 4–0 lead for New York. With Hernandez on third and Carter on second, Ray Knight bounced a squibbler down the third-base line. Wade Boggs fielded the ball as Hernandez broke for home. Boggs threw too quickly to catcher Rich Gedman in the attempted rundown play, enabling Hernandez to stop and lure Gedman into chasing him back to third.

As Gedman charged after Hernandez, he waited too long to throw to Boggs at third, and Hernandez was able to dive past Boggs and slide safely back to the bag.

Now Carter was trapped off second, and Boggs threw the ball to Spike Owen, the Red Sox shortstop. Owen took his eye off Carter momentarily to see whether Hernandez would try to dash for the plate—and it was just long enough to allow Carter to belly-flop back into second base safely.

The botched play prevented the Red Sox from keeping the game close as Danny Heep lined a single to center, scoring Hernandez and Carter. The four runs in the first were more than enough for Ojeda, who yielded his only run in the third inning on a walk and a pair of singles.

With the Series tied at two games apiece, the Red Sox recuperated in what would be their final appearance of the year at Fenway Park. They beat the Mets 4–2 in game five, once again behind the left-handed slants of Bruce Hurst, who went the distance while pitching shutout ball for the first seven innings. Gooden, who started for the Mets, lasted only into the fifth inning and was charged with all four of Boston's runs.

"The pressure was on," Mets catcher Gary Carter admitted. "We had to beat the Red Sox two games in a row." *(George Gojkovich)*

So it was on to New York for game six, which would be played at Shea Stadium on Saturday night, October 25, a date destined to serve as a reference point for one of the most unbelievable rallies in World Series history.

"The pressure was on," Carter admitted. "We had to beat the Red Sox two games in a row."

The Mets' catcher related how Lenny Dykstra loosened his teammates up as their plane was taxiing for its takeoff from Boston for the flight home after the fifth game. "It's over!" Dykstra proclaimed. "We're gonna win it. It's *over*, man. We're gonna go home and win two in a row! It's over!" Dykstra's bold prediction provoked laughter from his teammates, who nonetheless seemed to relax after hearing such reassurance.

A crowd of 55,078 fans jammed Shea Stadium for game six, with Clemens starting for the Red Sox and Ojeda for the Mets. Clemens felt refreshed after recovering from the flu. "I felt certain we would win that sixth game," he said. In only his third major league season, the 24-year-old right-hander was about to

be reminded that the only certainty about a forthcoming baseball game is its uncertainty.

Clemens, however, was given a quick 2–0 lead when the Red
Sox scored in each of the first two innings off Ojeda. The lead
could have been even bigger.

Wade Boggs started the first inning with a single off Ray
Knight's glove at third. With two out, Jim Rice walked. Then
Dwight Evans, on a 1-and-1 pitch, hammered the ball against
the wall in left center field for a double, scoring Boggs. If
Evans's drive had had a little more lift, it would have been a
homer, giving the Red Sox a 3–0 edge and a chance to blow
the game wide open before the Mets came to bat.

Instead the score remained 2–0 until the bottom of the fifth
inning when the Mets tied it as Clemens yielded his initial two
hits and runs after striking out six batters in the first four innings.

A powerhouse pitcher, Clemens was strong early in the game
but began to tail off by the fourth inning. The Mets were a
good fastball-hitting team, and they did not chase pitches that
ran up and out of the strike zone. In their first times up, batters such as Carter, Strawberry, and Santana extended Clemens
by fouling off numerous deliveries.

"I couldn't get the ball in on them the way I wanted to,"
said Clemens. "I didn't have the cross-seam fastball that runs
and usually gets my strikeouts."

Nonetheless the hard-throwing right-hander held the Mets
in check in the sixth inning, and the Red Sox moved in front
3–2 in the top of the seventh after Ojeda had been replaced by
reliever Roger McDowell.

Leadoff batter Marty Barrett walked, and Jim Rice reached
first after hitting a chopper toward third to Ray Knight, who
threw the ball too high to Keith Hernandez at first for an error.
Barrett eventually scored on an infield out. The Red Sox might
have scored another run when Rich Gedman lined a single to
left, but Rice was tagged out at home on a throw from Mookie
Wilson to Carter.

Clemens retired Knight, Wilson, and Kevin Elster in order
in the bottom of the seventh, but a tormenting twist of fate, so

feared by Red Sox fans, had already transpired before the inning ended.

In throwing a slider to Wilson, Clemens tore the fingernail off the middle finger of his pitching hand, and it started to bleed. The finger was also blistered. When he went to the Red Sox bench, pitching coach Bill Fischer was upset at seeing all the blood, but Clemens told John McNamara that he could go back out for the eighth inning.

"I can get you through the eighth, at least," Clemens said to his manager. "The only thing I can't do is throw a slider, but I can get another inning with my fastball, change of speed, and forkball."

It was not to be. McNamara sent in a pinch-hitter for Clemens in the top of the eighth, an inning in which the Red Sox filled the bases but were unable to score.

In the bottom of the eighth, the Mets tied the game at 3–3 against Calvin Schiraldi, who had come on in relief of Clemens. Schiraldi once belonged to the Mets, who had traded him to Boston after the 1985 season, so he had an added incentive to beat his former team in what could be the deciding game of the World Series.

Extra incentive or not, Schiraldi ran into immediate trouble in the eighth. Pinch-hitter Lee Mazzilli, batting for Jesse Orosco, singled to right. Dykstra then sacrificed Mazzilli to second, but both runners were safe when Schiraldi, on an attempted force play, bounced his throw to Spike Owen at second.

Wally Backman then sacrificed Mazzilli to third and Dykstra to second, forcing McNamara to order an intentional walk to Keith Hernandez to set up a possible inning-ending double play.

With Gary Carter at the plate, Schiraldi suddenly was unable to hit the strike zone. He threw three straight balls to Carter, the first two low, the last one wide. Davey Johnson passed the signal to let Carter swing away on the 3-and-0 count.

Schiraldi had to come in with a strike or force in the tying run, an almost no-win situation for a reliever.

Carter attacked Schiraldi's next pitch, slightly inside and a bit high, and slammed a line drive to deep left field where Rice caught the ball. Mazzilli scored after the catch to tie the game at 3–3. Strawberry flied out to end the inning.

Neither team could score in the ninth. The tenth inning produced a deliriously joyful finish for the Mets and an incredible setback for the Red Sox.

Rick Aguilera was on the mound for the Mets when Dave Henderson came to the plate to lead off the top of the tenth inning. Aguilera got ahead in the count 0-and-1, then delivered a fastball which Henderson drove into the left-field stands for a homer, giving Boston the lead again, 4–3.

Years later Henderson said he was surprised that Aguilera challenged him with a fastball, which came to the plate higher than Aguilera and Carter wanted it. "It was kind of weird," Henderson said, "because Mel Stottlemyre [Mets' pitching coach] was my coach when I was in Double-A ball, and he knew me like the back of his hand.

"No way should they have thrown me a fastball in that situation because I was hitting about .400 in the Series. Typically, you stay away from the guy who's swinging the hot bat."

After crushing the ball, Henderson bounded gleefully toward first on his trip around the bases. His Red Sox teammates were on their feet, cheering and waiting to give him a royal welcome when he reached the dugout.

Aguilera managed to regroup against the next two batters. He struck out Owen and Schiraldi, but then was touched for another run on a double to the wall in left center by Boggs and a single to right by Marty Barrett. When Aguilera finally closed out the inning, the Red Sox were on top 5–3 and only three outs away from becoming, at long last, world champions.

To start the bottom of the tenth inning, Schiraldi retired two tough left-handed batters in Backman and Hernandez. Backman hit an easy fly ball to Rice in left field. Hernandez drove the ball to center field where Henderson backpedaled and gloved it for the second out.

"After those two quick outs," Henderson recalled, "I figured this thing is over."

Carter was in the on-deck circle as Hernandez lost his battle to Schiraldi. "What I was seeing," Carter recalled, "was sort of like a dream every kid has—bottom of the ninth in the World Series, two outs, and your team needs a hit.

"When I went up to the plate, I kept saying to myself, 'I'm not going to make the last out, I'm not going to make the last out.' I almost felt a spiritual presence in me, calming me, giving me the confidence to succeed."

Schiraldi was so close to victory. The adrenaline was flowing through him. His eyes were big with excitement. Sweat shone on his face.

At that moment someone accidentally punched the wrong key, and the board at Shea Stadium lit up with the message: "Congratulations, Boston Red Sox, World Champions." It was quickly doused.

Schiraldi's first pitch to Carter was a good fastball which Carter fouled off. He then threw two balls, one high and one outside. With the count 2-and-1, Carter was sitting on another fastball, got it, and hit it off the end of his bat for a looping single to left field.

The burden to keep the Mets' hopes alive now passed to Kevin Mitchell, who pinch-hit for Aguilera. Mitchell looked bad on Schiraldi's first pitch, fouling the ball on a checked swing. Then Schiraldi threw a hanging slider that Mitchell lined to center for a single, moving Carter to second.

That brought Ray Knight to the plate. Schiraldi quickly threw two fastballs by him, both strikes. If Schiraldi could get one more strike, called or swinging, tens of thousands of fans in Boston and in other cities and towns in New England would have reason to go slightly mad.

With the count 0-and-2, Knight, using a short, quick swing, nudged an inside fastball from Schiraldi to center for a single, scoring Carter and moving Mitchell to third base with the tying run.

That was all for Schiraldi, and McNamara waved in Bob Stanley from the bullpen.

After making the second out in the inning, Keith Hernandez had retired in disgust to the Mets' clubhouse, where he popped open a beer and sat down in Davey Johnson's office to watch the finish of the game on television.

"I was very ticked," he admitted. "After seeing Gary and Kevin get their hits, I still wasn't sure about our coming back. But when Ray got the hit to score our first run of the inning, I grabbed my hat and glove. I was ready to go back to the dugout—but then I decided I'd go back to the chair in Davey's room. I figured that chair still had some more hits in it, so I didn't leave."

Shea Stadium was vibrating with noise as Stanley took his eight warm-up pitches before facing Mookie Wilson, a switch-hitter who was batting left-handed.

With the tying run on third in Mitchell and the winning run on first in Knight, the duel began. Wilson fouled off Stanley's first pitch, took a ball on the second, received another ball on the third, and fouled off the fourth pitch.

Stanley then threw an inside fastball that almost hit Wilson and shot past Gedman's glove. It was later ruled a wild pitch, though some press box observers thought it should have been a passed ball. As the ball bounced behind Gedman, Mitchell raced home with the run that tied the score, 5–5, while Knight moved to second on the play.

Now came one more shocking breakdown for the Red Sox. On a 3-and-2 count, Wilson slapped a grounder toward first base. As Bill Buckner stooped to get it, the ball bounced through his legs for an error, allowing Knight to score all the way from second base. The Mets had a stunning 6–5 victory.

"The ball went skip, skip, and didn't come up," said Buckner. "I can't remember the last time I missed a ball like that, but I'll remember that one."

As Knight jumped on home plate with the winning run, he was mobbed by his fellow Mets who were celebrating and yelling wildly as though they had been reprieved from a death sentence.

Although there was still one more game to play to bring the World Series to a conclusion, Buckner was so harshly criticized for his error that he could not escape being stigmatized for the rest of his baseball career, which came to an end in 1990. The criticism was not justified in the eyes of his teammates or, for that matter, in the opinion of umpire Dale Ford, who worked behind the plate in game six.

Bob Stanley (left) threw too far inside to Mookie Wilson, and catcher Rich Gedman missed the ball, allowing the tying run to score. *(Mitchel Layton, Clifton Boutelle)*

"That was my most memorable game," Ford said. "Schiraldi had Knight down two strikes and no balls, and he throws a fastball right down the middle. Then Stanley comes in and lets the tying run in from third on what was called a wild pitch to Wilson. But in my mind, it wasn't a wild pitch. The ball almost hit me in the head. I think it should've been a passed ball. Gedman didn't get his glove up. Then Wilson hit the ball that went through Buckner's legs.

"I think the fans criticized Buckner too much for losing the game. Schiraldi should've taken some blame for throwing that pitch down the middle to Knight when he was so far ahead in the count."

Gary Carter agreed with Ford in one respect, though he claimed the pitch to Knight was more to the inside than over the middle of the plate. He thought Gedman should have caught Stanley's pitch that forced Wilson to bend almost in half in trying to avoid being hit. He said the Red Sox catcher should have been charged with a passed ball.

"It wasn't an easy play," said Carter, "but Geddy should have made it. Maybe he lost sight of it for a split second. He didn't stick his mitt out far enough."

After the game, Stanley said, "I wanted to go inside, over the corner on Wilson, but the pitch didn't do what it was supposed to do and went too far inside." Interviewed many years after the fact, he did not blame Gedman for failing to knock down the pitch. "Yogi Berra used to kid me and tell me he would've blocked that pitch," Stanley said, "but Geddy is a good friend of mine, and it's all water over the dam.

"When Wilson hit that ball to Buckner, I thought we were out of the inning [tied at 5–5]. I felt sorry for Buckner for what happened to him on that play. He had a great career, but he's remembered for that error.

"It shouldn't be that way. We had chances to win that game. We left 14 runners on base, and in game three we had that screwed-up rundown play that helped set up the Mets' 4–0 lead right at the start. But people will always remember that missed play by Buckner."

Buckner was playing behind first base near the line and simply did not get his glove down low enough to scoop up Wilson's grounder, which bounced behind him out of reach. If he had fielded the ball cleanly, he still might not have been able to outrun Wilson to the bag on his gimpy legs. But would he have gotten the putout by throwing to Stanley who was running to cover first base? Probably.

McNamara was censured for not replacing Buckner with Dave Stapleton for defensive purposes in the tenth inning. The manager defended his inaction even though he had replaced Buckner with Stapleton in Boston's three previous victories over the Mets.

"But that was because we had put in a pinch-runner for Buckner," McNamara said. "I never thought about taking him out tonight. He has very good hands." McNamara did not dwell on the fact that Buckner had difficulty bending over for grounders.

During the season Stapleton had appeared in 29 games at

first base and had not committed an error in 86 chances. He was obviously a better defensive first baseman at that juncture than Buckner, who was playing hurt. Stapleton was upset that McNamara did not send him into the game. He was loosened up, ready to go. "He won't admit it," Stapleton said, "but he knows he messed up."

Stapleton did not fault Buckner for making the error. Neither did Ray Knight, who scored the winning run. "We felt badly for Buckner," Knight said after the game.

It was the 39th time the Mets had won a game in their last at-bat. "Somehow we came through," said Mookie Wilson. "How did we do it? Mirrors? I don't know."

In his post-game comments, McNamara likened the Red Sox loss to the defeat Boston hung on the Angels in the fifth game of the American League playoffs.

"As close as we came to winning the ball game," he said, "we couldn't do it. I guess you could associate it with what we did in California when we were down to our last out.

"There's disappointment, but at least we have another game tomorrow."

Heavy rain, however, forced postponement of game seven until Monday night, October 27. The Red Sox appeared to have recovered from their heartbreaking loss on Saturday night as they gained an early 3-0 lead, but they eventually crumbled, 8-5. There would be no victory parade in Boston, only memories of another crushing defeat.

Long after the 1986 World Series, former Red Sox players were asked to retrieve some of those memories.

"One of the things I remember about that sixth game," said Wade Boggs, "happened before the Mets rallied in the tenth inning. I was out at third base. There were two outs, we were up two runs and felt like we were in the driver's seat. Harry Wendelstedt, the third-base umpire, says to me, 'Hey, when this is over, can I have your cap? I collect all winning third baseman's caps.'

"I said, 'Harry, this game isn't over yet. I can't guarantee you I can flip you my hat.'

"After that, it became sort of a messy game. I watched people running by me at third base. I never touched a ball.

"Later on I had heard that somebody in our clubhouse had popped the cork on a champagne bottle when we had that 5–3 lead and needed only one more out. That was the kiss of death.

"We had a great club in '86, a close-knit club. It just wasn't our time. It was wrong for people to put blame on Buckner. We just couldn't close the deal."

Boggs, who was named batting coach for the Tampa Bay Devil Rays in 2000, finally did play on a World Series winner with the Yankees in 1996.

"Sometimes the best club doesn't win the World Series," he said in an oblique reference to the '86 Red Sox. "When I was with the Yankees in '96, we were maybe the fourth-best team on paper. The Braves were the best club, but we beat them in the Series."

Boggs added a fatalistic touch to his view on the mercurial nature of so many baseball games. "I'm a firm believer in what my father told me. He said, 'Everything happens for a reason. If it's in the cards, you reap the fruits of your labor. If it's not in the cards, then so be it.'"

Rich Gedman was asked about the pitch that escaped him when Mookie Wilson was at bat in the tenth inning.

"It was a sinkerball that Stanley threw. I was set up pretty much in the middle behind the plate. When he went to release the ball, I felt it was going to go in farther than anticipated. It was a fast pitch, and I couldn't move quick enough to stop it.

"All the hits the Mets got before that, none of them were hit hard, but they were hit in the right places. I was thinking, 'Gosh, can't anybody hit a ball right at one of our fielders?'

"Maybe that's what makes baseball so terrific. Sometimes it defies analysis. Anything can happen. We had that sixth game within our grasp, and we let it slip through our fingers. The only nice thing about it was that we had one more game to play and still had the opportunity to win a World Series."

Gedman played with the Red Sox until 1990, spent a little time with the Houston Astros, and then finished his career after the 1991–1992 seasons with the St. Louis Cardinals. He never had another chance to enjoy a World Series triumph. Does he ever reflect on that lost "opportunity" in 1986?

"From time to time," he said, "especially around October.

But I have no regrets. People, especially in Boston, made a big deal out of whether that was a wild pitch by Stanley or a passed ball. If you're not involved in a play like that, it's too easy to lay the blame on somebody, but losing that game was not my fault, not Stanley's fault, not Buckner's fault. It was all our fault.

"Everybody on the team had to deal with that loss in their own way. It formed a close, unique bond among us for having gone through it. It's a special bond that's still there today."

Dave Henderson had completed the 2000 season as a broadcaster for the Seattle Mariners when he was asked to recall his tenth-inning home run against the Mets in game six.

"The only thought I had was maybe that homer would win the World Series for us," he said. "That's what I was focused on—winning. As a baseball player, you're always taught that when you get beat by the best, you tip your hat and go get 'em next time. But losing the way we did still sticks in my craw. We gave the game away. As a team we gave it away.

"There was a lot of stress in that game, and what everyone seems to forget is that it took four plays that went against us to get to Buckner's error. So you can't pin that loss on one man."

Bill Buckner played 22 years in the majors, starting with the Dodgers in 1969, then moving on to the Cubs in 1977, the Red Sox in 1984, the Angels in 1987, the Royals in 1988, and one final turn with the Red Sox in 1990. He won a National League batting championship by hitting .324 for the Cubs in 1980. He was a driven competitor. He had to be after suffering a serious ankle injury in 1975 when he was with the Dodgers.

He damaged the ankle sliding into second base in a game against the Giants early in the season. He caught his left foot on the base, and his ankle was twisted beneath him, absorbing the weight of his body as he went down.

Despite surgery at the end of the season to correct the damage, Billy Buck, as he was nicknamed, never fully recovered from the injury, and for the rest of his career he was virtually a one-legged player.

In all he underwent four operations to fix the ankle. He played hurt and still wound up collecting 2,715 hits and 1,208 RBI while finishing with a respectable .289 batting average.

Boston Red Sox vs. New York Mets
at Shea Stadium, October 25, 1986

Boston Red Sox	AB	R	H	RBI	New York Mets	AB	R	H	RBI
Wade Boggs, 3b	5	2	3	0	Lenny Dykstra, cf	4	0	0	0
Marty Barrett, 2b	4	1	3	2	Wally Backman, 2b	4	0	1	0
Bill Buckner, 1b	5	0	0	0	Keith Hernandez, 1b	4	0	1	0
Jim Rice, lf	5	0	0	0	Gary Carter, c	4	1	1	1
Dwight Evans, rf	4	0	1	2	Darryl Strawberry, rf	2	1	0	0
Rich Gedman, c	5	0	1	0	Kevin Mitchell, ph (e)	1	1	1	0
Dave Henderson, cf	5	1	2	1	Ray Knight, 3b	4	2	2	2
Spike Owen, ss	4	1	3	0	Mookie Wilson, lf	5	0	1	0
Roger Clemens, p	3	0	0	0	Rafael Santana, ss	1	0	0	0
Mike Greenwell, ph (b)	1	0	0	0	Danny Heep, ph (a)	1	0	0	0
Calvin Schiraldi, p	1	0	0	0	Kevin Elster, ss	1	0	0	0
					Howard Johnson, ph-ss (d)	1	0	0	0
					Bob Ojeda, p	2	0	0	0
					Lee Mazzilli, ph-rf (c)	2	1	1	0
Total	**42**	**5**	**13**	**5**		**36**	**6**	**8**	**3**

(a) Grounded into a double play (with run scoring) for Santana in fifth inning; (b) Struck out for Clemens in the eighth inning; (c) Singled for Jesse Orosco in the eighth inning; (d) Struck out for Elster in the ninth inning; (e) Singled for Rick Aguilera in the tenth inning.

Boston	1	1	0	0	0	0	1	0	0	2	—	5
New York	0	0	0	0	2	0	0	1	0	3	—	6

Boston Red Sox	IP	H	R	ER	SO	BB
Roger Clemens	7.0	4	2	1	8	2
Calvin Schiraldi (L)	2.2	4	4	3	1	2
Bob Stanley +	0.0	0	0	0	0	0

New York Mets	IP	H	R	ER	SO	BB
Bob Ojeda	6.0	8	2	2	3	2
Roger McDowell	1.2	2	1	0	1	3
Jesse Orosco	0.1	0	0	0	0	0
Rick Aguilera (W)	2.0	3	2	2	3	0

+ Pitched to one batter in the tenth inning

E—Buckner, Evans, Gedman, Knight, Elster. **DP**—Boston 1, New York 1. **LOB**—Boston 14, New York 8. **2B**—Evans, Boggs. **HR**—Henderson. **SB**—Strawberry (2). **SH**—Owen, Dykstra, Backman. **SF**—Carter. **Wild pitch**—Stanley.
Umpires—Dale Ford, John Kibler, Jim Evans, Harry Wendelstedt, Joe Brinkman, Ed Montague.
Time—4:02. **Attendance**—55,078.

Buckner's fabled miscue
haunted him for a long
time. *(Mike Valeri)*

For a long time Buckner was hounded by reminders of his
error in the 1986 World Series. Today those reminders have
pretty much faded, except for an occasional reference by a
writer or mention by a baseball broadcaster.

Buckner lives 2,200 miles from Boston in a small town near
Boise, Idaho, where he moved in 1993.

"Do you ever think of that game and the missed ground
ball?" he was asked.

"I get tired of it," he said. "I just don't care to talk about
it."

His response is understandable, but it also indicates he has
never completely exorcised memories of that game and that
error.

In 2000 Bob Stanley completed his fourth season as a pitching coach in—irony of ironies—the New York Mets' farm sys-

tem. He had played his entire major league career with the Red Sox, primarily as a reliever from 1977 through 1989, finishing with 115 victories and 132 saves.

Shortly after he retired, he and his wife Joan learned that their nine-year-old son, Kyle, had cancer. A large tumor had developed behind the boy's right eye. A year of chemotherapy and radiation treatment reduced the tumor to a quarter of its original size. In January 1991 the rest of the tumor was removed by surgery, and the doctors declared Kyle free of cancer. The young patient still had to receive periodic checkups, but the long-term prognosis was heartening.

"Going through an experience like that as a parent puts everything in perspective," Stanley said. "There are more important things in life than the game of baseball.

"I prayed to God that Kyle would be cured, and when he got his health back, my wife and I couldn't have been happier. The disappointment we had in losing the '86 World Series? You can throw that right out the window."

1992

Pennant Eludes the Pirates for the Third Straight Year

"This is, without question, the toughest loss I've ever had to handle."—Jim Leyland

In 1992 the Pittsburgh Pirates fell a step short of winning the tenth pennant in the club's history, bowing to the Atlanta Braves in a heart-stopping seventh game of the National League Championship Series. It was the third consecutive year they had reached the league playoffs under manager Jim Leyland, only to come up empty-handed each time.

They were ahead 2–0 going into the bottom half of the ninth inning in the final game against the Braves at Atlanta–Fulton County Stadium on Wednesday night, October 14 when a little-used reserve player, Francisco Cabrera, put the cap on a 3–2 victory for the Braves with a pinch-hit single.

When it was all over, Leyland had a hard time restraining tears. "This is, without question, the toughest loss I've ever had to handle," he said. "It's tough, but it's life. I hope youngsters learn from this game. In life you learn to handle both the wins and the losses."

As in every year, there were "wins" and "losses" in 1992. California Angels manager Buck Rodgers was seriously injured on May 21 when one of the buses carrying the team from New York to Baltimore swerved out of control on the New Jersey Turnpike and crashed through a guardrail. In addition to 12 others who were less seriously hurt in the mishap, Rodgers suffered a broken knee, elbow, and rib, and did not return to manage until August 28.

During three days in late August, Hurricane Andrew stormed across southern Florida and then ripped through southern Louisiana before dying out, leaving an estimated 250,000 people homeless and causing $30 billion in damage. Homestead, Florida, was particularly hard hit.

Also on the losing side of the ledger was Fay Vincent, who on September 7 resigned under advisement as commissioner of baseball. Owners had voted no confidence in Vincent a few days earlier, and when he resigned they elected Bud Selig, head of the Milwaukee Brewers, as interim commissioner.

The owners in effect ousted Vincent because they felt he was not responsive to them and had exceeded his authority in several instances, including his attempt to realign the National League by shifting the Cardinals and Cubs to the West Division; his handling of the suspensions of Yankees' owner George Steinbrenner and pitcher Steve Howe; and his refusal to exclude himself from forthcoming negotiations with the Players' Association.

Among baseball figures who died in 1992 were Jean Yawkey, owner of the Boston Red Sox; Joe Burke, president of the Kansas City Royals; Hall of Fame second baseman Billy Herman; broadcaster Red Barber, who announced games for the Reds, Dodgers, and Yankees; and Sal Maglie, who earned the nickname "The Barber" for his pitches that gave batters a "close shave."

The baseball universe was speckled with many winning achievements, including the attainment of three thousand career hits by two future Hall of Fame players, Robin Yount of the Brewers and George Brett of the Royals. Pitchers Tom Seaver, Rollie Fingers, and Hal Newhouser, and umpire Bill McGowan were inducted into the Hall of Fame. Seaver was named on 98.8 percent of the ballots cast, most ever in the elections conducted annually since 1936 by the Baseball Writers Association of America.

In the American League, 1992's individual leaders included Edgar Martinez of the Mariners, who won the batting championship with a .343 average. Jack Morris of the Blue Jays and

Kevin Brown of the Rangers paced all pitchers as they each recorded 21 victories. Reliever Dennis Eckersley, who piled up 51 saves for the Oakland A's, received the league's Cy Young and Most Valuable Player awards.

Gary Sheffield of the Padres led National League batters with a .330 average while Tom Glavine of the Braves and Greg Maddux of the Cubs each won 20 games, most among league pitchers. The baseball writers named Barry Bonds of the Pirates as the senior league's Most Valuable Player and Greg Maddux as its Cy Young award winner.

Division champions in the American League were the Blue Jays in the East and A's in the West. Playing their home games in Toronto's spectacular SkyDome, the Blue Jays set a major league attendance record of 4,028,318 spectators.

In the National League the Braves topped the West Division with a 98–64 record, finishing eight games ahead of the runner-up Reds. The Pirates won the East Division title with a 96–66 mark, outrunning the second-place Expos by nine games.

It was the third year in a row Pittsburgh had won 95 or more games under Jim Leyland, who had succeeded Chuck Tanner as the club's manager in 1986. A native Ohioan, Leyland had spent 11 years managing in the Detroit Tigers' farm system and four seasons as a third-base coach for the Chicago White Sox before being appointed manager of the Pirates. He was hired by general manager Syd Thrift, and between them they helped rebuild a losing Pittsburgh team that had been embarrassed by drug scandals and was threatening to leave the city for financial reasons.

Leyland took over a team that had lost 104 games in 1985. With an infusion of young talent through trades executed by Thrift, the Pirates slowly began to improve in the next few years, recast as a resurgent, blue-collar team, an image that suited the city well. In 1990 Leyland and the Pirates won the East Division race, only to lose to the Cincinnati Reds in the League Championship Series, four games to two. They were back again in 1991 for another try at a pennant, but lost in seven games to the Braves, whose starting pitchers Steve Avery and John Smoltz shut them down, 1–0 and 4–0, in the final two contests.

Opportunity knocked again in 1992, even though the Pirates had lost Bobby Bonilla via free agency to the Mets and in a cost-cutting move had dealt away 20-game winning pitcher John Smiley in a trade with the Twins. Leyland made up for these losses with managerial leadership that kept the team focused and helped two position players, Barry Bonds and center fielder Andy Van Slyke, fashion excellent seasons. During spring training he straightened Bonds out in a heated shouting match that changed Bonds's self-centered attitude about the game.

He also showed a fine touch when it came to pitching decisions. "I've never seen anybody better at handling pitchers," said Ray Miller, who coached the Pirates' mound staff. Miller himself was highly respected for his ability to bring out the best in starters and relievers. He constantly preached the importance of pitchers getting ahead in the count and not wasting time between deliveries. During his coaching career with the Orioles, from 1978 through part of the 1985 season, and with the Pirates from 1987, Miller had added his touch to the work of seven 20-game winners, including Mike Flanagan, Steve Stone, Jim Palmer, Scott McGregor, Mike Boddicker, Doug Drabek, and John Smiley.

Drabek finished 22–8 for Pittsburgh in 1990, and Smiley was 20–8 in 1991, but he had been traded to the Twins before the start of the 1992 season for Denny Neagle, a young left-hander. Yet the Pirates marched to their third successive East Division title without the benefit of a 20-game winner. Drabek led the staff with a 15–11 record, followed by Randy Tomlin at 14–9 and 35-year-old Bob Walk at 10–6. No other staff member won more than eight games.

In all, the club used 21 pitchers during the season, and 18 of them won at least one game, an indication that Leyland and Miller got the most out of a rather undistinguished group of starters and relievers.

Three of their pitchers, Zane Smith, Vicente Palacios, and Walk, all were hampered and sidelined at times with physical ailments. After the mid-season break, Smith was out of action because of tendinitis in his left shoulder. Palacios was absent for most of the year with arm problems. Walk was on the disabled list twice with groin-muscle pulls.

In search of pitching sustenance, the club called up rookie right-hander Tim Wakefield on July 31 from its Buffalo farm team in the American Association. A knuckleball specialist, Wakefield soothed Leyland's concerns, posting an 8–1 record with a 2.15 ERA the rest of the way. He would make a strong impact in the league playoffs.

Despite question marks about their pitching, the Pirates posted 20 shutout victories during the season, second most in the league only to the 24 recorded by the Braves' talent-laden staff.

With the New York Mets tabbed as pre-season favorites in the East Division, the Pirates charged out of the starting gate with a 15–5 record in April, held first place for all but an eight-day period from May 24 through June 1, struggled a bit in July, then hammered out records of 19–8 in August and 21–8 in September to cruise home without much of a challenge from Montreal, their nearest rival.

Bonds and Van Slyke provided a potent thrust to Pittsburgh's championship drive. In his last year with the Pirates before moving on to the San Francisco Giants, Bonds, 27, batted .311 with 36 doubles, 34 homers, 103 RBI, and 39 stolen bases. He led the league in runs scored with 109, in bases on balls with 127, in on-base percentage with .461, and in slugging percentage at .624.

Troubled by a bad back, Van Slyke was forced to alter his swing yet hit .324 while scoring 103 runs and collecting 199 hits including 45 doubles, the latter two being the best marks in the league.

Van Slyke won a Gold Glove for fielding excellence in 1992 as did the Pirates' second baseman Jose Lind, who teamed up with shortstop Jay Bell to form the middle infield defense. Third-base chores were handled by versatile Jeff King; first base was usually occupied by Orlando Merced. Mike LaValliere and Don Slaught took turns catching.

The Pirates could hardly be described as a fearsome team, but they did score 693 runs, more than any of their rivals in the National League. And they were tenacious. They won 37 games by one run, and 14 games in extra innings.

In the National League Championship Series against the

Braves, they would be facing a strong starting rotation that included left-handers Tom Glavine, 20–8; Charlie Leibrandt, 15–7; and Steve Avery, 11–11, along with right-hander John Smoltz, 15–12. Atlanta manager Bobby Cox also had a deep bullpen that featured Mike Stanton, Marvin Freeman, Jeff Reardon, Kent Mercker, and Mark Wohlers.

On offense the Braves were led by third baseman Terry Pendleton, who hit .311 with 21 homers and 103 RBI. Joining Pendleton in run production were right fielder David Justice with 21 homers and 72 RBI; center fielder Otis Nixon, who hit .294 with 41 stolen bases; and left fielder Ron Gant, an 80-RBI man with 17 home runs.

With many of these same players, Cox had guided the Braves almost to the summit in 1991 when they lost the World Series to the Minnesota Twins, 1–0, in the tenth inning of game seven. Now, in 1992, his team again had to overcome the Pirates in order to reach the Fall Classic. Although the Braves owned a 7-to-5 edge in the 12 meetings between the two teams during the regular season, seven of those games were decided by one run and four by two runs. Only one contest was a blowout, by Atlanta.

"We weren't intimidated by them," recalled Doug Drabek. "We had played them good during the season, and though they beat us in the playoffs the year before, we thought we could take them this time."

Drabek complimented Leyland and Miller for the way they managed and coached during the 1992 season. "They worked well together," he said. "Leyland had the knack of knowing pitchers and their time, when to let them stay in a game and when to take them out. Miller always stressed getting the first pitch over for a strike. If I had control on my curve ball, I'd throw it on the first pitch. And, if it worked, I'd throw another one on my second pitch.

"Ray had some T-shirts made up for our starters. They were black and gold, with the lettering, 'Throw Strikes. Change Speeds. Work Fast.' I still have a bunch of them and wear them once in a while. He also had some shirts for the relievers with the lettering 'We Close the Deal.'"

The first two games of the League Championship Series were played in Atlanta and did little to substantiate the near-parity between the two pennant contenders. In the opener on Tuesday night, October 6, the Braves won handily 5–1 behind starter John Smoltz, who gave up only four hits and one run over eight innings. Reliever Mike Stanton closed out the ninth. Drabek started for the Pirates but lasted only into the fifth inning and was charged with four of Atlanta's runs.

In game two on October 7, the Braves destroyed Pirate pitching, 13–5, with a 14-hit barrage that made a winner of starter Steve Avery.

Through the first two games, the Pirates' key offensive players were virtually neutralized. Van Slyke had one hit in nine trips to the plate while Bonds produced one hit in six official at-bats. Assessing Bonds's post-season struggle to contribute, Leyland felt his left fielder was pressing. "I think Barry is trying to hit a five-run homer in every at-bat," the manager said.

Down two games to none, the Pirates needed a stalwart savior as the series moved to Pittsburgh's Three Rivers Stadium for game three on Friday night, October 9, and they found one in Tim Wakefield. The 26-year-old knuckleballer outdueled Tom Glavine and went the distance in earning a 3–2 decision over the Braves.

Wakefield surrendered five hits, two of them homers by former Pirate Sid Bream and Ron Gant. In throwing 109 pitches in all, 104 of them knuckleballs—which usually are difficult to control—he walked only one batter. "I was probably more nervous than he was," said Ray Miller, who was impressed with Wakefield's ability to throw his elusive flutterball for strikes.

"To be a rookie and get a chance to pitch in a game like this doesn't come along every day," said Wakefield. "I wanted to make the most of the opportunity."

The Pirates had inched away from the brink of defeat but were pushed back near the edge in game four when their nemesis, John Smoltz, beat them for the second time in four days. Despite a nagging muscle strain in his back, Smoltz pitched six-plus innings to gain a 6–4 decision. Drabek again was the loser, failing to last longer than five innings.

Now trailing the Braves three games to one, the Pirates faced an intimidating challenge: beat Atlanta three in a row or go home. They came close, ever so close, to meeting the challenge.

In game five at Three Rivers Stadium on October 11, they came away 7–1 winners behind the three-hit pitching of veteran right-hander Bob Walk, who went the distance. In 19 regular-season starts, Walk had recorded only one other complete game. He had also made 17 relief appearances in 1992.

"The starting assignment was a surprise," he said, "but a pleasant surprise. Winning that game was the highlight of my career. When you pitch a game like that in July it's one thing, but when you're down three games to one and do it in the play-offs, it's pretty special."

The teams flew back to Atlanta to resume their battle, and in game six on Tuesday night, October 13, the Pirates once again rattled Braves pitching, scoring a decisive 13–4 victory to even the series.

Bonds ignited an eight-run explosion by the Bucs in the second inning, hitting the first post-season home run of his career. He also singled in the same inning when Braves starter Tom Glavine simply lost it and was charged with all eight runs on six hits before Bobby Cox mercifully relieved him with Charlie Leibrandt, who finally retired the side.

It was no contest after the Pirates' outburst in the second inning. Tim Wakefield pitched his second complete game of the series in gaining the victory. With Pittsburgh in front, 13–1, nearly half the Atlanta–Fulton County Stadium crowd of 51,975 headed for the exits by the seventh inning.

After the game, reporters asked Leyland if he thought the two overwhelming wins by his team had swung the momentum in favor of the Pirates. "Momentum is very simple," he said. "It's your next day's pitcher."

So the struggle for the 1992 National League pennant came down to one game. Starters John Smoltz and Doug Drabek would be matched for the third time in eight days.

The Pirates jumped off to a 1–0 lead in the first inning when Alex Cole drew a walk on mostly high pitches by Smoltz, advanced to third on a double by Van Slyke and, after an intentional pass to Bonds, scored on a sacrifice fly by Orlando

Merced. They increased their edge to 2–0 in the top of the sixth on a leadoff double by Jay Bell and a single up the middle by Van Slyke.

In the bottom of the sixth, the Braves filled the bases with the help of a single by Jeff Treadway, who pinch-hit for Smoltz. But Drabek escaped without a scratch. The Pirate starter, pitching the game of his life, retired Jeff Blauser on a liner to third baseman Jeff King, who took three steps to the bag to force Mark Lemke for a double play. Drabek then ended the threat by getting Terry Pendleton to line out to left.

With Smoltz finished for the night, Bobby Cox went to his bullpen, calling in Mike Stanton, Pete Smith, and Steve Avery to hold the Pirates scoreless through the top of the eighth inning.

The Bucs almost added their third run in the eighth when Merced singled and King doubled into the right-field corner. Third-base coach Rich Donnelly waved Merced around, but David Justice unleashed a one-hop throw to catcher Damon Berryhill who made a sweeping tag on Merced.

In retrospect it was perhaps the most vital defensive play of the series for the Braves, who were still in the hunt after closer Jeff Reardon shut down the Pirates in the top of the ninth.

Drabek had kept the Braves off the scoreboard on five hits as he headed back to the mound with a two-run lead in the bottom of the ninth inning, needing three outs to assure the Pirates of the pennant. "Dougie still had good stuff at the start of the inning," recalled Mike LaValliere, "but it had been a long game for him."

Pendleton led off for the Braves. A switch-hitter, he was batting left-handed against Drabek who had set him down in his three previous trips to the plate. This time Pendleton doubled into the right-field corner.

"The ball Pendleton hit to right stayed straight," LaValliere noted. "Usually a left-handed hitter would hook a ball like that and it would go foul. This one didn't. It landed just fair in the corner."

With Pendleton on second base, Drabek then faced Justice, another left-handed batter, who hit a grounder to second base-

Jose Lind's rare defensive lapse put the tying run on base for Atlanta. *(George Gojkovich)*

man Jose Lind. Lind was called Chico by his Pirate mates, who admired his defensive skills. He had made only six errors in 745 total chances during the regular season, and was the top fielding second baseman in the National League. Inexplicably, he muffed Justice's easy grounder for an error, putting the tying run on base and giving the Braves an extra out in their attempt to even the score—or possibly win the game.

"It was just one of those things with Chico," said Drabek. "He tried to backhand it, and the ball hit the heel of his glove."

Sid Bream, who had played for the Pirates from 1985 through 1990, was the next batter. He also hit left-handed. He had been signed by the Braves as a free agent after the 1990 season.

Bream was on the disabled list for much of the 1991 season after injuring his right knee in a game with the Phillies on June 18. He underwent surgery to remove a bone chip and repair torn cartilage in the knee. He had also had surgery on his left knee in 1987, so when he bounced back to play 120 games at first base for the Braves in 1992, his ability to run had been considerably diminished. He was regarded as the slowest man on the team.

Still, Bream, who stood 6–4 and weighed 220 pounds, could

"Marsh squeezed us real bad," recalled catcher Mike LaValliere (right) about the umpiring of Randy Marsh as Doug Drabek (left) struggled to finish off the Braves. *(George Gojkovich)*

produce the long ball, and Drabek knew he had to be careful. "Dougie was just about out of gas. He was on his last legs," LaValliere recalled.

John McSherry, the umpiring crew chief, had left the game after the first inning because of illness. First-base umpire Randy Marsh moved behind the plate. "Marsh squeezed us real bad," LaValliere said. "As far as I'm concerned, we had a couple of guys struck out on pitches that definitely were strikes, but he called them balls."

LaValliere did not blame Marsh, however, for the walk that Drabek issued to Bream on four straight balls. "The first two pitches were pretty close," recalled Drabek, "but the last two I threw to Bream didn't come close to being strikes. I didn't want to lay one in there to Sid, and I wound up overthrowing.

"Up to the time I faced him, everything seemed normal. I wanted to close the game, but then I just lost it, and that's when Leyland came out to get me."

The walk to Bream loaded the bases, and Leyland waved

Stan Belinda in from the bullpen. Drabek headed for the dugout to watch the remainder of the contest. He had given the Pirates everything he had for 129 pitches and now was hoping the 26-year-old Belinda could save the game.

"Once on the bench," said Drabek, "it's all more difficult. There you are no longer in control."

Ron Gant hit Belinda's second pitch to the wall in left field. After Bonds made the catch, Pendleton scored from third to make it a 2–1 ball game.

Damon Berryhill, who had managed only four hits in 24 at-bats during the series for a .167 average, batted after Gant. He was walked by Belinda, who questioned the calls by Marsh after the game. The walk reloaded the bases. Justice was on third with the tying run and the hobbled Bream on second with the potential winning run.

"In the three years I've been here," said Belinda following the game, "I've never said anything like this, but I think two of those pitches to Berryhill were strikes, especially the three-and-one pitch." In a reference to Marsh, he added, "In a game like this, every pitch counts, but he's human."

With the bases packed and the pressure of an entire season weighing on him, Belinda gained momentary respite when he retired pinch-hitter Brian Hunter on a pop-up to Lind behind second base. Two outs. Had Lind not made his error earlier in the inning, the Pirates would have been celebrating a thrilling come-from-behind championship.

One final act of the drama remained, however, and it would be played out by a 26-year-old Dominican who had been recalled from the minors by the Braves on August 31 and had come to bat only ten times during the regular season.

A catcher and a .282 career hitter in the minors, Francesco Cabrera had been acquired by the Braves as the player to be named later in a trade with the Toronto Blue Jays on August 24, 1989. He had played sparingly for Atlanta in parts of three seasons while spending the rest of his time with Syracuse and Richmond in the International League. Now Bobby Cox sent him up to pinch-hit for reliever Jeff Reardon. A rangy, right-handed hitter who stood 6–4, Cabrera was about to send the home crowd at Atlanta–Fulton County Stadium into a state of delirium.

On a 2-and-1 count, Cabrera lined Belinda's next pitch between short and third for a single that was scooped up in left field by Barry Bonds. Justice scored easily on the play, but it looked as though Bream, churning around third with the winning run, could be cut down at home plate by Bonds's throw to LaValliere. It was going to be close.

"I thought they'd hold Sid at third," recalled LaValliere, "but he got a good jump at second and he made a good turn at third. Still, I thought I'd have time to make the play.

"Barry's throw came in slightly up the line on the first-base side. I couldn't block the plate and had to go get the ball. If I was 6–4 like Sid, I might've been able to make the swipe tag but I'm 5–8 and couldn't stretch that far."

Bream slid across the plate just before LaValliere could put the glove on him. A startling victory was completed as Randy Marsh spread his arms, signalling Bream safe. The Braves had won 3–2, with one of the most exciting rallies ever in postseason play.

LaValliere recounted the pitch sequence to Cabrera. "He was a dead fastball hitter," said the former receiver. "So we went with a breaking ball on the first pitch, but it was a ball. We came back with another breaking ball, but it missed too.

"With the bases loaded we couldn't risk forcing in the tying run, so we went with a fastball that Cabrera hammered foul. Then Belinda threw another fastball, a good pitch, down—but he connected on it."

"When you have two outs and the bases filled, you know you can't walk a guy," said Belinda. "That's probably worse than giving up a hit. I wanted to make him hit the ball, and I hoped he would hit it at somebody.

"He hit it too far from Jay for him to dive for the ball," Belinda added, referring to shortstop Jay Bell. "A little to his left and Jay could've stopped it, but it came off the bat hard and skipped through the infield pretty fast."

Before Cabrera applied the coup de grace, Bob Walk had gone out to the Pirates' left-field bullpen to warm up in case the game went into extra innings. Three days earlier he had started and pitched brilliantly in game five, giving up only three hits in beating the Braves. Like most every major league competitor, he was ready to march the extra mile if his team needed him.

"I had been on the bench during the game," Walk recalled, "but near the end, when we were ahead 2–0, I went beneath the stands for a while until I heard the fans yelling, so I went back out to see what was happening.

"The Braves had a couple of guys on base and nobody out when I heard Leyland tell Miller, 'Get Walk up.' So I started to loosen up in the bullpen, and that's where I had a good view of Bonds as he made the throw home after fielding Cabrera's hit.

"I thought Bream would be out. It all happened so quick. It was over—you couldn't call time out, and there was nothing you could do about it.

"It certainly was disheartening to me. I was going on 36 and had been in a World Series in 1980 when I was a rookie with the Phillies. I figured it was my last chance to get back to the World Series because Bonds and Drabek would be free agents after the season, and we had already lost Bonilla and Smiley the year before.

"It was tough for me, certainly the big disappointment of my career. It put me under for a while, and as the fall and winter wore on it was hard for me to forget because Sid Bream was my neighbor then. He lived four houses down from me in the Pittsburgh area. We've always been good friends, but every time I'd see him in those days, I'd be reminded of that play at home."

Reconstructing his dash from second base, Bream said, "I saw Frankie hit the ball and took off. When I saw Bonds charging in, there was some doubt. I tried to cut third base as hard as I could. I made a sweeping slide and that saved me. My foot touched the plate and then Spanky [LaValliere] tagged me. I was just glad I could take it the whole way."

After the Braves rushed onto the field from their dugout to pile on Bream—who had flipped on his back and wiggled his legs joyously—Atlanta fans turned their tomahawk chant into a tumultuous roar.

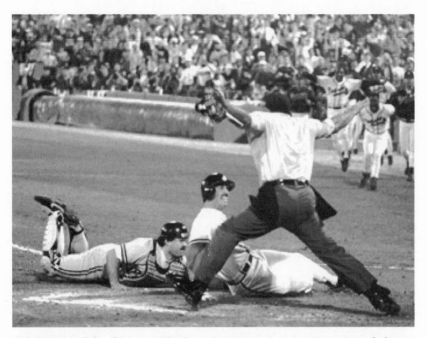

Sid Bream slides home with the winning run in game seven of the
1992 NLCS. *(Chris Hamilton)*

Bonds remained briefly in left field, kneeling on his left
knee, incredulous that within a space of 22 pitches by Drabek
and Belinda, he and his teammates were once again runners-
up in the chase for a pennant. After a minute Bonds rose and
walked slowly off the field to the Pirates' clubhouse, which Leyland kept closed to the media until he and his players had a
chance to recover a bit from their sudden and wrenching loss.

"I'm still in shock," Leyland said to reporters. "We felt this
game was ours. It was a real heartbreaker. This is a lesson for
all Little Leaguers. You have to learn how to lose. The Pirates
are walking tall tonight, but the Braves are walking taller.

"I have no reservations about anything that went on in the
game. The ball to Lind? What can you say? He's a Gold Glove
fielder. He makes that play ten out of ten times. But, it happens. That's baseball."

Recalling the clubhouse scene after the game, LaValliere
said, "There was no yelling or screaming or throwing things.
We were more stunned than anything. We just sat dumbfounded

Pittsburgh Pirates vs. Atlanta Braves
at Fulton County Stadium, October 14, 1992

Pittsburgh Pirates	AB	R	H	RBI	Atlanta Braves	AB	R	H	RBI
Alex Cole, rf	2	1	0	0	Otis Nixon, cf	4	0	1	0
Lloyd McClendon, ph-rf (b)	0	0	0	0	Jeff Blauser, ss	4	0	0	0
Cecil Espy, pr-rf (c)	0	0	0	0	Terry Pendleton, 3b	4	1	1	0
Jay Bell, ss	4	1	1	0	David Justice, rf	4	1	0	0
Andy Van Slyke, cf	4	0	2	1	Sid Bream, 1b	3	1	1	0
Barry Bonds, lf	3	0	1	0	Ron Gant, lf	2	0	0	1
Orlando Merced, 1b	3	0	0	1	Damon Berryhill, c	3	0	1	0
Jeff King, 3b	4	0	1	0	Mark Lemke, 2b	2	0	1	0
Mike LaValliere, c	4	0	1	0	Lonnie Smith, ph (d)	1	0	0	0
Jose Lind, 2b	4	0	1	0	Rafael Belliard, 2b	0	0	0	0
Doug Drabek, p	3	0	0	0	Brian Hunter, ph (f)	1	0	0	0
					John Smoltz, p	1	0	0	0
					Jeff Treadway, ph (a)	1	0	1	0
					Deion Sanders, ph (e)	1	0	0	0
					Francisco Cabrera, ph (g)	1	0	1	2
Total	**31**	**2**	**7**	**2**		**32**	**3**	**7**	**3**

(a) Singled for Smoltz in the sixth inning; (b) Intentionally walked for Cole in the seventh inning; (c) Pinch-ran for McClendon in the seventh inning; (d) Flied out for Lemke in the seventh inning; (e) Struck out for Avery in the eighth inning; (f) Popped out for Belliard in the ninth inning; (g) Singled for Jeff Reardon in the ninth inning.

Pittsburgh	1	0	0	0	0	1	0	0	0	—	2
Atlanta	0	0	0	0	0	0	0	0	3	—	3

Pittsburgh Pirates	IP	H	R	ER	SO	BB
Doug Drabek (L) +	8.0	6	3	1	5	2
Stan Belinda	0.2	1	0	0	0	1

Atlanta Braves	IP	H	R	ER	SO	BB
John Smoltz	6.0	4	2	2	4	2
Mike Stanton	0.2	1	0	0	0	1
Pete Smith	0.0	0	0	0	0	1
Steve Avery	1.1	2	0	0	0	0
Jeff Reardon (W)	1.0	0	0	0	1	1

+ Pitched to three batters in the ninth inning

E—Lind. **DP**—Pittsburgh 1. **LOB**—Pittsburgh 9, Atlanta 7. **2B**—Bell, Van Slyke, King, Lind, Pendleton, Bream, Berryhill. **SB**—Nixon. **SH**—Drabek. **SF**—Merced, Gant.
Umpires—John McSherry, Randy Marsh, Steve Rippley, Gary Darling, Gerry Davis, Ed Montague. (Note: McSherry left game after the first inning due to illness and was replaced by Marsh behind the plate)
Time—3:22. **Attendance**—51,975.

over the way it happened. For the first five or ten minutes you could hear a pin drop.

"Then, after the shock wore off, I guess you could say we were pissed off. We thought we could take them. We were both very good teams. We were fully confident, but we knew we had to make every run count.

"We did a lot of little things right that year, like bunting a guy over, hitting the sacrifice fly, working the hit-and-run play, catching the ball on defense. That was probably our biggest thing, defense. And our pitchers didn't give up many walks.

"As a manager, Leyland was a master. He always got the right matchups."

LaValliere was among about 30 former Pirate players from the 1970s, 1980s, and 1990s who attended ceremonies following the final baseball game at Three Rivers Stadium on October 1, 2000. "Dougie, Bream, and I, we all sat together," he said.

Did they talk about that historic play at the plate eight years earlier?

"No," he laughed.

After the defeat by the Braves, Drabek admitted, "I didn't want to think about it too much, but everybody kept bringing it up. I can talk about it easier now.

"I was getting a little tired there in the ninth, but I didn't think I was at the time. In that situation you don't feel anything. You just want to keep going and going as long as you can.

"When Sid was called safe at home, I left the bench and was one of the first guys in the clubhouse. A few men there were removing a small wooden platform that would have been used for a stage for the post-game interviews if we had won. It was like a knife in the back. I wanted to rip that stage up with my bare hands."

Drabek and Bream have remained good friends. "We exchange Christmas cards and phone calls," said Drabek. "We stay in touch. I always remember and appreciate how Sid's wife, Michelle, helped my wife, Kristy, when I first went to Pittsburgh in 1988."

Ball players who have gone through the wars usually enjoy deflating their peers with good-natured verbal jabs when the opportunity arises. Drabek is no exception. "I like to tell Sid he was out at the plate," Drabek chuckled.

John Smoltz of the Braves, like Drabek, watched the last part of the game from the bench after he had been relieved, and saw Jeff Reardon get credit for the victory. "We kept fighting," Smoltz said. "It was a miracle win."

He was named MVP of the series for his 2–0 record and 2.66 ERA, even though he allowed the Pirates their only runs in the final game. He said he felt his most valuable contribution to the team was his moving around on the bench. "I sat on every seat until I found the lucky one," he said of the spot where he was sitting when Cabrera produced the winning hit.

In the Braves' clubhouse afterward, Smoltz was soaked in champagne and bubbled over with excitement. "This is what athletics are all about," he said. "Somebody losing a heartbreaker and somebody winning a heartbreaker."

In the runway beneath the stands, a touching moment occurred when Cox embraced Leyland. "If Jimmy's not the best manager in baseball," Cox said, "I don't know who is. He had his team ready for every inning."

Leyland was 47 when he led the Pirates in 1992. He stayed with the club through the 1996 season, then in 1997 moved on to take over as manager of the Florida Marlins, who would bring him the joy of winning a World Series.

In 2000 he was no longer engaged in the front-line duties of the game. "I'm doing some scouting for the St. Louis Cardinals and watching the kids grow up," he said.

He talked briefly about the seventh-game loss to the Braves in 1992. "I remember asking the press for a few extra minutes before opening the clubhouse to them after the game," he said. "I was almost in a fog. I didn't know what to say.

"We had a real good ball club, but we just couldn't get it done. We were not a big power team, but we had excellent defense and our pitching was pretty good.

"I thought Bonds made a good throw," Leyland concluded, "but it just wasn't meant to be. Atlanta was a little better."

1997

The Indians Are Ambushed by the Marlins in Extra Innings

"We were so close. Then it all got taken away from us."—Omar Vizquel

Almost three years after the deed was done, Sandy Alomar, Jr., was recalling a line-drive single up the middle that Edgar Renteria of the Florida Marlins hit to beat the Cleveland Indians in game seven of the 1997 World Series.

Alomar was crouched behind the plate for the Indians in Pro Player Stadium in Miami on that warm Sunday night, October 26, when Renteria positioned himself in the batter's box to face Charles Nagy in the 11th inning.

The score was tied 2–2, there were two outs, and the bases were filled with Marlins.

"Renteria's an inside-out hitter who likes to hit up the middle or the other way," Alomar said. "So we wanted to keep the pitches away from him. Nagy threw him a split-finger fastball that hung over the plate a little, and Renteria lined it just over the glove of Nagy and through the middle for a single that scored the winning run.

"When he hit that ball, it was the worst feeling I ever had in my life. It was heartbreaking. It felt like a dagger in my heart. I didn't want to accept what had happened. I just couldn't believe it."

Alomar had summed up the climax of the Indians' 3–2 loss as they tried to gain their first World Series championship in

Sandy Alomar wanted the
pitch away from Renteria.
(Jeff Carlick)

49 years. In contrast, the Marlins walked away with the winner's share of money—$188,467 per player—in only their fifth
year of existence.

While the '97 Series commanded fervid regional interest, it
failed to capture a respectable measure of national attention
until its dramatic seventh game because neither team was the
most dominant force in its own league.

The Marlins, under new manager Jim Leyland, were the first
wild-card entrant in the World Series. They had finished the
regular season with a 92–70 record in the National League East
Division, nine games behind the first-place Atlanta Braves
whose 101–61 mark was the best in the majors.

The Indians had won the American League Central Division
title, but their 86–75 record was not as good as the final totals
posted by the Orioles and Yankees in the East Division and the
Mariners in the West Division, all of whom stacked up 90 or
more victories.

Other quirks distinguished the 1997 World Series. Four

games were played in the humid weather blanketing the Miami area, and three in the frigid air hovering over Jacobs Field in Cleveland. In fact, the 38-degree temperature with a wind chill factor of 18 degrees on Wednesday night, October 22, during game four, was the coldest ever recorded for a Series contest. Snow fell before the game started.

Rookie pitchers won three games in the Series, two by Livan Hernandez of the Marlins and one by Jaret Wright of the Indians. None of the teams' four leading starters won a single game. They included Alex Fernandez (17–12)—out of action with a torn right rotator cuff—and Kevin Brown (16–8) of the Marlins, and Charles Nagy (15–11) and Orel Hershiser (14–6) of the Indians.

The championship struggle set a record for most walks issued (76) in a seven-game Series, with 40 of them being charged to Cleveland pitching, and it tied a record for the most errors (three) by one team—the Indians again—in one inning.

For the first time in baseball history, two teams that did not have the best records in their respective leagues were the last-standing survivors of an extended pennant march which now grinds down the hardiest of pitching staffs because it includes additional rounds of playoffs.

It featured blowouts and nail-biting games decided by one run.

It produced a surprise young hero in the Marlins' shortstop Edgar Renteria, and an unlikely veteran fall guy in Cleveland second baseman Tony Fernandez.

It showcased a pitcher, Chad Ogea of the Indians, who proved he could hit, collecting a two-RBI single and a double in game six, an effort that not only evened the series but served as a rebuttal to arguments favoring the designated hitter rule.

It brought forth a dazzling catch by Gary Sheffield against the right-field wall in game three, a tremendous 438-foot homer by Charles Johnson into the upper deck at Pro Player Stadium in game one, and a redeeming seventh-game four-bagger by Bobby Bonilla who was playing on a damaged leg.

It displayed the sound, managerial strategies exercised by Jim Leyland of the Marlins and Mike Hargrove of the Indians who made all the right moves, particularly in the final game when they deployed their troops astutely, reminding some viewers of master chess players.

It was a Series in which Latin-American players made their greatest impact on the October post-season scene.

These players, born outside the continental United States, included Renteria, who was only the fourth Colombian to reach the majors; Livan Hernandez, a Cuban defector; Moises Alou, Tony Fernandez, Manny Ramirez, Felix Heredia, Jose Mesa, and Antonio Alfonseca, all of the Dominican Republic; Omar Vizquel of Venezuela, Devon White of Jamaica, and Sandy Alomar, a native of Puerto Rico.

The Series ended with one of the lowest TV ratings since such records were begun in 1959, but it attracted the largest total attendance ever (403,617), thanks largely to the crowds of 67,000-plus vociferous fans who jammed Pro Player Stadium each night for the Marlins' four home games that stirred baseball passions in South Florida to a high pitch.

When it was all over, perhaps Hargrove best capsulized the intriguing skirmish between his Indians and the Marlins. "If you enjoy baseball," said the Cleveland manager, "you had to enjoy this Series."

For impartial observers, his comment was on target. It was a most unusual World Series, topped off by a spectacular finish.

The story of the Marlins' success in 1997 begins with owner Wayne Huizenga, and a strange story it is, for Huizenga as early as June had announced he wanted to sell the club. He claimed by season's end he had lost more than $30 million that year on his baseball venture.

Huizenga, 59, had originally made his fortune as a co-founder of Waste Management, Inc., and then as director of Blockbuster Entertainment Corporation which was sold in 1994 to Viacom for $8.5 billion. He was a leading force in bringing major league baseball to South Florida in 1993. Through wise free-agent signings and trades by general manager Dave Dombrowski, he was able to hold a World Series trophy in his hands four years later as compensation for committing millions of

"You had to enjoy this Series," said Cleveland manager Mike Hargrove— even though he was on the losing side. *(John Williamson)*

dollars in contracting for such players as Alex Fernandez, Bobby Bonilla, Gary Sheffield, and Moises Alou as well as his manager Jim Leyland, who came over from the Pittsburgh Pirates.

During the offseason preceding the 1997 pennant race, Huizenga committed $89 million in salaries to free agents.

After the Marlins went through the traditional ritual of spraying champagne around the clubhouse following their World Series victory, Huizenga admitted he had mixed emotions about what it cost him to build a championship team.

"Every week when I write the checks, I regret it," he said, "but this is worth it. It has pulled the community together. We wanted to find out if baseball could succeed in South Florida, and the fans have shown us they will attend games."

On November 6, however, Huizenga was ready to bail out. He reached a tentative agreement to sell the club to a group represented by Marlins president Don Smiley. It was the first step in dismantling what might have become a new baseball dynasty.

In cost-cutting moves by the Marlins, key players from the pennant team wound up performing for other clubs in 1998, including Moises Alou with the Astros, Devon White with the Arizona Diamondbacks, Jeff Conine with the Royals, Robb Nen with the Giants, Kevin Brown with the Padres, and Al Leiter with the Mets.

Looking back on the breakup of a championship club, Dombrowski said, "A love affair had just started between the fans and the team, crossing many cultures. Those players would have been celebrities here for years to come. This place would have been alive with baseball."

The Marlins' swift rise to the heights was among the significant baseball stories in 1997, the year that marked the fiftieth anniversary of Jackie Robinson breaking down racial barriers in the major leagues. Robinson took the field for the first time in a regular season game for the Brooklyn Dodgers on April 15, 1947. In 1997, in his honor, all clubs were asked to retire uniform number 42 which Robinson had worn during his Hall of Fame career.

The year also marked the beginning of interleague competition during the regular season, a move that upset more than a few baseball purists.

Mark McGwire, who started the season with the Oakland A's and finished it with the St. Louis Cardinals, fell short in his quest to match Roger Maris's home run record of 61 set in 1961. McGwire hit 58 homers, 34 with the A's, before being traded to the Cardinals on July 31.

In April the Cardinals and Padres took major league baseball to Hawaii for the first time, playing a three-game series in Honolulu.

On June 10, Kevin Brown of the Marlins crafted a 9–0 no-hitter against the Giants, losing a perfect game with two out in the eighth inning when he hit a batter with a pitch.

The American League won the All-Star game 3–1, at Jacobs Field on July 8, with Sandy Alomar delivering a decisive two-run homer in the seventh inning and thereby earning the game's

MVP award. "To have the game-winning home run in your hometown is a once-in-a-lifetime dream," said Alomar. "I was flying around the bases. I don't think I've ever run so fast around the bases."

In mid-summer, knuckleball pitcher Phil Niekro, second baseman Nellie Fox, former Dodger manager Tom Lasorda, and Negro League shortstop Willie Wells were inducted into the baseball Hall of Fame.

Among outstanding, season-long individual performances were those turned in by Tony Gwynn of the Padres and Roger Clemens of the Blue Jays. Gwynn hit .372 to win the National League batting championship for the eighth time. Clemens led the American League with 21 victories, 292 strikeouts, and a 2.05 ERA to claim the "triple crown" of pitching and earn his fourth Cy Young award.

Deaths of notable baseball figures during the year included those of Curt Flood, 59; Richie Ashburn, 70; Johnny Vander Meer, 82; and Buck Leonard, 90. Flood had gained notoriety by challenging in court major league baseball's reserve clause that restricted players in their movements from one club to another. Ashburn and Leonard were Hall of Famers, and Vander Meer had made headlines in 1938 when he pitched consecutive no-hitters for the Cincinnati Reds.

Unlike the Marlins, who won three straight games in sweeping the Giants in the 1997 National League division playoffs, the Indians had to fight for their lives in turning back the Yankees in the American League division playoffs. Down two games to one, they eked out two more victories, 3–2 and 4–3, and moved on to the league championship series in which, once again, they were stretched almost to the limit, this time by the Orioles.

Baltimore had a strong pitching staff led by starters Jimmy Key, Scott Erickson, and Mike Mussina, but the Indians endured, winning four games by one run, two of which went into extra innings.

After their 1–0 decision in 11 innings in game six at Camden Yards, Hargrove told reporters, "You guys don't have to write this one. This one writes itself."

The Indians prevailed on an 11th-inning home run hit by

Tony Fernandez off reliever Armando Benitez. They were headed back to the World Series after a year's hiatus, hoping to make up for their loss to the Braves in the 1995 Fall Classic.

"Playing a series like this, against a very good team like the Orioles, it gets you ready for the World Series," said Cleveland first baseman Jim Thome.

The Marlins had clinched the National League pennant the night before, beating the favored, pitching-rich Braves 7–4 in the sixth game of the championship series at Turner Field in Atlanta.

Kevin Brown had gone the distance in defeating the Braves, limiting them to four hits. He scoffed at the idea the Marlins were able to reach the World Series because of Wayne Huizenga's open checkbook. "They talk about the money we spent, that we bought a championship," he said. "The money is not what won this series. Heart, determination, and pursuit of the right goal got us there."

Intangibles aside, both teams brought an array of knives and forks to the World Series table. The Indians' starting lineup was loaded with home-run power. Thome hit 40 homers during the regular season; left fielder David Justice, 33; third baseman Matt Williams, 32; right fielder Manny Ramirez, 26; and catcher Sandy Alomar, 21. Their shortstop Omar Vizquel committed only ten errors in 684 total chances and was considered the game's best defensive player at his position.

The Marlins had some long-ball punch themselves, represented by left fielder Moises Alou with 23 home runs; right fielder Gary Sheffield with 21, and catcher Charles Johnson, 19. Third baseman Bobby Bonilla also had some pop in his bat. And their bullpen closer, Robb Nen, scorched opposing batters with an intimidating fastball that helped him average more than one strikeout per inning pitched and collect 35 saves. Some of his fastballs were clocked at close to 100 miles an hour.

So the elements were in place for a World Series destined to be cherished by baseball fans in South Florida and remembered ruefully by loyal Indian partisans living not far from the shores of Lake Erie and in many other areas of Ohio.

The noise created by a crowd of 67,245 spectators was deafening at Pro Player Stadium as game one got under way on Saturday night, October 18. Fans were waving banners and Cuban, Dominican, and Colombian flags. They were holding handmade signs reading "Go Fish!" and "We Belong!" An eagle was released during pre-game ceremonies and soared over the field before returning to its trainer, drawing loud cheers from the crowd.

The atmosphere was electrifying, and the stadium was rocking as Livan Hernandez, 22, the hero of Miami's Little Havana, stepped to the mound and began throwing his warmup tosses.

Orel Hershiser, 39, was the starter for the Indians. He had joined the Tribe in 1995 after spending 11 years with the Dodgers. The game was tied at 1–1 until the bottom of the fourth inning when Alou, on an 0-and-2 count, reached Hershiser for a three-run homer that bounced off the left-field foul pole. Johnson followed with a monstrous home run to give the Marlins a 5–1 lead that eventually turned into a 7–4 victory.

The home run by Johnson stunned Hershiser, who jerked his head to the right as he watched the ball take flight into the left-field upper deck. The Indians' starter looked like a man who had just seen his house rising in the air from a gas explosion. The crowd reacted with an ear-splitting roar.

Afterward Leyland resurrected an old cliché. "There's no defense for the home run," he said. "They came at the right time, and we broke it open a little bit.

"Johnson's hitting got this club going in the second half of the season. When you get a catcher who has great defense and he hits a homer like that, it's like finding gold."

In game two the Indians scratched the dirt at Pro Player and uncovered a "gold nugget" of their own in starter Chad Ogea, who came away a 6–1 winner against Kevin Brown.

During the regular season, Ogea had spent two months on the disabled list with a strained ligament in his right elbow. After a 30-day rehab assignment with Buffalo in the International League, he returned to the Indians on September 1, finishing the season with a 4–5 record and an unimpressive 4.66 ERA.

Starting Ogea against Brown seemed like an invitation to a mismatch, but Brown coughed up ten hits, all six Cleveland runs, and did not pitch beyond the sixth inning. Ogea came away the winner with the late-inning help of relievers Mike Jackson and Jose Mesa.

The Series now moved north where the temperature ranged in the 40s at Jacobs Field for game three on Tuesday night, October 21. It turned out to be a long, draining game, filled with six errors and an astounding 17 bases on balls. It took four hours and 12 minutes to complete, with the Marlins chopping up Cleveland pitching for 16 hits and a 14–11 victory.

"It was as ugly a game as you'll ever see," Hargrove said later. "It wasn't the weather. It was just poor play."

Gary Sheffield sparkled for the Marlins, collecting three hits including a homer in five at-bats while driving in five runs. And he made a superb catch against the right-field wall in the seventh inning on Jim Thome's long smash that had extra bases stamped all over it.

Snow flurries were descending on Jacobs Field when newly inducted Hall of Fame member Phil Niekro, who once pitched for the Indians, threw out the ceremonial first ball before the start of game four. With most of the 44,877 fans bundled up in winter clothing, Jaret Wright, 21, only a few years out of high school, took the mound for the Indians.

A son of Clyde Wright, who pitched for the Angels, Brewers, and Rangers in the 1960s and 1970s, the young rookie right-hander had been called up from the minors by the Indians in late June. He finished with an 8–3 record in 16 regular-season starts, then won two big games against the Yankees in the American League division playoffs. He threw hard, employing a sinking fastball, curve, and occasional change-up. How fast did he throw? "There were a few times," he laughed, "when the planets were aligned just right that I got up to 98, 99 miles an hour."

He was throwing in the mid-90s against the Marlins, and although he was often behind in the count, he held the Florida team in check despite issuing five walks through the six innings he pitched. He left the game with the Indians in front 6–3, a lead that jumped to 7–3, then 8–3, and finally to a triumphant 10–3 score in what was turning out to be a punch-counterpunch World Series.

Wright was credited with the victory. "It was the coldest weather I've ever pitched in," he said. "I was just fortunate we got ahead early." He referred to the Indians' first inning 3–0 lead, fashioned with the help of Manny Ramirez's two-run homer off loser Tony Saunders, another rookie pitcher.

The seesaw struggle between the two teams continued in game five, the last to be played at Jacobs Field in 1997, with starters Livan Hernandez and Orel Hershiser matched against each other again. In another slugfest the Marlins won 8–7, even though Hernandez was roughed up and relieved in the ninth inning by Robb Nen, who narrowly escaped with a save as the Indians scored three final runs before the game ended.

The teams headed back to Florida for game six. The way the Series was going, Cleveland fans could not be reproached for claiming it was the Indians' turn to win. It was.

Game six was played at Pro Player Stadium on Saturday night, October 25, and it belonged to Chad Ogea. The Indians' pitcher beat the Marlins from the mound and from the batter's box, where he slapped a two-run single and then a double, leading to another run.

Since the designated hitter was not used in Series games played in National League parks, Ogea went into the cage to tone up his stroke before the game. "I was watching him take batting practice," said Hargrove, "and from what I saw, I was willing to bet that he wouldn't make contact with the ball when he came to the plate during the game." Hargrove was happy his analysis of Ogea's hitting ability had to be trashed.

Ogea swung from the right side. He had had exactly two at-bats in his major league career when he stepped in to face Kevin Brown the first time with the bases filled in the second inning. His single to right just past the outstretched glove of first baseman Jeff Conine scored Matt Williams from third and Jim Thome from second, giving the Indians a 2–0 lead.

Then, as the leadoff hitter in the top of the fifth, Ogea rapped a hard grounder between Conine and the first-base line. The ball skipped along the line and Ogea slid into second with a double, eventually scoring, once he reached third, on a sacrifice fly by Manny Ramirez. After the game, Ogea laughed about the strawberry that marked his knee from sliding into second.

He was so proud of his battle wound, he later took a photograph of it.

That was all the offense of the Indians needed as they went on to win 4–1 before a crowd of 67,498 fans, largest attendance of the Series. Ogea, supported by relievers Mike Jackson, Paul Assenmacher, and Jose Mesa, received credit for the victory, his second against the Marlins.

Marlins manager Jim Leyland paid a compliment to Ogea on his hitting. "He was very aggressive at the plate. I'm very impressed," he said.

"Those two base hits I gave up to Ogea, that really killed us," Kevin Brown said.

"I think Chad is available to pinch-hit in game seven," twitted pitching teammate Brian Anderson.

Besides Ogea's contributions as a pitcher and hitter, shortstop Omar Vizquel made one of the great defensive plays of the Series in the sixth inning. With two outs, the Marlins had runners on second and third. Jackson had been summoned from the bullpen and was trying to protect the Indians' 4–1 lead.

Charles Johnson hit a hard grounder into the hole off Jackson. Vizquel made a diving stop on the ball, righted himself, and threw Johnson out, preventing two runs from scoring. If the runs had scored, the momentum of the game might have changed in favor of the Marlins.

"I was getting a drink of water in the dugout when the ball was hit," said Hargrove. "I looked up in time to see Omar make the play, and I almost choked."

Later, Vizquel said he had made similar, defensive maneuvers six or seven times over the years, but he admitted, "It was the most important play of my career."

Starting assignments for the deciding seventh game of the World Series on the following Sunday night went to Al Leiter and Jaret Wright.

Why did Hargrove go with Wright instead of the more experienced Nagy in the most important game of the year? "I decided to start Jaret," the Cleveland manager said, "because he had pitched so well under a lot of pressure against the Yankees in the division series.

"And after seeing the way he handled himself in game four against the Marlins, I felt very good about him coming back on short rest."

"I was going on three days' rest, but I wanted the ball," said Wright. "I felt lucky to be asked to pitch in the seventh game of a World Series. How many guys get a chance like that? It was the most exciting time of my life."

Through the first six and a third innings, the young right-hander used his three basic pitches expertly, holding the Marlins to two hits and one run while striking out seven batters.

The Indians had pounced on Al Leiter for two runs in the third inning on a walk to Thome, a single by Marquis Grissom, a sacrifice by Wright, and another single by Tony Fernandez, scoring Thome and Grissom.

With Cleveland in front 2–0, the lone run off Wright came on Bobby Bonilla's leadoff homer in the seventh inning. After Wright struck out Charles Johnson and walked Craig Counsell, he was relieved by Assenmacher, who closed out the inning without further damage.

Wright was asked about his matchup with Bonilla, whose homer squeezed the Indians' lead to 2–1.

"He hit the first pitch, a change-up," Wright said. "After he did that, I put that pitch away for a while."

It was now gut-wrenching time. Neither team scored in the eighth. The Indians threatened to push over another run in the top of the ninth but were thwarted. With Alomar on third base, Thome on first, and only one out, Grissom hit a grounder to shortstop Edgar Renteria who threw home to get Alomar as he attempted to score on the play.

The next batter, pinch-hitter Brian Giles, flied out to end the inning, and the Indians, wearing their dark blue jerseys with red lettering outlined in white, were only three outs away from the club's first world championship since 1948.

In the ninth, Mesa, pitching in relief for Cleveland, gave up a leadoff single to right center by Moises Alou. He then fanned Bonilla. Only two more outs and baseball fans in Cleveland would start celebrating.

The next batter, Charles Johnson, chilled thoughts of such a celebration by hitting an opposite field single to right, advancing Alou with the tying run to third base. Counsell then hit a sacrifice fly to Ramirez in right, scoring Alou, knotting the score at 2–2, and sending the game into extra innings.

Johnson's clutch single was perhaps the most important hit of the Series. When he was interviewed late in 2000, Hargrove grimly recalled the action. "Mesa had Johnson down in the count, 1-and-2," he said. "We could've had two outs, but Johnson slashes that easy liner to right. I've played that inning over in my head a thousand times, thinking what might have been."

The game moved on to the tenth inning with neither team scoring. Charles Nagy, making his first relief appearance since his rookie year in 1990, came in from the bullpen to get the final Marlin out in the bottom of the inning.

The 30-year-old right-hander was back on the mound in the 11th inning after the Indians had been set down without much difficulty in the top of the inning.

Once again Bonilla led off, and once again he came through for Florida with a single to center. Catcher Gregg Zaun, who had come into the game to pinch-run for Johnson in the ninth inning, popped up to Nagy for the first out.

Then Counsell hit a grounder that skipped under Tony Fernandez's glove between first and second for an error, advancing Bonilla to third with the winning run.

It was a cruel twist of fate for Fernandez, who had singled home the Indians' two runs in the third inning. "I don't want to make any excuses," Fernandez said after the game. "It was a play I could have made." He had to range far to his left for the ball, and with one out he wanted to keep Bonilla from reaching second. "I wanted to get him," Fernandez said. "I think that was my mistake. I know Bobby wasn't running well. That's why I wanted to go to second."

Fernandez declined to blame Bonilla for distracting him on the play as he moved toward first to field the ball. He also said the ball did not take a bad hop. "I just missed it," he admitted.

With Bonilla on third and Counsell on first, Hargrove ordered Nagy to walk Jim Eisenreich intentionally, filling the bases and setting up a possible double play.

In game seven, Cleveland's Jaret Wright (left) got the call as starting pitcher. Tony Fernandez made a crucial error in the 11th inning—"a play I could have made," he said.

Devon White, the next batter, hit a grounder to Fernandez who fired the ball home to nail Bonilla on a forceout. The bases remained loaded with two outs as Renteria came to the plate.

Nagy had an 0-and-1 count on Renteria when the right-handed batter from Baranquilla, Colombia, slapped a line drive that ticked off Nagy's glove and zoomed over the infield near second base to score Counsell from third with the winning run and a final 3–2 victory for the Marlins.

When Counsell jumped on home plate, the crowd at Pro Player Stadium erupted with wild cheers, high-fives, and embraces. Marlin players swarmed onto the field. Fireworks were soon splashing their colors high in the darkened sky. Jim Leyland was weeping and blowing kisses everywhere. He made a victory lap around the field, saluting the fans. Livan Hernandez was shouting, "I love you *Mee-ah-mee!*" as he accepted the Most Valuable Player trophy. Hernandez's mother, who had been given a special visa to leave Cuba for the Series, looked on in amazement.

At the game's end, Jim Thome crouched on the field with his head bent down and his hands covering his face. Omar Vizquel sat in the Indians' dugout watching the Marlins yell, dance, and celebrate.

"I wanted to know what the feeling was like on the other side," said Vizquel. "We didn't have anywhere else to go. We had played 190 games to get to this point. I wanted to see what they felt.

"No question this is tougher than losing to the Braves in '95. We were so close, and then it all got taken away from us."

Thome created a new word in describing his feelings after the game. "It's disheartaching to come that close," he said.

In the Indians' subdued clubhouse, Hargrove said, "I don't think there are words to describe how this feels. You feel bad for the guys who lost. You feel bad because you know how hard they worked."

Hargrove was marking his 48th birthday, but there was little cheer in him as he responded to reporters' questions. He was asked about Nagy. "I thought Charlie had good stuff tonight," Hargrove said. "He made a great pitch to Devon White to jam him and get the ground ball out at home plate. He made a great pitch to Renteria, but he hit it where nobody was standing. Those are the breaks of the game."

After receiving hugs from Vizquel and Orel Hershiser, Fernandez stood by himself and waved reporters over to his locker. He knew he had to speak about his 11th-inning error.

"It's still painful," he said as he lowered his head. "I know something good is going to come of this, but things like this happen in baseball.

"I'm glad I contributed. I gave my best, gave a great effort, but unfortunately it didn't work out for me."

"I feel worse than Tony," said Marquis Grissom. "You can't blame Tony. Blame the whole team."

Nagy agreed with Vizquel that the loss to the Marlins was more devastating than the defeat the Indians had suffered against the Braves in the 1995 World Series. "This is harder," he said. "It's just crushing. I was warming up from the fifth inning on, and I finally got my chance to go into the game. I got out of one jam, but I couldn't get out of the other."

Years later Sandy Alomar confirmed what every competitive major leaguer knows. "We weren't playing for the money in that Series," he said. "We were playing for the ring, and for the pride it would give us in winning it."

Reminiscing about the Series loss, Hargrove said, "About a year and a half ago, a guy asked me how long it took me to get over that last game. I told him, 'As soon as it happens, I'll let you know.'"

Hargrove said he felt bad for what happened to Tony Fernandez. "It's a shame people were blaming Tony for losing that game. Without him, we wouldn't have gotten as far as we did that year. He hit real good for us in the postseason [.357], and maybe they forget that he won game six for us in the League Championship Series with his 11th-inning home run against the Orioles."

What did Hargrove say to the players after the Series ended?

"I told them, 'You have no reason to hang your heads. You played as good as you could. Sure, there's a lot of heartache and disappointment, but let's take a positive feeling away from this. I've seen a lot of winners on losing teams, and a lot of losers on winning teams, but there isn't a guy in this room that isn't a winner.'"

Hargrove was asked if he ever had any second thoughts about his tactical moves in the Series.

"No," he said. "When I look back on it I know I wouldn't have done anything differently. I know we didn't lose because of lack of effort or execution."

What did Jaret Wright do after he came out of game seven? "I sat on the bench. There was no need for me to go to the clubhouse to ice my arm," he said. "On the bench I turned into a fan, I wanted our team to win so badly."

How about Renteria's game-winning hit? "It was heartbreaking," Wright said. "It was such a great game, it was unfortunate someone had to lose."

Clyde and Vicky Wright flew in from California after learning that their son would pitch the final game of the Series. They were in the stands.

"My father was probably more nervous than I was," said young Wright. "He played ten years in the majors and never

Cleveland Indians vs. Florida Marlins
at Pro Player Stadium, October 26, 1997

Cleveland Indians	AB	R	H	RBI	Florida Marlins	AB	R	H	RBI
Omar Vizquel, ss	5	0	1	0	Devon White, cf	6	0	0	0
Tony Fernandez, 2b	5	0	2	2	Edgar Renteria, ss	5	0	3	1
Manny Ramirez, rf	3	0	0	0	Gary Sheffield, rf	4	0	1	0
David Justice, lf	5	0	0	0	Darren Daulton, 1b	3	0	0	0
Matt Williams, 3b	2	0	0	0	Jeff Conine, ph/1b (c)	1	0	0	0
Sandy Alomar, c	5	0	1	0	John Cangelosi, ph (f)	1	0	0	0
Jim Thome, 1b	4	1	1	0	Moises Alou, lf	5	1	1	0
Marquis Grissom, cf	4	1	1	0	Bobby Bonilla, 3b	5	1	2	1
Jaret Wright, p	2	0	0	0	Charles Johnson, c	4	0	1	0
Brian Giles, ph (d)	1	0	0	0	Gregg Zaun, pr/c (e)	1	0	0	0
					Craig Counsell, 2b	3	1	0	1
					Cliff Floyd, ph (a)	0	0	0	0
					Kurt Abbott, ph (b)	1	0	0	0
					Jim Eisenreich, 1b	1	0	0	0
Total	**36**	**2**	**6**	**2**		**40**	**3**	**8**	**3**

(a) Announced to pinch-hit for Dennis Cook in the seventh inning; (b) Flied out for Cliff Floyd in the seventh inning; (c) Fouled out for Daulton in the eighth inning; (d) Flied out for Brian Anderson in the ninth inning; (e) Ran for Johnson in the ninth inning; (f) Struck out for Robb Nen in the tenth inning.

Cleveland	0	0	2	0	0	0	0	0	0	0	0 — 2
Florida	0	0	0	0	0	0	1	0	1	0	1 — 3

Cleveland Indians	IP	H	R	ER	SO	BB
Jaret Wright	6.1	2	1	1	7	5
Paul Assenmacher	0.2	0	0	0	1	0
Mike Jackson	0.2	0	0	0	1	0
Brian Anderson	0.1	0	0	0	0	0
Jose Mesa	1.2	4	1	1	2	0
Charles Nagy (L)	1.0	2	1	0	0	1

Florida Marlins	IP	H	R	ER	SO	BB
Al Leiter	6.0	4	2	2	7	4
Dennis Cook	1.0	0	0	0	2	0
Antonio Alfonseca	1.1	0	0	0	1	1
Felix Heredia	0.0	1	0	0	0	0
Robb Nen	1.2	1	0	0	3	0
Jay Powell (W)	1.0	0	0	0	0	1

E—Ramirez, Fernandez. **DP**—Cleveland 1, Florida 2. **LOB**—Cleveland 8, Florida 12.
HR—Bonilla. **SB**—Vizquel 2. **SH**—Wright. **SF**—Counsell.
Umpires—Ed Montague, Dale Ford, Joe West, Greg Kosc, Randy Marsh, Ken Kaiser.
Time—4:10. **Attendance**—67,204.

Jim Leyland, so often heartbroken in the post-season, finally won it all with the Marlins. *(Florida Marlins)*

got into the post-season. After the game he told me he was proud of me and the team because we gave it all we had."

Although he appeared in five World Series games in 1997, reliever Paul Assenmacher had only a limited role in game seven, retiring both batters he faced after replacing Wright in the seventh inning.

"Pitching in the seventh game of a World Series," he said, "is like a dream you have as a kid playing baseball in the back-yard or in some field. How many people have a chance to do that in real life?

"It was a nerve-wracking game. It could have gone either way. When I came out I was going back and forth to the locker room and the dugout, and even to the bullpen to encourage the guys. I was more nervous because I couldn't do anything about it.

"While I was in the game, my wife, Maggie, was sitting in the stadium, and one of the kids asked her, 'When Daddy gets his World Series ring, can he retire?'

"Well, I was 36 years old, and I knew my chances of getting a World Series ring were pretty slim.

"When they tied the game in the ninth inning it was disheartening, and it was very disappointing to lose that last game, but I'm a realist and I was able to put it in perspective. There are more important things in life than losing a World Series."

Although market-conscious television executives would have preferred to see the Yankees or Braves or Orioles in the 1997 World Series, the Marlins and Indians earned the right to fight it out for baseball's highest team honor. They did not reach the pinnacle by luck.

On Monday, October 27, one day after the end of the World Series, the Dow Jones industrial average plunged 554 points, erasing more than 7 percent of the market's value.

It might not be stretching the truth to say that startling drop in the stock market matched a similar decline in spirit among many Cleveland players and fans the night before as Renteria's hit sailed over the outstretched glove of Charles Nagy into short center field.

Index of Names

A NOTE ON THE AUTHOR

John Kuenster is editor of *Baseball Digest* and executive editor of Century Publishing Company in Evanston, Illinois. A former staff writer and columnist for the *Chicago Daily News*, he has spent his life in journalism and has written extensively for newspapers and magazines. A former president of the Chicago Chapter of the Baseball Writers Association of America, he edited and contributed to *From Cobb to Catfish*, a baseball anthology, and with David Cowan wrote *To Sleep with the Angels*, a widely praised account of the Our Lady of the Angels school fire in Chicago.